CONFIRMATION

IN THE LUTHERAN CHURCH

CONFIRMATION

IN THE LUTHERAN CHURCH

ARTHUR C. REPP

CONCORDIA PUBLISHING HOUSE

Saint Louis, Missouri

Concordia Publishing House, St. Louis, Missouri

Concordia Publishing House Ltd., London, W. C. 1

© 1964 Concordia Publishing House

Library of Congress Catalog Card No. 64-19897

Reprinted in the Concordia Heritage Series, 1986,
by Concordia Publishing House.

ISBN: 978-0-7586-1818-4

TO MY STUDENTS AND COLLEAGUES

CONTENTS

ABBREVIATIONS ix

PREFACE 3

PROLOG 9

I. CONFIRMATION IN THE REFORMATION CHURCH 13
Confirmation Before the Reformation 13
Luther and the Confessions 15
The Developing Types of Confirmation 21
The Catechetical Type 22
The Hierarchical Type 28
The Sacramental Type 37
The Traditional Type 44
Summary Conclusions 55

II. THE DEVELOPMENT OF CONFIRMATION IN EUROPE 61
The Period of Orthodoxy 61
The Pietistic Type 68
The Rationalistic Type 76
The 19th Century 84

III. CONFIRMATION IN THE UNITED STATES 95
The Colonial and Early National Period 95
The Americanization of the Lutheran Church 106

IV. RECENT DEVELOPMENTS 139
Developments in Europe 139
Developments in the United States 147

V. THE THEOLOGICAL IMPLICATIONS OF CONFIRMATION   155

    Holy Baptism   156

    The Lord's Supper   167

    What, Then, Is Confirmation?   177

VI. THE STRUCTURE OF CONFIRMATION   181

    The Age of the Catechumen   182

    Age Levels Proposed for Confirmation   185

    The Educational Frame for Confirmation   193

    Objectives for Confirmation Instruction   196

    Cooperating with the Home and Enlisting Its Support   204

    The Congregation's Part in Working with Its Youth   206

VII. THE CONFIRMATION SERVICE   211

    The Examination   211

    The Hymns   213

    The Lection   214

    The Sermon   214

    The Rite of Confirmation   215

    Confirmation Certificates   223

    Memory Verses   224

    Song by the Catechumens   224

    The Confirmation Day   225

    First Communion   226

    External Preparations   226

EPILOG   229

BIBLIOGRAPHY   233

INDEX   253

ABBREVIATIONS

A	Agenda, altar book, church book, formulary, or liturgy.
BS	*Die Bekenntnisschriften der evangelisch-lutherischen Kirche, herausgegeben im Gedenkjahr der Augsburgischen Konfession 1930.* 4th, rev. ed. Göttingen: Vandenhoeck & Ruprecht, 1959.
BC	*The Book of Concord: The Confessions of the Evangelical Lutheran Church,* trans. and ed. Theodore G. Tappert in collaboration with Jaroslav Pelikan, Robert H. Fischer, Arthur C. Piepkorn. Philadelphia: Muhlenberg Press, 1959.
CO	Church Order or *Kirchenordnung.*
CT	*Concordia Triglotta: Die symbolischen Bücher der evangelisch-lutherischen Kirche, deutsch-lateinisch-englisch, als Denkmal der vierhundertjährigen Jubelfeier der Reformation, anno Domini 1917, herausgegeben auf Beschluss der evangelisch-lutherischen Synode von Missouri, Ohio und andern Staaten.* St. Louis: Concordia Publishing House, 1921.
CR	*Corpus Reformatorum.*
Graff	Graff, Paul. *Geschichte der Auflösung der alten gottesdienstlichen Formen in der evangelischen Kirche Deutschlands.* 2d, rev. ed. 2 vols. Göttingen: Vandenhoeck & Ruprecht, 1937—39.
LW	*Luther's Works.* American ed. Jaroslav [Jan] Pelikan and Helmut T. Lehmann, general eds. St. Louis: Concordia Publishing House; Philadelphia: Muhlenberg [later Fortress] Press, 1955— .
TLH	*The Lutheran Hymnal.* Authorized by the Synods Constituting The Evangelical Lutheran Synodical Conference of North America. St. Louis: Concordia Publishing House, 1941.
R-G	Rietschel, Georg. *Lehrbuch der Liturgik.* 2d ed., rev. Paul Graff. Göttingen: Vandenhoeck & Ruprecht, 1952.
Rich	Richter, Ae[milius] L[udwig]. *Die evangelischen Kirchenordnungen des 16. Jahrhunderts.* 2 vols. Weimar: Landes-Industriecomptoirs, 1846.
ReuC	Reu, [Johann] M[ichael]. *Catechetics or Theory and Practice of Religious Instruction.* 2d, rev. ed. Chicago: Wartburg Publishing House, 1927.
ReuK	————. *D. Martin Luthers Kleiner Katechismus: Die Geschichte seiner Entstehung, seiner Verbreitung und seines Gebrauchs.* Munich: Chr. Kaiser Verlag, 1929.
ReuQ	————. *Quellen zur Geschichte des kirchlichen Unterrichts in der evangelischen Kirche Deutschlands zwischen 1530 und 1600.* 8 vols. Gütersloh: C. Bertelsmann, 1904—35.

Abbreviations

Seh   Sehling, Emil. *Die Evangelischen Kirchenordnungen des XVI. Jahrhunderts.* 6 vols. Leipzig: O. R. Reisland, 1902—13. 3 vols. Tübingen: J. C. B. Mohr (Paul Siebeck), 1955— .

SBH   *Service Book and Hymnal of the Lutheran Church in America.* Authorized by the Churches cooperating in The Commission on the Liturgy and The Commission on the Hymnal. Music ed. Minneapolis, Minn.: Augsburg Publishing House; et al., 1958.

SL   *Dr. Martin Luthers Sämmtliche Schriften,* ed. Joh[ann] Georg Walch. New, rev. ed. 25 vols. St. Louis: Lutherischer Concordia-Verlag, 1880—1910.

WA   *D. Martin Luthers Werke: Kritische Gesammtausgabe.* Weimar: Hermann Böhlau and Hermann Böhlaus Nachfolger, 1883— .

CONFIRMATION

IN THE LUTHERAN CHURCH

A book is never the product solely of the person whose name decorates the title page. A book is the result of the interaction of many minds, forces, and experiences with the one who is finally regarded the author. *Confirmation in the Lutheran Church* is no exception. This is no attempt to pass the responsibility for its contents to others, for the final work must remain the sole responsibility of the author. It should serve, however, as an acknowledgment of thanks to the many persons, too many to mention individually, who have directly or indirectly contributed to the making of this book.

Perhaps my first real concern about confirmation may be traced to a superintendents' conference of The Lutheran Church — Missouri Synod in 1950, which suggested that a major study be made on confirmation. In the interest of stimulating someone to take over this task I was asked by the Synod's Board of Parish Education to draw up a prospectus for such a study. This appeared as a brief study in *Concordia Theological Monthly*, XXII (August 1951), 600—607. But no one came forward to volunteer for the assignment. Whether this was due to a lack of interest or because the task was too formidable, I could not tell at the time.

I became more personally involved in the subject by invitations to conduct workshops on confirmation in Austin, Tex. (1953), and St. Louis, Mo. (1954). Still little happened. It was not till August 1954, when I had undergone the stimulating and rigorous experience of the seminar conducted by the Lutheran Intersynodical Committee on Parish Education in Racine, Wis., that I felt I should take up my own proposal and make a serious study of the history and practice of confirmation. Additional

3

requests to conduct workshops at River Forest, Ill. (1955), St. Louis, Mo. (1956), and Buffalo, N. Y. (1957), served to whet my interest and made me realize more fully the general interest in the subject as well as the broad scope of the problem. A four-month sabbatical leave from Concordia Seminary, St. Louis, served as a welcome opportunity to make this serious study into the historical and theological background of confirmation. In preparation for my leave I received the assistance of a graduate fellow, Mr. Richard G. Maassel, now pastor in Glenview, Ill., who did some invaluable spadework in the Lutheran periodical literature of the United States. Further assistance was given me in the same area some time later by Mr. Harold J. Teuscher, a graduate fellow, now pastor in Milpitas, Calif.

It should be said that from the very start the Board of Parish Education of The Lutheran Church — Missouri Synod, especially its Executive Secretary, Dr. Arthur L. Miller, showed much interest in the study and encouraged me to write this book. The first draft, called "Strengthen Them," completed in 1960, was therefore submitted to the board and to a number of pastors in the field for critical analysis. It was generally agreed that there was too much material for one volume and that eventually two books might be published, one setting forth the general principles and the structure of confirmation, the other dealing with the application, emphasizing such matters as the curriculum, teaching methods and activities, and evaluation. Meanwhile the section on the theological implications of confirmation appeared in *Concordia Theological Monthly,* XXXI (March and April 1960).

A condensation of the proposed book was presented to the convention of the Iowa District East of The Lutheran Church — Missouri Synod in 1960 and later duplicated under the title "Reconstructing Confirmation for Our Day." The following year it was presented to the convention of the Western District, which resolved to print and circulate it among its congregations for further study. "Reconstructing Confirmation for Our Day," or parts of it with some elaborations, has been presented to many conferences, institutes, workshops, and congregations since then, so that by now more than 2,000 pastors, teachers, and laymen have heard major portions of the book. It has been no end of surprise that my basic theses have been so well received and have elicited so much interest. The constructive criticism which these meetings elicited have been an invaluable aid in the revision of the manuscript.

The original manuscript, "Strengthen Them," has been used as a tentative text for an elective course in confirmation instruction at Concordia Seminary since 1960. This use has given me additional opportunity to evaluate and refine the views expressed.

It soon became evident that the confirmation rite, as commonly found among the Lutherans in America, needed some drastic revisions if my theses were correct. After a presentation to the Commission on Worship, Liturgics, and Hymnology of the Synodical Conference, I was encouraged to prepare a more suitable rite which might be included in a revision of the agenda of the Synodical Conference. A proposed rite was later accepted as a working basis, and the commission arranged to have it appear in a clergy edition of *Advance,* IX (April 1962). The rite was later printed in a separate pamphlet. Many of the pastors expressed their interest in the proposed rite, used it, and made some valuable suggestions for its improvement. As a result of these suggestions and the commission's own recommendations the rite was revised and has been included in Chapter vii.

One of the most difficult tasks of the study was to draw up a set of objectives for confirmation instruction. Here again the help of others needs to be acknowledged. Because the curriculum commission of the Board for Higher Education was interested in describing what a Lutheran student should be when he enters a synodical high school for its ministerial training program, the commission requested me to submit my objectives for confirmation as a possible contribution to its study. A subcommittee of the commission — Dr. Walter Wolbrecht, Dr. Carl S. Meyer, and myself — carefully reviewed the objectives again. In their revised form they will be found in Chapter vi. In a slightly modified form these objectives were adopted by the commission and later by The Lutheran Church — Missouri Synod to describe what may be expected of freshmen enrolling in one of its synodical high schools.

This brief sketch of the background of this book should show conclusively that when I acknowledge the help of many others in its writing, my acknowledgment is not prompted by humility. It is offered merely in the interest of the truth. It should serve also to explain to my former parish, Mt. Olive Lutheran Church, San Antonio, Tex., why I could not have practiced then what I propose now. The book tries in its own way to make amends to them for making in their midst all the mistakes which I now view with alarm.

The book is dedicated to my students and colleagues for their encouragement and help. A final expression of gratitude must be made to my colleague, Harry G. Coiner, who was always interested in having me address myself to the current situation, or to use his expression, to the spot "where the rubber hits the road."

ARTHUR C. REPP

ALMIGHTY GOD, the Father of our Lord Jesus Christ, who hath begotten thee again of water and of the Spirit and hath forgiven thee all thy sins, strengthen thee with His grace unto life everlasting. Amen.

The Postbaptismal Prayer

DISCOVERING THE PROBLEM

FOR RECONSTRUCTING CONFIRMATION

Lutheran clergymen generally regard the instruction of the catechumens for confirmation as one of the most important responsibilities of their ministry. However, even the more conscientious pastor is ready to admit that the completed task frequently fails to give him deep satisfaction. The apparent cause often lies in that other concerns in the parish have forced him to neglect this task. The truth may well be that he might not have permitted himself to be forced into neglecting his catechumens if he had not been uneasy about his responsibilities in the first place. He is frequently haunted by a series of questions that in combination leave him with a sense of frustration. What is he really trying to do with his confirmation class? Does he have a clear picture of his purpose? If the curriculum were improved or if the pastor used some of the newer teaching techniques, would the results be more satisfying? Because of questions like these much time and effort has been expended for the improvement of the curriculum and of teaching methods. While the changes have no doubt brought some temporary relief, most pastors soon realize that improvements of this type do not get at the heart of the problem.

What in fact is the problem in the current practice of confirmation? Is there perhaps a basic problem underlying those usually discussed? Can it be isolated from those problems stemming from it? If there is a basic problem, it should be found in the meaning and purpose of confirmation itself. What constitutes the practice of confirmation as it comes to us from preceding generations? What are the theological presuppositions on which our confirmation practice rests? Are we certain of the answers to these questions, at least to some of the more important ones? If not, then we have isolated the problem. If an examination shows that we are not certain what the function of confirmation is and what the goals should be, it should be evident that we cannot begin to solve the secondary but nonetheless important problems related to the curriculum and to teaching methods, to mention only two. This study therefore proposes to make a historical and theological approach to the reconstruction of confirmation for our day. In this approach we will examine the relation of confirmation to the means of grace, the Gospel and the sacraments, and from this relation determine what the function and goal of confirmation should be. The historical examination will further seek answers to important related questions. What has been the development of confirmation during the long history of the Christian church? Has confirmation uniformly served the same purpose in the Lutheran Church? Are all the emphases and constituent parts as presently observed in harmony with the basic tenets of Lutheran theology? How much of our practice is hallowed by tradition rather than by the Holy Scriptures?

One European theologian has observed: "Confirmation is one of the strongest if not the strongest component of the church's customs. At the same time confirmation is most seriously burdened by the danger and the reality of being untruthful."[1] What is "untruthful" in our practice? Is the church untruthful when it requires a vow? Is it untruthful when it speaks of a renewal of the baptismal covenant? an acceptance into membership in the Lutheran Church or in a congregation? or when it practices the laying on of hands? Do pastors unwittingly preach some of this untruth in their sermons or reflect it in their Sunday bulletins and periodicals? Do Lutherans witness untruthfully in

---

[1] Martin Schmidt, "Konfirmation im Lichte von Schrift, Bekenntnis und Geschichte der Kirche," *Evangelisch-Lutherische Kirchenzeitung*, XIII (April 15, 1959), 125.

their hymns on the day of confirmation? Even the man who is not interested in the history of confirmation, perhaps because he prefers to be rootless and regards tradition as unimportant when discussing practical problems of the parish, needs to know whether his proposed reforms or curricular changes are theologically sound and Lutheran in practice. The historical and theological approach to confirmation will soon isolate the basic problem facing the Lutheran Church and will help it find many of the answers it seeks in reconstructing confirmation for present-day conditions.

CHAPTER I

CONFIRMATION IN

THE CHURCH OF THE REFORMATION

Confirmation Before the Reformation

L utheran confirmation is not a continuation of confirmation as practiced in the early church, nor as it is found later in the Greek Orthodox and Roman Catholic churches. The Lutheran tradition has only the name "confirmation" in common with these churches. In the early church, confirmation was a part of the rite of Baptism.[1] After the candidates were baptized on Easter Eve, they were "confirmed" with chrism, prayers, the sign of the cross, and the laying on of hands, and on Easter morning they were permitted to make their first Communion.[2] Candidates who for one reason or another could not be initiated at this time were given a second opportunity on Pentecost Eve. A remnant of this early practice of confirmation has survived in liturgical form in the Lutheran Church through Martin Luther's *Taufbüchlein* (1526). It is found in the prayer offered immediately after the Sacrament of Baptism has been administered.[3] We know it as the postbaptismal prayer, which reads in part: "Almighty God, the Father of our Lord Jesus Christ, who hath begotten thee again of water and of the Spirit and hath forgiven thee all thy

[1] The question of a confirmation in the apostolic age is discussed at length by G[eoffrey] W[illiam] H[ugo] Lampe, *The Seal of the Spirit* (London: Longmans, Green and Co., 1951), pp. 64—94.

[2] One of the earliest orders is found in Hippolytus' *Traditio apostolica* (ca. 220); so also in Tertullian's *De Baptismo*. For a discerning treatment of the subject compare Lampe, pp. 128—142.

[3] The original ed. (1523) contained the words "anoint thee with the salutary ointment unto eternal life." This was changed in the 1526 ed. WA 12, 46; 19, 541; SL, X, 2143, 2147.

13

sins, strengthen [confirm] thee with His grace unto life everlasting. Amen."

With the growth of the Christian church and especially with the increased number of infant baptisms, bishops began to delegate their authority to parish priests, permitting them to baptize at any time. In the Eastern churches priests were permitted also to confirm, provided they used chrism which had been blessed by the bishop. In the Western churches, however, Rome forbade the administration of confirmation except by the bishop. Where the Roman liturgy came into use, Baptism and confirmation became distinct and separate rites.[4] Because of this separation the idea gradually emerged during medieval times that confirmation was a complement to Baptism. At first the rite was greatly to be desired because it gave the Christian the added gift of the Holy Spirit, but later it was deemed necessary for salvation. To summarize broadly, one may say that in the Western churches Baptism was intended for the forgiveness of sins and confirmation for the bestowal of the Holy Spirit, though many Roman theologians believed that the Spirit was bestowed also in Holy Baptism.

Already in the first half of the 12th century Hugo of St. Victor (d. 1114) referred to confirmation as the second sacrament. Similar thoughts were expressed by Alexander of Hales (d. ca. 1245), William of Auxere (d. 1230), Bonaventura (1221–74), Aquinas (ca. 1224–74), and other medieval teachers.[5] There-

---

[4] Baptism and confirmation were performed together far into the early middle ages, although Faustus of Riez (d. end of 5th century) employed the term "confirmation," which had first emerged in the first Council of Orange (441), in the sense of confirming the baptismal grace. Wilhelm Maurer, "Geschichte von Firmung und Konfirmation bis zum Ausgang der lutherischen Orthodoxie," in *Confirmatio: Forschungen zur Geschichte und Praxis der Konfirmation,* ed. Kurt Frör (Munich: Evang[elischer] Presseverband für Bayern, 1959), p. 11. Hereafter this essay by Maurer is referred to as *Geschichte.*

[5] Kilian F. Lynch, *Texts.* Vol. I in *The Sacrament of Confirmation in the Early-Middle Scholastic Period,* Franciscan Institute Publications, Theology Series, No. 5, ed. Eligius M. Buytaert, O. F. M. (St. Bonaventure, N. Y.: The Franciscan Institute, 1957). The Decretals of Gratian (ca. 1150) cite the Pseudo-Isodorian Decretals (ca. 847—52) to show that confirmation at that time was not so much a strengthening of Baptism as a strengthening of the individual for the battle of life. Rhabanus Maurus (d. 856) took over this militant motif from Pseudo-Isodore. Maurer, *Geschichte,* p. 13.

fore when in November 1439 the Council of Florence designated confirmation a sacrament through the papal decree *Pro Armenis* of Eugene IV, the doctrine had already been generally accepted.[6]

Confirmation now became a part of the Roman sacramental system and was said to bestow grace and a "certain spiritual and indelible sign" necessary for salvation, equal in power to all other sacraments. Confirmation was regarded as a complement to Baptism and was accompanied by the sacred chrism and the laying on of hands. It could be conferred only by the bishop.[7] Considered an objective rite, it was said to be effective *ex opere operato* and was not necessarily associated with a period of instruction.[8] Later, at the Council of Trent in March 1545, Session VII, the Roman Catholic Church fixed the doctrine while anathematizing the Protestant substitution for confirmation.[9]

Luther and the Confessions

Luther and the Confessions vehemently rejected the Roman concept of confirmation. With his usual vehemence against any teaching which he believed to be contrary to the Scriptures, Luther referred to the sacrament as monkey business *(Affenspiel)*, fanciful deception *(Lügentand)*,[10] and mumbo-jumbo *(Gaukel-*

[6] Joseph Gill, *The Council of Florence* (Cambridge: University Press, 1959), p. 307. The Council of Lyon (1245) reaffirmed the exclusive right of the bishops to confirm. The Council of Florence, for all practical purposes, merely made official what the teachers of the church had long accepted.

[7] In special circumstances priests were granted permission by the pope to confirm, e. g., on the mission field. Maurer, *Geschichte*, p. 11.

[8] The question whether confirmation should precede first Communion has been a knotty one in the Roman Catholic Church. At different periods and places, particularly in Latin American churches, first Communion has preceded confirmation on the premise that the Eucharist is supernatural food, whereas confirmation is supernatural growth. In general the hierarchy has favored the precedence of confirmation, especially since instruction has become a part of preparation for the rite. Leo XIII regarded the right order a matter of importance and stated that confirmation should normally precede first Communion. J. P. Kenny, S. J., "The Age for Confirmation," *Worship*, XXXV (Dec. 1960), 4—15.

[9] The usually cited Scriptural bases for confirmation are Acts 8:4-20; 19:1-7; Heb. 6:1-6. Burkhard Neunheuser, O. S. B., *Taufe und Firmung*, in *Handbuch der Dogmengeschichte*, ed. Michael Schmauss, Josef Geiselmann, and P. Aloys Grillmeier, IV, 2 (Freiburg im Breisgau: Verlag Herder, 1956), 19—23.

[10] *Uom Eelichen Leben* ("Sermon on Married Life"), 1522, in *WA* 10 II, 282; SL X, 606; *LW* 45, 24. It should be stated that earlier, in 1518, Luther

15

werk).[11] He warned that confirmation must be avoided because
it had no Scriptural basis. It lacked both the command and the
promise of our Lord. The reformer's prime concern centered in
the Romanists' denial that the Holy Spirit was given at Holy
Baptism and in their insistence that He was given in confirmation
through the chrism and the laying on of hands.[12] Since confirmation was said to complete Holy Baptism, Luther could not
tolerate it. To him any abridgement of Holy Baptism was
blasphemous.

The Lutheran Confessions followed Luther's lead. The Augsburg Confession rejected the Roman view by implication when
it did not include confirmation in the enumeration of the sacraments. The Apology rejected it directly because it lacked God's
express command and clear promise of grace.[13] Veit Dietrich's
(1506—49) German translation of Philipp Melanchthon's (1497
to 1560) Treatise on the Power and Primacy of the Pope (1537),
inserted one of Luther's invectives, "humbug," in rejecting
this rite.[14]

In spite of Luther's strong judgment against confirmation,
we find him ready to permit a reformed type of confirmation if he were assured that it would not infringe on Holy
Baptism or be regarded a sacrament. In *The Babylonian Captivity of the Church* (1520) he thought it "sufficient to regard
confirmation as a certain churchly rite or sacramental ceremony,
similar to other ceremonies, such as the blessing of water and

spoke of Baptism and confirmation as both being unrepeatable and on the same
level. He cited John Chrysostom, without reproof, who made the imparting
of the Spirit in Baptism dependent on the experience of the laying on of hands.
Divi Pauli apostoli ad Hebreos epistola ("Lectures on Hebrews"), 1517—18, in
WA 57 III, 180; *Luther: Early Theological Works*, trans. and ed. James Atkinson
(Philadelphia: The Westminster Press, 1962), p. 120.

[11] *Wilche person verpoten sind tzu ehlichen ynn der heyligenn schrifft beyde
der freundschafft und Mogschafft, Leuit. 18* ("The Persons Related by Consan-
guinity and Affinity Who Are Forbidden to Marry According to the Scriptures,
Leviticus 18"), 1522, in WA 10 II, 266; SL X, 629; LW 45, 8.

[12] *Zu der frue Christmess Epistell Pauli Tit. iii* ("Sermon for Early Christmas Matins"), Titus 3:4-8, 1522, in WA 10 I 1, 117; SL XII, 143.

[13] XIII 6, in BS, p. 293; BC, p. 212; CT, pp. 308—311.

[14] 73 (German), in BS, p. 493; BC, p. 332 and n. 9; CT, pp. 524, 525.

the like." [15] In a sermon in 1522 he conceded, that he "would permit confirmation as long as it is understood that God knows nothing of it, and has said nothing about it, and that what the bishops claim for it is untrue. They mock our God when they say that it is one of God's sacraments, for it is a purely human contrivance." [16] The following year he said: "Confirmation should not be observed as the bishops desire it. Nevertheless we do not find fault if every pastor examines the faith of the children to see whether it is good and sincere, lays hands on them, and confirms them.[17]

Luther did very little to encourage an evangelical type of confirmation even though he approved Johannes Bugenhagen's Brandenburg Church Order (1540) and later subscribed to the Wittenberg Reformation (1545). While the Brandenburg church prescribed an evangelical type of confirmation, to be discussed more fully later,[18] Luther's approval of the church order was not as wholehearted as one is sometimes led to believe. In a letter to Prince Joachim II of Brandenburg (1505—71), dated Dec. 4, 1539, Luther did approve of the church order in a general way but indicated that he had some misgivings about the Romanizing emphases which he characterized as *Witzelisch*.[19] True, he did not single out confirmation, but in a letter written the following year in response to a pastor who had some misgivings about confirming an adult, Luther advised him to feel free to refuse to confirm if he had conscience scruples. He

[15] *De captivitate Babylonica ecclesiae praeludium,* in WA 6, 50; SL XIX, 91; LW 36, 92. Concerning the laying on of hands Luther said: "Would that there were in the church such a laying on of hands as there was in apostolic times, whether we chose to call it confirmation or healing!" WA 6, 549; SL XIX, 91; LW 36, 91.

[16] *Uom Eelichen Leben* ("Sermon on Married Life"), 1522, in WA 10 II, 282; SL X, 606; LW 45, 24, 25.

[17] *Predigt am Sonntag Lätare Nachmittags* ("Sermon for Laetare Afternoon"), March 15, 1523, in WA 11, 66

[18] See below, p. 45.

[19] Luther wrote from Wittenberg. *WA Br* 8, 622, 623; *Dr. Martin Luthers Briefe, Sendschreiben und Bedenken,* ed. Wilh[elm] Martin de Wette, V (Berlin: G. Reimer, 1828), 233; SL XIX, 1022—1025. *Witzelisch* refers to Georg Witzel (1501—73), who had come under the influence of Luther and Melanchthon but who still had some strong Romanizing views. Witzel later returned to Roman Catholicism.

further expressed the thought that for the time being he would be willing to confirm since the prince had acknowledged that confirmation was not a sacrament.[20] From this it appears that Luther's approval of confirmation as prescribed in the church order was a concession he was ready to make for the time being as long as no compromise was involved.

Both Luther and Bugenhagen subscribed to the Wittenberg Reformation which had been drawn up by Melanchthon. Among other things, this document suggested an evangelical type of confirmation, though somewhat different from the Brandenburg CO, placing greater emphasis on a promise of loyalty. As will be shown later, the Wittenberg Reformation reflected the views of Martin Bucer (1491–1551) that had influenced Melanchthon at the time.[21]

These few references exhaust Luther's views on confirmation. Actually confirmation did not play an important role in his thoughts. His interest took a different tack. He was concerned primarily with catechetical instruction. To understand Luther we must hear what he has to say about Christian instruction. There were a number of reasons for his emphasis. The initial sacrament of Holy Baptism carried with it the obligation for the parents and the sponsors to see to it that the child was instructed, because its faith, generated by the sacrament, needed to be kept alive and nurtured by the Word. "As long as there is no special congregation, this instruction [i. e., the Ten Commandments, the Creed, and the Lord's Prayer] must be given from the pulpit at stated times or daily as may be needed and repeated or read aloud evening and morning in the homes for the children and the servants, if we want to train them as Christians." [22] Thoughtful instruction on the part of the parents would result in better understanding of sermons and of Bible reading.

Perhaps of even greater importance was Luther's emphasis that all Christians, young and old, needed to be instructed so

[20] Luther to Gregor Solinus [Keel, Krele] in Tangermünde, Wittenberg, Sept. 13, 1540, in *WA Br* 9, No. 3534; De Wette, V, 307; SL XXI II, No. 2709.

[21] Seh. I, 1, 211. See below, p. 47.

[22] *Deudsche Messe und Ordnung Gottesdiensts* ("German Mass and Order of Service"), 1526, in *WA* 19, 76; SL X, 230.

that they could partake of the Lord's Supper in a worthy manner. In his Latin Mass, Luther suggested that everyone who desired to commune first be examined and asked to give an account of his faith. He should, in particular, be able to indicate what he believed concerning the Lord's Supper and what he expected to receive from the Sacrament.[23] This same requirement was set forth in the *Instructions to Visitors to Saxony* (1528), which Melanchthon drew up under Luther's direction.[24]

Both catechisms of Luther emphasized the importance of instruction in preparation for the Lord's Supper. "If any refuse to receive your instructions, tell them that they deny Christ and are no Christians. They should not be admitted to the sacrament, be accepted as sponsors in Baptism, or be allowed to participate in any Christian privileges. On the contrary, they should be turned over to the pope and his officials, and even to the devil himself." [25] While this referred to both young and old, specific directions were included for the instruction of children.

Similarly the Large Catechism emphasized the importance of instruction as a duty to be carried out by the father.

> Therefore let every head of a household remember that it is his duty, by God's injunction and command, to teach or have taught to his children the things they ought to know. Since they are baptized and received into the Christian church, they should also enjoy this fellowship of the sacrament so that they may serve us and be useful. For they must all help us to believe, to love, to pray, and to fight the devil.[26]

Luther's emphasis on instruction, especially in preparation for the Lord's Supper, is his major contribution to a new type of confirmation, for now it was to be associated not merely with Holy Baptism, as it had been in the past, but also with the Lord's Supper. The place given private confession and absolution underscored further Luther's concern for proper preparation for

[23] *Formula missae et communionis pro ecclesia Wittembergensis* ("Formula of Mass and Communion for the Church of Wittenberg"), 1523, WA 12, 215; SL X, 2247, 2248.

[24] Rich, I, 91.

[25] SC Preface 11, in *BS*, p. 503; *BC*, p. 339; *CT*, pp. 534, 535.

[26] LC V 87, in *BS*, p. 725; *BC*, pp. 456, 457; *CT*, pp. 772, 773.

the Lord's Supper. The prerequisite instruction for private confession and absolution became a major element in a Lutheran type of confirmation. Luther's emphasis became the first step toward a new form of confirmation without, however, actually establishing the rite. Those who regard instruction as the most important element in confirmation consider Luther the founder or at least a cofounder of a Lutheran confirmation.

Such an appraisal of Luther's contribution can hardly be maintained if the full practice of confirmation is meant. Recent investigations have made it evident that the idea of a catechetical type of instruction culminating in a rite has humanistic roots and stems to a great degree from Desiderius Erasmus (1466 to 1536). In his *Paraphrase of Matthew* (1522) Erasmus proposed that during Lent baptized boys be required to hear catechetical sermons that explained to them their baptismal profession. Thereafter they should be examined to determine how many had properly applied this profession to themselves. Whoever was prepared to assume the duties implied in the baptismal vow was publicly to renew his confession in a solemn ceremony.[27]

The public ceremony suggested by Erasmus was not to imply a repetition of Baptism but to help all realize what Baptism had done and what it should mean. Similar thoughts were expressed by Erasmus in his *Symbolum sive Catechismus* (1533).[28] With this he was not suggesting a reform of the Roman sacrament of confirmation but was proposing an extended rite of Baptism to precede confirmation.[29]

Erasmus' views influenced Bucer, and through Bucer both the Lutheran and the Anglican practices were affected.

[27] Walter Caspari, *Die evangelische Konfirmation, vornämlich in der lutherischen Kirche* (Erlangen, Leipzig: And. Deichert, 1890), p. 20. Wilhelm Maurer, *Gemeindezucht, Gemeindeamt, Konfirmation* (Kassel: Johannes Stauda-Verlag, 1940), pp. 44—50; hereafter referred to as *Gemeindezucht*.

[28] E[rnst] Chr[istian] Achelis, *Lehrbuch der Praktischen Theologie*, II, 3d ed. (Leipzig: J. C. Hinrich'sche Buchhandlung, 1911), 309.

[29] Carl-Gustav Andrén, *Konfirmationen i Sverige under medeltid och reformationstid* (Lund: Berlingska Boktryckeriet, 1957), pp. 202—205, 288; Lukas Vischer, *Die Geschichte der Konfirmation* (St. Gallen: Evangelischer Verlag AG., Zollikon, 1958), pp. 64, 65.

The Developing Types of Confirmation

From the evangelicals' universal rejection of the Roman Catholic confirmation, and their felt need for religious instruction to strengthen the faith created by Holy Baptism and to prepare the Christian for a worthy participation of the Lord's Supper arose a natural situation which in time led to the present rite of confirmation. In some instances it was not a conscious development; for a long time, centuries in some cases, the very name confirmation was an offense to a large section of Lutheranism. In such circumstances the practice arose chiefly out of confession and absolution and preparation for the Lord's Supper. In other cases there was a conscious effort to establish either a new form of confirmation or a substitute for the Roman sacrament. Therefore the gradual development of confirmation in the Lutheran Church followed no uniform pattern. Local conditions, with their varying theological climates, might permit a type of confirmation to appear at once in full bloom as it happened in Hesse in 1539, or the introduction might be delayed as in Hamburg, where confirmation was not publicly observed until 1832, when it finally appeared in a form quite different in structure from any that appeared in the 16th century.

Out of the tangled mass of influences and counterinfluences one may discern no less than six different major types of confirmation within the Lutheran Church. These may be characterized, for want of better terms, as catechetical, hierarchical, sacramental, traditional, pietistic, and rationalistic. The first four made their appearances in the 16th century, while the last two appeared in the 17th and the 18th century. In practice it is difficult to find these types in pure form, except perhaps in the initial stages. In a given instance it is more likely that a particular practice was influenced by more than one tendency. In the latter part of the 19th and particularly in the 20th century it is not unusual to see the impact of at least five of the six types on confirmation as practiced in a particular area, especially in the United States, which has been a melting pot also in this respect.

21

The Catechetical Type

For reasons of chronology and extensiveness of practice we may well begin with the catechetical type of confirmation, which originated largely through the personal influence of Martin Luther, Johann Brenz (1499–1570), and Johannes Bugenhagen (1485–1558). Strictly speaking, this form should be regarded not a type but a prototype of confirmation. Where it was practiced, there was at first no thought of confirmation or an accompanying rite of any type. The catechetical form was most common where Luther's pupils were most influential. Far into the second half of the 16th century most of them questioned whether Lutherans should attempt to maintain confirmation even when it was given a new interpretation and form. They believed quite generally that the old rite should be discarded completely.[30]

The catechetical type arose from the need to prepare Christians for the Lord's Supper. It was not necessarily limited to those contemplating first Communion. Because the average communicant was so poorly instructed, he was to become in effect a catechumen each time he went to Communion. The Goslar CO, 1531, prescribed that persons indicating their intention to partake of the Lord's Supper be examined in the Ten Commandments, the Lord's Prayer, and the words of Holy Baptism and the Lord's Supper. Each was to confess his faith, be questioned as to what he desired to receive in Holy Communion, and be examined in respect to his Christian life.[31]

As time went on, several of the church orders stated that a practice of this type should be instituted as a substitute for confirmation, without necessarily implying that it be called confirmation or be practiced with a rite. So great was the fear of a Romanizing tendency, a majority of the church orders that established the practice avoided the term confirmation. Instead the practice was referred to as catechetical instruction *(Catechismus)*, confessional examination *(Beichtverhör)*, admission to

[30] Martin Doerne, *Neubau der Konfirmation* (Gütersloh: C. Bertelsmann, 1936), p. 18.

[31] Rich, I, 155. Also Hesse CO, 1532, in Rich, I, 164; Brandenburg-Nürnberg CO, 1533, in Rich, I, 203; Bremen CO, 1534, in Rich, I, 244; Prussia Befehl, 1543, in Seh, IV, 59—68; Wittenberg Consistorialordnung, 1542, in Seh, I, 202.

22

the Lord's Supper,[32] profession of Baptism,[33] or some similar name to avoid using the term confirmation. Till the middle of the 18th century one still spoke not so much of confirmation as of *Beichten* or *Communiciren der Kinder*.[34]

The catechetical approach was simple and often without liturgical form. Pastors were expected to preach a short series of catechetical sermons several times a year, often four times, perhaps daily or several times a week.[35] These sermons were intended for the entire congregation and were part of the general educational program for the parish.[36]

In addition to the catechetical sermons, the catechism itself was often read from the pulpit, usually before the Gospel for the day, so that the congregation, especially the children, might become accustomed to the text.[37] It was partly for this reason that Luther urged pastors to "adopt one form, adhere to it, and use it repeatedly year after year" and to "adhere to a fixed and unchanging form and method" in their instruction of the young.[38] Familiarity with the texts was to be cultivated and confusion avoided through pastoral consistency in catechetical instruction.

Congregations were also expected to conduct catechetical instruction for the young people and servants, who were sometimes expected to attend until they were 20 years old or until they married.[39] Frequently older persons, especially the unlearned,

---

[32] Erkki Kansanaho, *Konfirmaatio: Liturgishistoriallinen tutkimus konfirmaatioaktista* (Helsinki: Suomalainen Teologinen Kirjallisuusseura, 1956), p. 284.

[33] Cited from the Denmark *Act. Eccles.*, II, 1086, 1087, by Caspari, p. 101.

[34] Joh[ann] Wilh[elm] Friedrich Höfling, *Das Sakrament der Taufe*, II (Erlangen: Palm'schen Verlagsbuchhandlung, 1848), 353.

[35] Wittenberg CO, 1533, in Rich, I, 220, 221; Synod of Greifswald in Pomerania, 1544, in Jac. Henr. Balthasar, *Erste Sammlung Einiger zur Pommerischen Kirchen-Historie gehörigen Schriften*, Part I (Greifswald: Andreas Bussen, 1723), 25. See also a series of such sermons by Luther in *LW* 51, 133—193.

[36] Emil Hansen, *Geschichte der Konfirmation in Schleswig-Holstein* (Kiel: n. pub., 1911), pp. 10, 11.

[37] Saxony CO, 1580, in Seh, I, 1, 423; Württemberg CO, 1533, in ReuQ, I, 1, 287, 288.

[38] SC Preface 7, 9, in *BS*, pp. 502, 503; *BC*, p. 339; *CT*, pp. 532—535. So also the Württemberg CO, 1533, in ReuQ, I, 1, 287, in reference to Brentz's catechism. The catechism was primarily an oral process. Its association with a book was just beginning to come into use. ReuC, p. 87.

[39] Balthasar, p. 25; ReuQ, I, 2, 1, 258, 259; Höfling, p. 353.

were also admonished to attend *Catechismus*. This type of instruction was the most important means of keeping alive the spiritual life created by Baptism.[40]

Catechetical instruction was also conducted in connection with confession or preparation for the Lord's Supper. The catechization might be made annually,[41] whenever the visitor came to the parish,[42] or at stated intervals during the year.[43]

As schools were established, they assumed an additional important place in the instruction of children in Luther's or Brentz's catechism and the preparation for first Communion.[44]

From these various procedures arose the practice that when a child seemed to have sufficient understanding and to be able to examine himself properly for his first Communion, his pastor declared him ready.[45] The initiative might also be taken by the parents and sponsors, who then presented the child to the pastor or congregation for an examination to determine whether he was indeed ready. Since parents and sponsors were held primarily responsible for the instruction, they were often given the right to initiate this step.[46]

Before the children were actually admitted to the second sacrament, the pastor took several candidates and gave them a brief review, usually lasting several days or a few weeks (*Beichtwochen*). Georg Karg (1512–70) described such a special preparation in the Preface to his catechism, 1564.

> Such an examination and exercise takes place here at Onoltz-bach [in Ansbach] on weekdays for the city children at twelve o'clock, one hour each day, between Easter and Pentecost, and for the village children who belong to this parish, on Sundays

[40] Brandenburg-Nürnberg CO, 1533, in Rich, II, 203; Stadt Braunschweig CO, 1528, in Seh, VI, 1, 362.

[41] Saxony CO, 1580, in Seh, I, 1, 424, 425.

[42] Kansanaho, p. 284.

[43] Similar *Examen* were conducted with bridal couples before marriage. The *Examen* covered their Christian life and the doctrine of matrimony. Hansen, p. 13.

[44] Mansfeld A, 1580, in Seh, I, 2, 233, 234; Lauenburg CO, 1585, in Seh, V, 458.

[45] Württemberg CO, 1533, in ReuQ, I, 1, 287, 288.

[46] Strassburg CO, 1534, in Rich, I, 236; Liegnitz CO, 1535, in Seh, III, 436; Synod of Greifswald, Pomerania, 1551, in Balthasar, p. 74.

and the festivals at one o'clock during the period of Reminiscere and Exaudi. In this way all may receive the Lord's Supper together on Pentecost after each one has made his confession privately on the previous day.[47]

Thereupon the pastor examined the children either privately in his home [48] or in the presence of the congregation.[49] When it was done in the parsonage, the parents and sponsors were usually present.[50]

Obviously such a casual procedure could take place several times a year,[51] though in time it was limited to specific seasons of the church year.[52] The Saxon CO of 1580 prescribed a catechetical type of instruction without any liturgical form. The date for the church order is significant. It was the same year in which the Book of Concord was accepted and, as Weissgerber points out, showed the effect of the crypto-Calvinistic controversy on the one hand and the beginning of the early orthodox influence on the other.[53]

The emphasis throughout the Saxon CO was on the pedagogical or catechetical. It required pastors annually to preach catechetical sermons. It prescribed that Luther's catechism be used exclusively both in the schools and in the churches. The catechism was to be read without explanation every Sunday in the villages so that all might learn to know it well. The church

---

[47] ReuQ, I, 1, 580.

[48] Strassburg CO, 1534, in Rich, I, 236. This practice continued for some time in many areas. Johann Fr. Bachmann, *Die Confirmation der Catechumenen in der evangelischen Kirche* (Berlin: Wilhelm Schultze, 1852), pp. 63, 72, 73.

[49] Liegnitz CO, 1535, in Seh, III, 436.

[50] Schwäbisch-Hall CO, 1615, in Graff, I, 314.

[51] [Hieronymous] Mencel's [1517—90] *Zirkularschreiben,* Mansfeld, 1571, in ReuQ, I, 2, 1, 258.

[52] Reussischen Herrschaften Burggräfliche CO, 1552, in Seh, I, 2, 156; Sächsische Generalartikel, 1557, in Rich, II, 185. The Pfalz-Neuburg CO, 1543, prescribed that about a week before Easter, Pentecost, and Christmas notice should be given of persons who wish to partake of the Lord's Supper for the first time on the coming feast day. They should be presented on the eve of the holiday and publicly examined at vespers. If they are sufficiently prepared, a common prayer should be offered in their behalf that they grow in faith and doctrine and continue therein to the end. Then the Lord's Prayer should be prayed, after which they may go to the Lord's Supper. Rich, II, 27.

[53] Hans H. Weissgerber, "Zur Geschichte der Konfirmation im 16. Jahrhundert," *Evangelisch-Lutherische Kirchenzeitung,* IX (May 15, 1955), 160.

order further authorized catechetical instruction for young people and servants. The parents and masters were urged to send them to the instruction and were asked to review carefully with them what they had learned and further to instruct them.[54]

Concerning those who had not yet partaken of the Lord's Supper the church order closed the section on the catechism with the requirement:

> Fifth, the pastors are diligently to examine in the catechism especially those who are going to the blessed Sacrament of the body and blood of Christ for the first time, to determine whether they have learned the catechism and to inform themselves whether they are in the position to partake of Communion.

Nothing is said as to where the examination was to take place and whether the congregation was to be present.[55]

The Saxon CO had a special section in which it described in detail the annual catechization to be held during Lent. The annual catechization was called "the genuine Christian confirmation," that is, the confirmation of the faith in which the Christian had been baptized. In place of this "the papists had substituted a superstitious spectacle which should be avoided and shunned by all pious Christians." [56] It must be noted that the confirmation here referred to in the Saxon CO is not the concluding act which admitted a child to his first Communion but the annual catechization which was intended for all communicants.

The catechetical type of confirming without a closing ceremony was the normal practice in all Scandinavian countries for a long time. The church order of Denmark formulated under Bugenhagen's direction became law in 1539, two years after he had been called to that country to establish the Reformation. This church order combined the examination of children and other communicants without a rite.[57] In Sweden the question of

---

[54] Seh, I, 1, 423, 424.

[55] Seh, I, 1, 423, 424.

[56] Seh, I, 1, 425.

[57] E[dmund] Belfour, "The History of the Liturgy in the Lutheran Church in Denmark." *Memoirs of the Lutheran Liturgical Association,* II (Pittsburgh: Lutheran Liturgical Association, 1906), 68, 69.

confirmation was not debated till 1528, and the Roman form continued for a short time. In 1529 at the Council of Örebro the anointing with chrism was given a Lutheran interpretation. By 1535 there were no longer any indications that confirmation in any form still took place.[58] The church order of 1571 gave directions for the instruction of children but recognized no particular type of confirmation.[59] For a short time the *Nova ordinantia,* 1575, reintroduced a traditional form of confirmation. When this was canceled in 1593, the last trace of a liturgical rite for confirmation vanished for more than a century.[60] A purely catechetical type of examination was introduced similar to the one described above. This procedure was called "the admission to the Lord's Supper." As orthodoxy became stronger, the catechetical forms also grew in strength.[61]

In this stage of the development of the catechetical type, three important elements were present: the instruction, the examination to determine the understanding of the catechumen (also regarded as a profession of faith), and the prayers of the congregation. After the candidates were accepted for Holy Communion, it was understood that they would continue to attend the *Kinderbericht* or the *Catechismus* even though they were regarded as "confirmed Christians."[62]

It is important to remember that the catechetical type of preparation for first Communion was the method most widely employed in the Lutheran Church during the 16th and the greater part of the 17th century. It was the normal practice and usually without a closing ceremony, especially among the Gnesio-Lutherans in Germany and in the Scandinavian countries. Where church orders with a decided catechetical pattern had a confirmation ceremony, the orders were drawn up later, and all showed a marked influence from other types of confirmation

58 Andrén, p. 290.
59 Kansanaho, p. 284.
60 Andrén, p. 291.
61 Kansanaho, p. 284.
62 Reussischen Herrschaften Burggräfliche CO, 1552, in Seh, I, 2, 156.

by way of the Hessian church orders.[63] In time the catechetical form was fused with Chemnitz' views, which gave a stronger emphasis to the confession of a personal faith. Other influences affected it also, especially after Pietism became widespread. But the churches espousing the catechetical pattern during the first two centuries of Lutheranism were reluctant to develop the private examination into a formal religious rite in which a group of children was publicly presented to the congregation in festive manner. However, the catechetical type may nevertheless be regarded as the historic bridge to a distinctively Lutheran confirmation even though it was not an independent act intended to replace the Roman confirmation.[64]

Reluctance to introduce a public ceremony persisted in some parts of Germany, especially in several larger cities, till the beginning of the 19th century. Among those holding off till a very late date were Leipzig, 1803; Regensburg, 1803; Russia (the Lutheran Church), 1805; Gera, 1806; Dresden, 1812; Frankfurt on the Main, 1813, only when conducted on a weekday; Nürnberg and Augsburg, 1813; Lübeck, 1817; and Hamburg, 1832. In a number of these places, private confirmation was permitted at a somewhat earlier date.[65]

The Hierarchical Type

Those who trace confirmation back to Luther through the catechetical pattern do so either by hindsight or by regarding the instruction as confirmation itself, the rite then becoming a sort of unessential appendage. But if the rite is given the importance that it presently has in the Lutheran Church, at least in the popular mind, then it is more accurate to trace confirmation to the Hessian church, where it was first introduced

[63] Wilhelm Diehl considers the Pomeranian CO, 1569, the only exception. *Zur Geschichte der Konfirmation: Beiträge aus der hessischen Kirchengeschichte* (Giessen: J. Ricker, 1897), p. 51. However, this church order may be classified better as traditional than as catechetical; see below, p. 50. As examples of church orders influenced by the Hesse CO see Mansfeld A, 1580, in Seh, I, 2, 233, 234; Lauenburg CO, 1585, in Seh, V, 458—460. The latter church order still served as a pattern in the 16th century as far away as Iceland. Maurer, *Geschichte*, p. 36.

[64] Doerne, p. 19.

[65] R-G, II, 642, 643.

by Martin Bucer in 1538. The form in which it appeared in Hesse may be described as hierarchical or disciplinary because of two elements which were found in the rite but were lacking in the catechetical form even when a public ceremony of some kind was observed. Both elements were disciplinary in nature: a surrender to Christ in the form of a confession of faith and a vow of obedience to the church.[66] The Hessian ceremony also had certain sacramental overtones which contributed to the development of still another form of confirmation.

Bucer had served at Strassburg before Philip (1504—67) called him to Hesse. While at Strassburg, Bucer had been seriously vexed by the Anabaptists and the followers of Kaspar Schwenkfeld because they had an entirely different concept of a Christian congregation. Instead of recognizing that sin and grace live side by side in the Christian community, they operated with principles that attempted to create a pure church by eliminating all those who did not measure up to their standards of purity.[67]

The Anabaptists vehemently opposed the doctrine of infant baptism and accused Bucer, among other things, of encouraging moral laxity with this teaching. They maintained that little children were not capable of giving a promise of purity and obedience and that later as adults they were inclined to rely on their baptism without feeling an obligation to live the Christian life. Bucer fought their criticism of infant baptism on Scriptural grounds, but he also recognized that the impact which the Anabaptists made indicated that they were meeting some real need. Consequently he himself looked for means to meet the same need.[68] He countered Anabaptist arguments by showing

66 Rich, I, 290—295.

67 Strassburg was known as a city of "religious vitality, variety, and toleration" even before the Reformation. As early as 1518, dissenters against Romanism found Strassburg a friendly city. After 1529, when the Mass was abolished, many radical reformers, especially Anabaptists of various persuasions, were drawn to the city. From their leaders Bucer experienced much opposition particularly on Baptism. George Huntston Williams, *The Radical Reformation* (Philadelphia: The Westminster Press, 1962), Ch. x.

68 Hastings Eells, *Martin Bucer* (New Haven, Conn.: Yale University Press, 1931), p. 155. At the Marburg Anabaptist disputation of 1538, Bucer's oppo-

that he, too, was concerned about church discipline, for as he said, "Where there is no discipline and no ban, there is no congregation." [69] Since the Anabaptists maintained that vows should not be exacted from persons till they had reached the age of discretion and had been instructed, Bucer devised a plan by which children, who had been baptized in infancy and for whom a promise of loyalty had been given by sponsors, were required to take a vow of loyalty to Christ after they had reached the age of discretion. Such a vow was to follow a period of careful instruction. The result was a form of confirmation planned as a polemical device.

The plan was not wholly original. Bucer had undoubtedly gotten some of his ideas from the Anabaptists at Strassburg and from the Bohemian Brethren. The latter had an initiation rite for those who had previously been instructed and examined in private. The rite included a confession of faith and a vow of loyalty, followed by the laying on of hands and a prayer that God would give the necessary strength to maintain such loyalty.[70] While the right to attend Holy Communion was not mentioned in the ceremony, it may well be assumed, since all members of the brotherhood partook of the Lord's Supper.[71]

Bucer's views were set forth in *Ad monasterienses*, 1534, in which he urged that confirmation be revived according to the ancient custom whereby "bishops laid their hands on the baptized and thereby gave them the Holy Spirit according to the example of the apostle in Samaria, Acts 8." [72]

There is no conclusive evidence that Bucer suceeded in

nents — George Schnabel, Leonard Fälber, Herman Bastian, and Peter Lose — stressed the need for instruction as well as explicit faith before Baptism. In response, Bucer acknowledged the need for formal religious instruction and for having the implicit baptismal vow of infancy made explicit in a ceremony of confirmation. Williams, p. 449.

[69] Gustav Anrich, *Martin Bucer* (Strassburg: Karl J. Truebner, 1914), p. 77.

[70] Achelis, p. 308. Franklin H. Littell believes the original suggestion came from Schwenkfeld during the Strassburg debates of 1533. *The Anabaptist View of the Church*, 2d ed., rev. (Boston: Stan King Press, 1958), p. 36.

[71] Caspari, pp. 21, 22.

[72] Achelis, p. 315.

having his plan adopted while he was pastor in Strassburg. Soon after he was called to Hesse in 1538, however, he was able to put his ideas into effect with the Ziegenhain Order of Church Discipline (adopted in 1538 and published in 1539).[73] Since the Anabaptists were creating serious disturbances in Hesse, Philip invited Bucer to come to his territory. Bucer's previous success in Strassburg gave the landgrave a measure of assurance that some semblance of order might again be achieved. Bucer accepted Philip's invitation, and a synod was called at Ziegenhain soon after Bucer's arrival. There an order of church discipline was drawn up with the hope that it would help the Hessian congregations. The Ziegenhain Order of Church Discipline, as the order was called, was designed to regulate the whole life of the congregation, especially its sacramental life. Through a detailed program of church discipline, Bucer believed he could meet the major criticism of the Anabaptists.

Within this purpose the order authorized the first confirmation, in the modern sense, in Lutheran history. According to it the public rite was to be a means whereby baptized children would be received into the *Gottesdienstgemeinde*, that is, the congregation assembled to receive the Word and the sacraments. The ceremony for confirmation as authorized in the order read:

[73] Whether Strassburg had a confirmation before Hesse is a moot question. The Strassburg synods of 1533 and 1539 do not refer to confirmation. The official church orders make no mention of such a rite. Nor do Bucer's catechisms of 1534, 1537, and 1539 refer to the practice. ReuQ, I, 1, 23—90. In 1548 Bucer said that he had proposed a form for confirmation some 28 years earlier in Strassburg, but there is no evidence that his proposal was accepted. That anyone in Strassburg practiced confirmation soon after Bucer established the practice in Hesse is also in doubt. A revision of Bucer's earlier catechisms, published in Strassburg in 1543 and 1544 but used also elsewhere, has a reference to a *Bestetigung in den Christlichen Glauben* which may be identified with confirmation, but this is little evidence that the practice was adopted. ReuQ, I, 1, 93, 94. In fact, Strassburg does not seem to have had a confirmation till perhaps the end of the 18th century, except around 1550 in St. Nikolaus Church under Superintendent Marbach. Even then the other pastors of the city did not follow Marbach's lead. Some of them preached against confirmation as *ein halbes Papstum*. See also various views expressed by Achelis, p. 315; Caspari, pp. 16, 17; August Ernst and Johann Adam, *Katechetische Geschichte des Elsasses bis zur Revolution* (Strassburg: Fr. Bull, 1897), pp. 63, 64, 194, 195; Diehl, pp. 10—13; Wilhelm Rott, *Konfirmation: Ein Studienbuch zur Frage ihrer rechten Gestaltung* (Berlin: Burckhardthaus-Verlag, 1941), pp. 27—32.

31

Such children who through catechetical instruction *(Catechismos)* are sufficiently advanced in Christian knowledge to be permitted to go to the Lord's Table shall on a high festival such as Christmas, Easter, and Pentecost, at the instance of the elders and preachers, be presented by their parents and sponsors to the pastors in the presence of the congregation in a place designated in the churches for that purpose. The elders and all other ministers of the Word shall stand about the pastor, who shall then examine these children in the chief articles of the Christian faith. When they have answered the questions and publicly surrendered themselves to Christ the Lord and His churches, the pastor shall admonish the congregation to ask the Lord, in behalf of the children, for perseverance and an increase of the Holy Spirit, and conclude this prayer with a collect.

Finally the pastor shall lay his hands upon the children, thus confirming them in the name of the Lord, and establish *(bestetigen)* them in Christian fellowship. He shall thereupon also admit them to the Table of the Lord, adding the admonition that they continue faithfully in the obedience of the Gospel and readily receive and faithfully heed Christian discipline and reproof from each and every Christian, especially from the pastors.[74]

This authorization of a confirmation rite is of interest for a number of reasons. Here Bucer was influenced also by Erasmus in establishing a confirmation rite. But he did not limit himself, as did Erasmus, to a rite in which the youths themselves made a confession of the faith which their sponsors had made for them; under Luther's influence he associated the rite also with first Communion. This is the first formal association of the rite of confirmation with the Lord's Supper. Together with the privilege of partaking of the Lord's Supper, the confirmands voluntarily surrendered themselves to the discipline of the churches.[75] Such a "surrender" appeared to be an initial act and went beyond that which was implied in the daily repentance and forgiveness growing out of Baptism. The discipline was given a special place of importance and left room for more than the

[74] Rich, I, 291.

[75] The voluntary element of the rite was lost when confirmation later became obligatory in Hesse by its association with the state schools.

normal church discipline. The vow of obedience to the churches implied a submission also in matters not governed by the Word, i. e., a discipline imposed by the pastor and the elders of the congregation.

Philip hesitated to introduce some of the ideas embodied in the order, especially the parts relating to the ban.[76] The section on confirmation is nevertheless of great importance because many church orders were later based on it. In fact, the main ideas of the Ziegenhain order were used and formulated experimentally by the pastors of Cassel in the 1539 CO [77] and therein prescribed the first rite for confirmation as it is known today.

The rubrics of the Cassel CO required every catechumen to be examined publicly by the pastor in the presence of the elders, after which the catechumen was to answer certain prescribed questions pertaining to the Christian articles of faith. He was also required to promise to remain in the fellowship of the church. Concerning this fellowship the following question and answer are of special interest:

> What does such fellowship of the church of Christ imply?
>
> That I practice strict obedience to the Word of God by hearing it at the appointed times, particularly on Sundays when proclaimed by the ordained ministers of the church; also by submitting with due humility to the reproof for sin on my part when administered by the elders or any other Christian and by making proper amends. Moreover, that I instruct and restore my fellow Christian whom I may find in some sinful conduct or inform some other good Christians of the matter, who in my judgment are able to help those in error. Should these in error refuse to hear the church in the person of these pastors and elders, and are put in the ban in consequence, I will likewise treat them as excommunicated or heathen people.

In addition to the promise to remain in this fellowship, the catechumen promised to use the means of grace and live a Chris-

---

[76] Luther was pleased with the "Hessian ban" and in a letter of April 2, 1543, recommended to Anton Lauterbach (d. 1560) in Pirna that, if possible, he too establish it. *WA Br* 10, No. 3861; SL XXI II, No. 3004.

[77] Diehl, pp. 8, 9.

tian life.[78] When Bucer revised his *Short Catechism* in 1543, he inserted a section on confirmation called "The Reaffirmation of the Christian Faith" *(Die Bestedigung)*. Here Bucer referred to the promise as a vow and illustrated all the more the prominent place church discipline was to have in confirmation and the somewhat subordinate place assigned to the Lord's Supper.[79]

It cannot be determined to what extent the Ziegenhain Order of Discipline was used in Hesse outside of Cassel before the introduction of the Hessian CO of 1566. Perhaps there was very little use since Philip hesitated to enforce it. Nevertheless, complaints were heard that some pastors were most eager to introduce church discipline as suggested by Bucer, so that many little popes were created.[80]

The Hessian CO of 1566 included a section on confirmation which for the first time authorized the rite for all of Hesse. This order leaned heavily on the Cassel CO and was similarly intended to "stop the mouths" of the Anabaptists.[81]

The Hessian order contained both a longer and shorter form for confirmation. The shorter is the more important because it was included with minor changes in the order of 1574 and remained a part of the Hessian church orders for more than 200 years. The longer form found favor in the Austrian A of 1571, and a few parts found their way into a number of other orders.[82] Both forms contained a public examination, an important part of the Hessian confirmation ceremony. The examination contained a series of prescribed questions on Luther's Small Catechism without explanation, interspersed with questions pertaining to the Christian fellowship. The examination was regarded a public confession of faith. It put into effect the confession made by the sponsors in behalf of the child at the time of Baptism. The catechumen was now publicly confessing the faith for himself.[83]

[78] Rich, I, 303, 304.
[79] ReuQ, I, 1, 93, 94.
[80] Diehl, p. 30.
[81] ReuQ, I, 1, 2, 430.
[82] Diehl, pp. 37, 48—51.
[83] ReuQ, I, 2, 1, 428.

The shorter form of confirmation concluded with two questions. The first asked the catechumen whether his answers in the examination were a confession of his faith. The second asked whether he promised to submit himself to the discipline of the church. The questions were followed by the laying on of hands.[84]

The disciplinary element so prominent in the Cassel order was deemphasized somewhat in the Hessian CO of 1566, and the instructional element, with its appeal to the understanding rather than to the will, was given greater prominence. Thus some of the more wholesome effects of Bucer, who associated confirmation with confession and absolution, were weakened while the more humanistic emphases of Erasmus were strengthened.[85]

The Hessian CO of 1574, which was slightly revised, contained additional details of interest. It directed the pastor to announce to his congregation about three or four weeks before one of the three high festivals that those children who had been sufficiently instructed and who wished to partake of their first Communion should be presented by their parents to the pastors for intensive instruction. About two or three days before confirmation the children were examined in the presence of the elders, parents, and sponsors by the catechist who had instructed them. Those who were unprepared were dismissed and kindly asked to wait till a future festival. The rest were instructed on the meaning of confirmation and how they were to answer in the presence of the congregation. They were admonished to remember the day of their confirmation, especially the "solemn oath" then made. On confirmation day the children were publicly catechized as indicated above. One of the more adept children answered for all and at the end each child was asked to give his personal assent to what had been answered.

One of the many church orders influenced by the Hessian church orders was that of Waldeck, 1556. In it some of the ideas latent in the Cassel CO came clearly to the fore. As in

[84] Ibid., I, 2, 2, 1083.
[85] Maurer, *Gemeindezucht*, p. 100.

the latter order, the catechumen was required to surrender himself to the obedience of Christ and "His holy church," in a measure identifying the local congregation with the church.[86]

The public rite which was formulated and attached to the catechetical instruction by the Cassel CO influenced all public rites in the Lutheran Church after 1539, except that of Pomerania, 1563, even in those Lutheran provinces or countries which were otherwise orthodox. The modifications which from time to time affected the confirmation ceremony over the centuries, even radically in some areas, did not change the basic liturgical structure of the Cassel CO. Bucer has therefore rightly been called the father of Lutheran confirmation. It should again be emphasized that with his ceremony Bucer added two elements which had not been present in the catechetical approach: a surrender to Christ in the form of a confession of faith and a submission to the discipline of the church, both elements firmed up with a vow. While Holy Baptism and the admission to the Lord's Supper together had an important place, church discipline was really the focal point in Bucer's approach to confirmation. From his point of view, such an emphasis was needed because of his intention to use confirmation as a polemical device against the Anabaptists. Yet it would be an injustice to Bucer not to remind that his basic interest grew out of a deep pastoral concern for the catechumens. The intercession of the congregation in behalf of the confirmands served to point up for them that they were wholly dependent on the grace of God throughout life.

Church discipline can, of course, be defended on theological grounds. But by giving it such a prominent place in confirmation, as viewed in the light of subsequent history and the intended polemical purpose, Bucer gave confirmation an emphasis more congenial to Zwinglian than to Lutheran theology. Thereby Bucer, perhaps unwittingly, introduced a foreign element into preparation for first Communion.[87]

[86] Rich, II, 174.

[87] Hans H. Weissgerber takes issues with Mahrenholz, who in *Begleitwort zur Ordnung der Konfirmation* (Berlin: Lutherisches Verlagshaus, 1952), p. 157, gives the impression that the Hessian type of confirmation introduced a foreign tendency. Weissgerber argues that since this type is the oldest rite, those who

In the succeeding section it will be pointed out that Bucer's form for confirmation had not only hierarchical overtones but sacramental implications as well.

The Sacramental Type

A third type of confirmation to appear in the 16th century may be termed sacramental. In this form certain sacramental accents were retained in reflection of Roman Catholic tradition. One of these was the implication that the Holy Spirit was given in the laying on of hands or that this act was needed to complete Holy Baptism. A second stress was that confirmation conferred a new or fuller membership not previously given in Baptism.

The sacramental type was not formulated independently but was attached to an existing rite. The earliest appearance of this set was in the confirmation rite established by Bucer in Hesse. Already there the interpretation of the laying on of hands reflected a sacramental leaning. While the Ziegenhain Order of Discipline had spoken of a laying on of hands in a general way, the Cassel CO, 1539, which was based on it, became more explicit in its description of the practice. Because of the tremendous influence of the Cassel CO in Lutheranism, it is important to consider it somewhat carefully also in this respect. The order spoke of three sacramental ceremonies, the first of which was known as "the order of confirmation and the laying on of hands," a name indicating the importance attached to the imposition. It came in prayer form immediately after the vows of surrender to Christ and of obedience to the discipline of the church. The prayer closed with these words:

> Grant unto them also, as we now in Thy name lay our hands on them and therewith assure them of Thy gracious hand and of Thy Holy Spirit, the Spirit of all strength and help for a proper Christian life, that they may not despair; that Thou wilt continue to uphold them with Thy divine hand, protect

differ are actually the ones introducing new elements. Doerne, p. 35, believes that a confirmation designed for disciplinary purposes is not genuinely Lutheran. He takes the position not so much for theological as for historical reasons. Since the disciplinary element became a focal point, it may also be regarded a foreign element theologically.

them against all harm, direct and guide them to all good, nor ever take Thy Holy Spirit from them . . .[88]

The accompanying rubric states that the pastor shall lay his hands on the child and say, "Receive ye the Holy Spirit, Refuge and Protector against all harm, Strength and Help for all good, from the hand of God the Father, Son, and Holy Spirit." [89]

This formula has been the center of much controversy. Bucer is blamed not only for having burdened the church with a foreign element by his overemphasis on church discipline in confirmation but also for introducing here a sacramental element.[90] The case against Bucer is not as clear as one might at first believe. The mere fact that the church order calls the laying on of hands a sacramental ceremony is not conclusive when one interprets the expression sacramental ceremony as it was meant in Bucer's day. In *The Babylonian Captivity of the Church,* Luther carefully distinguished between sacramental ceremonies, such as confirmation and the blessing of holy water, and the sacraments of faith.[91]

The prayer's reference to the laying on of hands is more striking. The "therewith" seems to imply that the laying on of hands is the means by which the Holy Spirit is bestowed on the child. This the formula also clearly seems to indicate. To argue, as Diehl does, that the formula does not say, "Receive ye *now* . . ." seems to be very weak.[92] However, it is true, that the prayer

[88] With minor changes this portion of the prayer was adopted by Johannes Konrad Wilhelm Löhe, and Johannes Deinzer in the agendas of 1844, 1859, and 1884, but it was omitted in the Iowa A, 1919.

[89] Rich, I, 304.

[90] Doerne, pp. 27, 28.

[91] *De captivitate Babylonica ecclesiae praeludium,* 1520, in WA 6, 549, 550; SL XIX, 91; *LW* 36, 91, 92. See also Ap XIII 12, in *BS,* p. 293; *BC,* p. 212; *CT,* pp. 310, 311. Nevertheless it is a fact that Bucer did refer to the laying on of hands as a sacrament in his Alsatian (Strassburg) catechism of 1534. Here he referred to Jesus' blessing of the children as a sacrament *(mit dem Sacrament des hend vfflegens gesegnet),* adding the thought that Jesus regarded one sacrament the same as the other, whether it was the imposition of hands or Baptism *(so ist doch bey jm ein Sacrament wie das ander, des hend vfflegen als fil als der tauff).* ReuQ, I, 1, 42. This view was modified in his catechism of 1543. ReuQ, I, 1, 93. See below, p. 39.

[92] Diehl, p. 26.

does ask God to grant His Spirit and strengthen the work done in the children. The formula may therefore be interpreted as merely symbolizing what God will do in answer to the prayer. The prayer as such does not bestow the Spirit, who comes only through the Word and the sacraments.

Additional complications arise when it is pointed out that the term "Strength" as used to describe the Holy Spirit seems to be taken directly from the *ad robur* used by the Council of Florence in 1439, where it had definite sacramental implications.[93] However, Diehl questions whether Bucer here borrowed from the Roman Catholics, because it is an expression which he used frequently in various forms.[94]

Bucer's catechism of 1543 explained the purpose of the laying on of hands in confirmation. He admitted that the Lord did not command it, but since Jesus and His disciples did find blessing in its use, it was proper that the church continue to use it in His name. "The Lord would be present also with His Spirit and work, and as the church entreated Him according to His Word, He would richly strengthen such children for His kingdom." [95]

While Bucer maintained that Baptism needed no complement to become valid, his emphasis on imparting the Spirit laid him open to the charge that either the laying on of hands was necessary to make Baptism valid or the Spirit was directly received in the act.[96] Even Diehl admits that the formula could be and was misunderstood, although he does not believe that Bucer shared the sacramental implications.[97]

The Hesse CO of 1566, referred to above,[98] was in part drawn

[93] Graff, I, 316. Maurer, *Geschichte*, p. 11, cites Peter Lombard (d. 1164) as teaching in his *Sentences*, IV, 7, 1—5, that the use of chrism in confirmation completes Baptism. Chrism is said to augment forgiving grace in Baptism through the gift of the Holy Spirit to power *(ad robur)*. Aquinas held a similar view. Maurer, *Geschichte*, p. 16.

[94] Diehl, p. 26. Rott, pp. 35, 36, is not alone in seeing the sacramental emphasis in this expression, though Bucer may not have recognized the implications.

[95] ReuQ, I, 1, 93.

[96] Vischer, p. 66.

[97] Diehl, p. 26.

[98] See above, p. 34.

up by Andreas Hyperius (1511—64).[99] Through Hyperius the Cassel formula was taken over into the Hessian church. In the Hessian order, too, the ambiguity continued. However, the order did state explicitly that the laying on of hands was not a sacrament as were Baptism and the Lord's Supper, nor was it instituted by Christ. The laying on of hands was rather an ancient custom and, quoting Augustine, nothing more than a prayer over people.[100]

That Hyperius' personal views went beyond Bucer may be seen in his *De catechesi* (1570) and *Elementa Christianae Religionis* (1563). In these he explained that in Baptism only the forgiveness of sins was given but that in the laying on of hands the Holy Spirit was imparted for the strengthening of the individual.[101] Through Hyperius' influence the ambiguous formula of the Hesse CO came to be understood sacramentally, as more than a prayer over people (Augustine), and with the sacramental understanding the ambiguous formula spread into many parts of the Lutheran Church, little matter Bucer's original intention.

The formula, "Receive ye the Holy Spirit . . ." was retained in the Hessian A till 1896 (though with some modification, e. g., in 1842), when other formulas were added as alternatives.[102] The Hessian formula was widely used in the Lutheran Church both in Europe and in America.[103] Since some recognized the ambiguity of the formula, it was occasionally rephrased as a prayer, "We pray Thee, strengthen N. with Thy Holy Spirit," continuing with the same general thought but avoiding any sacramental implications.[104]

[99] Achelis, p. 316. Hyperius, the Marburg theologian, is known as the founder of practical theology as a scientific discipline.

[100] ReuQ, I, 2, 1, 428.

[101] Achelis, pp. 316, 317; ReuQ, I, 2, 1, 421; Theo[dor] Kliefoth, *Die Confirmation*, in *Liturgische Abhandlungen*, III, 1 (Schwerin: Stiller'schen Hof-Buchhandlung, 1856), 71; R-G, II, 648. *De catechesi* was published posthumously by Hyperius' pupil Heinrich Vietor. ReuQ, I, 2, 1, 419.

[102] Achelis, p. 316.

[103] For a partial list of European church orders influenced by the Hessian rite see Graff, I, 316.

[104] So the Cologne Reformation, 1543, in Rich, II, 41; Waldeck CO, 1556, in Rich, II, 175. Both otherwise borrowed directly from the Cassel CO.

In the Calenberg-Göttingen CO, 1542,[105] an interesting attempt was made to draw up an order of confirmation which might use some of the important features from both the Brandenburg CO, 1540, and the Cassel CO without adopting any of the questionable emphases. In the order for confirmation it was pointed out that unless the ceremony was preceded by instruction, there was danger that it would revert to the papal *Affenspiel*.[106] There were two important parts in the rite itself: the examination, which was at the same time a confession of faith, and the laying on of hands. The order stated explicitly that the laying on of hands was only an outward ceremony, for the Holy Spirit came only through the Word. In spite of its clear statement at this point, the order was somewhat ambiguous earlier when it cited Jerome, saying that the laying on of hands "has no other meaning than that God wants to give to those persons upon whom the hands are laid eternal help and support through His Spirit, for to extend the hands means the same as help." [107] The Cassel formula was used without any change.[108]

The practice of laying on hands continued to be considered papistic in many areas of the Lutheran Church. Matthias Flacius (1520—75) was vehement in his opposition. Brenz believed that the time was past when it could be employed without offense. Erasmus Sarcerius (1501—59) shared his misgivings and changed the Cassel formula to read: "We pray thee, strengthen this *N.* with Thy Holy Spirit." Hyperius, as already shown, championed the practice as both Scriptural and necessary.[109] Martin Chemnitz (1522—86) believed that the ancient custom should be maintained if it could be done without superstition.[110]

When Chemnitz and Jacob Andreae (1528—90) were asked to draw up a church order for Braunschweig-Wolfenbüttel in

---

[105] Also called the Braunschweig CO.

[106] Seh, VI, 2, 839.

[107] Seh, VI, 2, 839.

[108] Seh, VI, 2, 843.

[109] Sarcerius' *Pastorale* (1559 [1565?]), cited by Caspari, pp. 43—45.

[110] *Examen Concilii Tridentini*, II, 3, 25; ed. Ed[uard] Preuss (Berlin: Gust. Schlawitz, 1861), p. 297 A.

41

1569,[111] Chemnitz used his influence to include a form for a Lutheran confirmation, which ancient custom, he argued, should be revived according to the true apostolic tradition. The rite was to be preceded by instruction for those who desired to make their first Communion. Chemnitz suggested that when the parents have presented a number of eligible children to the pastor, he record their names and notify the superintendent in time for his annual visitation. On the day of the rite the superintendent should briefly review the purpose of confirmation and admonish the congregation about its continued responsibility. The children were to be reminded of their baptismal covenant and asked to confess the faith which had been professed in their behalf at the time of their baptism. Furthermore, they were to promise to continue in this confession till the end of their life. Thereupon the superintendent should admonish the entire congregation that all, not only the parents, must help the children realize the importance of their promises. The rite was to be closed with a prayer and the laying on of hands, where this could be done without offense.[112]

While this order reflects Bucer's influence, it avoids sacramental and hierarchical overtones. The superintendent was to perform the ceremony primarily as a representative of the church making sure that the instruction of the children was not neglected and that the congregation was properly prepared for Communion.

As Maurer points out, Chemnitz also displays a humanistic-Erasmian tradition without minimizing Baptism.[113] Although Chemnitz speaks of remembering the baptismal covenant rather than of renewing the covenant, he speaks of it as one which God made with the catechumens and which they established with God in their baptism. The emphasis on having children make for themselves the profession of faith which was made for them at their baptism further exhibits the Erasmian tradition.[114]

111 Also called Braunschweig and Lüneburg CO or Calenberg CO.

112 Seh, VI, 1, 164—166.

113 *Geschichte*, p. 37.

114 The Braunschweig-Wolfenbüttel CO speaks of "reminding" the children of their baptismal covenant; in his *Examen* Chemnitz speaks of their "perseverance" in the covenant.

While Chemnitz added nothing new, he did work out one of the most detailed confirmation forms of the 16th century. His personal influence helped quiet some of the fears concerning the practice of laying on hands. In his *Examen* Chemnitz further elaborated his views and so continued to exert an influence for several centuries, sometimes almost with confessional authority.[115]

That confirmation confers a kind of church membership not previously held is expressed in the Waldeck CO, 1556. This order declares that while Baptism puts one into fellowship with God, confirmation makes one a member of the fellowship of the church. The order contains such references as being "accepted as a member of the Christian church" (*für eyn Gliedmass der Christlichen Kirchen angenommen*) or the "Christian congregation" (*zur Christlichen Gemeynschafft angenommen werden*).[116] After the vows the pastor says: "I receive you therefore in the name of our Lord Jesus Christ and in the place of the holy Christian church into the fellowship of the grace and glory of God, our heavenly Father, into the fellowship of the blood of Jesus Christ, His beloved Son, and into the fellowship of the Holy Spirit." [117]

Such stress on membership was no doubt intended to give a legal frame of reference permitting the congregation to exercise church discipline. But at the same time the church order further confused membership in the Christian church and the

[115] See Bachmann, p. 47; Hansen, p. 108; Caspari, p. 43.

[116] Rich, II, 174.

[117] Rich, II, 175. This prayer was taken over from Johannes Hefentreger's handwritten agenda of 1534 and does not reflect Bucer's influence. ReuQ, I, 3, 1, 2, 1091. So also Victor Schultze, who was the first to refer to it, in "Ein unbekanntes lutherisches Konfirmationsbekenntnis aus dem Jahre 1529," *Neue Kirchliche Zeitschrift*, XI, (1900), 232—242.

Achelis doubts that Johannes Hefentreger (1497—1542) intended his rite for the confirmation of children and argues that it was for mature persons who had come over from the Roman Catholic Church. Hence the prayer was not originally intended to be used as adopted in the Waldeck CO, 1556. "Bemerkungen zu dem Waldeckschen Konfirmationsbekenntnis aus dem Jahre 1529," *Neue Kirchliche Zeitschrift*, XI (1900), 423—427. Schultze's answer is found in "Ein Nachwort zur waldeckischen Konfirmationsordnung vom Jahre 1529," *Neue Kirchliche Zeitschrift*, XI, (1900), 586—589. See also Maurer, *Gemeindezucht*, pp. 62 ff.

organizational structure of the congregation. The result was some strange ideas concerning the doctrine of the church.

The sacramental type continued to exert an influence in the centuries to follow, particularly in respect to the laying on of hands. Throughout the history of the Lutheran Church there were some who, while rejecting confirmation as a sacrament, believed that the Holy Spirit was imparted through the laying on of hands and insisted that the church therefore maintain it as an important part of the rite. Confusion regarding church membership continued to be felt and increased during the period of Rationalism, when fellowship was stressed to an even greater degree and was identified more closely with the organization of the church. Because of these sacramental emphases the fear of Romanizing tendencies, which some saw reflected here, kept parts of the Lutheran Church from accepting confirmation in any form for a long time.

The Traditional Type

It was natural that within the conservative genus of Lutheranism there were those who sought to preserve the old order as much as possible. Some within this conservative element felt that a Lutheran type of confirmation could be developed — one that retained as many traditional features as possible without denying any confessional principles. While many others doubted that this was possible and preferred to drop confirmation altogether, the more conservative element persisted in efforts to fashion a substitute of some kind or, to use a favorite expression, to develop a Lutheran confirmation "according to tradition" *(nach dem alten brauch)*. Attempts to develop a traditional type failed to produce a uniform pattern except in one respect, in that confirmation was not directly associated with first Communion. As in the Roman rite, the traditional type of confirmation was associated only with Holy Baptism, though in some cases confirmation might be a prerequisite for later participation in the Lord's Supper.

The traditional type of confirmation was first exemplified in the duchy of Liegnitz in 1535, where the church order set forth the following article under the section on Holy Baptism:

VII. When children have matured in age and grace, they shall again be presented by the parents and sponsors to the ministers in the presence of the congregation that they may make a public confession of their faith. This is to take the place of confirmation.[118]

This is the earliest date for a ceremony of any type in Lutheran territory. The ceremony was obviously somewhat informal and in this respect was similar to a later development in the catechetical form. However, it differed in this that the Liegnitz "confirmation" was not associated with the Lord's Supper. In fact, the church order's next section, on the Lord's Supper, makes it clear that the "confirmed" were still required to receive instruction before they partook of the Lord's Supper (Article I) and were to give an account of their faith (Article IV).[119]

An outstanding example of the traditional type is found in the very conservative Brandenburg CO, 1540, drawn up by Bugenhagen and approved by Luther.[120] While much in the order was dependent on the Brandenburg-Nürnberg CO of 1533, the 1540 order struck out on its own path by authorizing a confirmation "which they wished to have observed according to tradition." The Brandenburg CO retained the name confirmation, spoke of the old ceremonies, especially the laying on of hands, and reserved the performance of the ceremony, including the examination, as the right of the bishop or his substitute. This confirmation was intended for baptized children who had reached

[118] Liegnitz CO, 1535, in Seh, III, 436, 437. R-G, II, 632, and Rich, I, 239, date the order 1534, but Sehling gives 1535. Some early MSS give the year 1542, which Seh, III, 419, says is the date of a renewal of the 1535 order with some minor changes. According to Doerne, p. 23, the Liegnitz CO may have been influenced by the Schwenkfeldians, who had marked influence on Bucer. See above, nn. 68, 70.

Caspari, p. 172, believes the first Lutheran confirmation rite was introduced in Strassburg in 1534—39, but see above, n. 73. Caspari assigns the date 1542 instead of 1535 to the Liegnitz CO. Diehl, pp. 8, 9, assigns the same date and regards 1539 in Hesse the earliest. Schultze, as indicated above, n. 117, believes that Johannes Hefentreger's 1534 agenda for Waldeck was the first confirmation rite.

[119] Liegnitz CO, 1535, in Seh, III, 437.

[120] See above, p. 17.

the age of understanding what they believed and who had learned from the catechism how they were to live as Christians. The order further required that their Christian life be attested.[121] From the section on confession it is clear that no one was permitted to go to the Lord's Supper without prior instruction. As in Liegnitz, this was required of all, even of those who had already been confirmed.[122]

The Brandenburg CO, 1540, later exerted some influence in Sweden with the adoption of the *Nova ordinantia,* 1575, which introduced a Lutheran form of confirmation in Sweden for the first time. The form was taken partly from the Brandenburg CO and from the Waldeck CO of 1556 but followed the Brandenburg CO in that it did not link confirmation with first Communion.[123] There is little evidence to show to what extent the rite of confirmation was used in Sweden at this time, though it was ardently championed by Erasmus Nicolai, the bishop of Västerås. Because the *Nova ordinantia* contained many Roman tendencies throughout the rest of the form, it was strongly opposed and was in effect for only a short time. It was canceled by the synod in 1593, and with it the rite of confirmation was abolished in Sweden.[124]

During the 1540s the practice of confirmation became part of a bitter dispute when the Romanists attempted to force their sacramental views on the Lutherans. An early attempt was made at the Ratisbon Colloquy of 1541. The Lutherans, led by Melanchthon, Bucer, and Johannes Pistorius (1502—83), expressed their willingness to retain the rite if confirmation were understood to comprise admonition, prayer, blessing, and the giving of thanks and would be administered only to those who were of sufficient age and who had been well instructed before their first Communion. The Lutherans were ready to accept the practice of laying on hands and the use of the sign of the cross in the blessing, since both were unobjectionable and might suggest

121 Seh, III, 59.
122 Seh, III, 50.
123 Andrén, p. 291.
124 Ibid., p. 291.

many pious thoughts.[125] Although some of the Romanists were ready to make the implied concessions, the extremists among them refused to accede, and nothing came of the colloquy. Since the emperor did not feel sufficiently strong to impose his will, the Roman demands were not enforced.

In 1545, Melanchthon drew up the Wittenberg Reformation, in which he included a section on confirmation immediately after one on Holy Baptism.

> It is deemed most necessary that catechetical instruction be held on specific days in all the churches, at which time the children be instructed in all the necessary articles of the Christian faith. To such instruction confirmation might be added, namely, that when a child has reached the age of discretion, he be required to make a public confession of faith and be asked whether he will remain in this one divine doctrine and church. Upon making the confession and promise, a prayer should be offered, accompanied by the laying on of hands. This would be a valuable ceremony, not merely for appearance' sake, but much more to serve in the maintenance of pure doctrine, a proper understanding, and good discipline.[126]

Bucer's influence on Melanchthon is apparent in the inclusion of "good discipline" as one of the values of confirmation. His influence may also be partly responsible for the subjective element in the proposed form and the inclusion of a vow at confirmation.

In this form the document was signed by Luther, Bugenhagen, Caspar Cruciger (1504–48), Georg Major (1502–74), and Melanchthon. However, the Wittenberg Reformation exerted little influence on the development of confirmation in the Lutheran Church, because the political and religious climate changed suddenly.

By 1548, less than two years after Luther's death, the emperor felt strong enough to reject any concession to the Lutherans. Both the Augsburg (May 15, 1548) and the Leipzig (Dec. 21, 1548) interims demanded acceptance of a confirmation which was in essence papal. The interims required the Lutherans

---

[125] Cha[rle]s Theo. Benze, "The Liturgical History of Confirmation," *Memoirs of the Lutheran Liturgical Association,* III (Pittsburgh: Lutheran Liturgical Association, 1907), 14.

[126] Seh, I, 1, 211.

to recognize the apostolic institution of confirmation and to accept it as a sacrament necessary for salvation and as a rite which could be administered only by the bishop.[127]

While the interims were being drawn up, Melanchthon and others for a time were willing to accept some of the features demanded by the Romanists. Melanchthon would not concede that confirmation was necessary for salvation, but he did not want to argue about it.[128] To this Bugenhagen, Cruciger, Johann Pfeffinger (1493—1573), and Major agreed.[129] Repeated efforts were made to have them alter their position, but little was conceded. Melanchthon, with the help of others, drew up a report at Meissen on July 6, 1548, in which he agreed that confirmation was a valuable practice though not required by Christ and not necessary for salvation. Under those conditions Melanchthon was ready to institute confirmation as a valuable ceremony.[130]

On Oct. 19, 1548, Melanchthon recommended that mature young people who wish to partake of the Lord's Supper be examined of their faith by the bishop or their pastor, confess the faith which their sponsors confessed in their stead at Baptism, renounce the devil, and be confirmed with the laying on of hands and Christian prayer.[131]

At the conclave of theologians at Celle on Nov. 16, 1548, there was considerable discussion of confirmation. Melanchthon accepted confirmation and set forth at length what it should be. He stressed the importance of instruction, of public confession of faith, and the prayers of the congregation. Parents were advised that children who had reached the age of 14 be brought to the pastor, who was to designate a Sunday or other day on which the children might be publicly examined. On that occasion they were to recite the Apostles' Creed, the Ten Commandments, and the Lord's Prayer and then be examined in the Christian doctrine. After a brief talk the pastor should lay his hands

[127] Bachmann, pp. 33—41.
[128] April 1, 1548; *CR*, VI, 840, 844.
[129] April 24, 1548; *CR*, VI, 869. June 16, 1548; *CR*, VI, 932.
[130] *CR*, VII, 32.
[131] *CR*, VII, 179.

on their heads and pray over them, whereupon the congregation should sing "Come, Holy Spirit." This was to be followed by a prayer, after which the children were to partake of the Lord's Supper with their parents.[132]

But an interesting note is added.

> The aforementioned age is not to be understood as though children of younger years who have been instructed in the catechism may not be brought by their parents to confession and the Sacrament in accordance with the passage, Let the children come to Me, for such belong to the kingdom of God. But confirmation shall take place at an age of discretion when the children better understand their faith and their affirmation.[133]

Accordingly Melanchthon and those with him at Celle were ready to have first Communion precede confirmation.[134]

When war became imminent in December 1548, Melanchthon and many others were ready to make additional concessions concerning confirmation and other adiaphora even though they had a Roman ring to them.[135] Because Melanchthon had gained some concession on the doctrine of justification, he said he could bear "harsh bondage" on other matters.[136]

Melanchthon's concessions were strongly opposed, especially in the northern areas of Germany. Johann Aepinus (Höck; 1499—1553) and Matthias Flacius were adamant in their stand against a Romanizing confirmation. Aepinus stated that he had no objections to confirmation as an edifying ceremony that could

---

[132] *CR*, VII, 199—201.

[133] *CR*, VII, 201. Hansen, pp. 86, 87, strongly contends that under the circumstances the separation of confirmation and first Communion was a concession to the Romanists. Caspari, p. 37, n. 21, believes that it may have been a concession for those who did not have confirmation. Höfling and Von Zezschwitz cite Melanchthon in evidence that a separation was already practiced at the time. Hansen, pp. 87, 373. In the light of practice in Liegnitz, Brandenburg, and Pomerania, it should be conceded that they have a point.

[134] In a further explanation on Dec. 28, 1548, they indicate that the children should be confirmed between age 12 and 15. *CR*, VII, 268.

[135] *CR*, VII, 252.

[136] *CR*, VII, 258. For an extensive study of the controversy see Clyde L. Manschreck, "The Role of Melanchthon in the Adiaphora Controversy," *Archiv für Reformationsgeschichte*, XLVIII (1957), 165—181.

49

be used to strengthen faith, but a confirmation as practiced in the Roman church was an "offensive abuse" and *ein lauter Affenspiel*. He regarded elevation of confirmation an offense against the sacrament of Baptism.[137] Flacius was so fearful of compromise that he rejected confirmation in any form, even when it was not regarded a sacrament. He supposed that even a purely Lutheran type of confirmation might be misunderstood by the people. If it was found desirable to have some type of ceremony in connection with the catechetical form, Flacius insisted it be made clear that the rite was not a confirmation and that the practice as such was not dependent on a ceremony and could be omitted if necessary.[138]

The bitter experiences of 1548 and the years following proved to be a major factor in retarding the growth of the practice of confirmation in the Lutheran Church, particularly in the Scandinavian countries and in northern Germany where the Gnesio-Lutherans were strongest. Particularly the practice of laying on hands was a stumbling block. The Brandenburg CO of 1572 dropped confirmation entirely.[139] Later almost every introduction of confirmation in these areas had to meet successfully the charge "papal" before it was eventually introduced. The strongholds of Lutheranism finally adopted confirmation when neither "papal" nor "Lutheran" were deemed important, namely, during the period of Rationalism.

Perhaps the most outstanding example of the traditional type of confirmation is found in Pomerania, both because of its uniqueness and because of its almost unbroken history well into the 19th century. While the Pomeranian confirmation has been recognized as unique,[140] it has usually been classified as catechetical rather than traditional. Furthermore, it is often said that confirmation was introduced into Pomerania by Bugenhagen, for it was he who drew up the church order of 1535.

[137] *Bekenntniss unnd Erklerung auffs Interimo* (Magdeburg: Christian Rödinger, 1548), fol. 35.

[138] Caspari, p. 38.

[139] Seh, III, 96.

[140] Diehl, p. 51. See also n. 63 above. Rott, p. 46, comments on the objective nature of the rite with its emphasis on the acts of God and His gifts.

But there is no direct evidence of introduction by him. Neither the church order of 1535 nor that of 1542, which Bugenhagen reviewed before publication, authorized confirmation.[141]

The first clear reference to confirmation in Pomerania is found in the records of the general synod at Stettin in 1545.[142] The synod resolved: "The catechism shall be reviewed briefly four times each year. At the end the catechumens who have not yet attended the Sacrament of the Altar are to be examined. Those who are shown to know the catechism are to be confirmed before the altar with the laying on of hands and thereafter (*postea*) admitted to the Sacrament, which custom was begun among the apostles in Acts." [143]

At first the wording does not seem to warrant classifying it as a traditional type of confirmation, for there seems to have been no separation between confirmation and first Communion — at least not in 1545. However, in the light of the 1563 church order and the 1569 agenda the "thereafter (*postea*) is not to be considered conclusive evidence that first Communion followed immediately after confirmation. It may have, but the chronology is not at all clear. In the earlier years, especially during the interim period of 1548 and 1549, practice changed rapidly because of Roman Catholic pressures. During that period a theological conclave at Stettin even accepted a sacramental form of confirmation setting forth the principle that confirmation was

---

141 The church order of 1535 states that children who had been properly instructed and examined need no confirmation but should be regarded as having been confirmed. Seh, IV, 332. The church order of 1542 was drawn up by Paul von Rode and Johann Knipstro and revised by Bugenhagen. Seh, IV, 322. It makes no reference to confirmation. Seh, IV, 354—370. Bachmann, p. 80, believes that confirmation was introduced through Bugenhagen's influence, though not through the church oiders.

142 R-G, II, 638, say that the Greifswald synod of 1544 had already authorized a ceremony but cite no authority. William Nagel states also that the 1544 synod spoke of confirmation, quoting Gregorio Langemack, *Histor: Catecheticae, oder Gesammleter Nachrichten*, III (Stralsund, 1729), 405: "The catechumens who desire to be permitted to partake of first Communion are, prior to this, to be given a Christian consecration in the church before the altar and confirmed with prayer and the laying on of hands." *Probleme der Konfirmation* (Berlin: Evangelische Verlagsanstalt, 1959), p. 11; hereafter cited as *Probleme*. So also Bachmann, p. 80. Balthasar, p. 25, who edited Supt. Johann Knipstro's minutes for 1544, notes only a resolution authorizing a catechization without a ceremony.

143 Balthasar, p. 50.

to be retained according to the apostolic example in which Christians received the Holy Spirit through the laying on of hands.[144]

In 1551 the synod of Greifswald again urged that confirmation be restored where it was no longer a custom, so that no one might go uninstructed. The sacramental element evident in 1548 was still there, for the Holy Spirit was said to be received to confirm the catechumen's baptism. The resolution is of special interest because it includes this significant statement: "Thereupon [*Demnach,* i. e., after confirmation] they shall be permitted, following confession and absolution, at a proper time to partake of the Sacrament of the Altar of the body and blood of Christ upon the counsel of the parents." [145] Thus it is clear that should the parents so advise, some time might elapse between confirmation and first Communion.

Although the Stralsund CO, 1555, rejected "papistic confirmation with chrism and a light blow on the cheek *(mundschlach),*" [146] it set forth a substitute confirmation, again separated from first Communion. "When children know the catechism and have recited it, they are to receive the blessing from their pastors and thereupon *(darna)* they are to be invited to the Sacrament and all Christian matters, upon the advice of their parents and pastors." [147] A more distinct confirmation pattern emerges with the church order of 1563 and the agenda of 1569. The church order makes it clear that the form prescribed was not new but mainly the one customarily followed in Pomerania. In the cities confirmation was to be held annually and twice a year if necessary, during Lent and on St. Michael's Day. The confirmation was regularly to be performed by the superintendent as overseer, but in emergencies the qualified pastors of the vicinity might officiate.[148]

---

[144] Ibid., p. 56.

[145] Ibid., pp. 73, 74.

[146] The *Backenschlag,* as it was also called, was taken over from the knighting ceremony during the 13th century to emphasize that in confirmation the Christian, as a soldier of Christ, receives spiritual power against the enemies of his faith. Maurer, *Geschichte,* p. 16.

[147] Seh, IV, 550.

[148] Seh, IV, 385, 386.

The 1569 agenda outlined the ceremony in detail, even as to the parts and content of the sermon. It stated that the first part of the sermon was to deal with the meaning and value of confirmation and to emphasize that the custom was maintained in the church for the sake of the instruction and the intercessions of the congregation, so that the children might attend the Sacrament without offense. The instruction, prayers, and the blessing were to help the children to be more appreciative of their baptism and to derive greater benefits from it.[149] After confirmation the children should be permitted to partake of the Lord's Supper "when their parents with the pastors approve it *(vor gut anseen)*." [150] Therefore when the confirmed should partake of the Lord's Supper became a pastoral concern.

No additional rite was prescribed for first Communion, but the children participated, as did all communicants, in private confession before partaking of the Sacrament.

Nagel calls attention to the statutes of the Greiffenhagen synod of 1574, which indicate that the association of confirmation with first Communion could not have been close when they state under Article III, Part 2: "They are to examine the children in the catechism four times a year and prepare for the rite of confirmation. Nor shall they admit children to the Lord's Supper unless they are confirmed." [151]

The agenda places the confirmation emphasis on Holy Baptism, not on the Lord's Supper, and links the sermon and the prayer with Baptism. The children are reminded that God gave them His Spirit in Baptism and made them temples of God. The first part of the sermon assures them that all those who are in God's kingdom possess all His benefits.[152] Presumably this means that also the right to the Lord's Supper is a gift of Holy Baptism and therefore not a right conferred in confirmation. The intercession speaks only of Baptism and its gifts.[153] Even the postscript of the long rite addresses itself to the importance

[149] Seh, IV, 443.
[150] Seh, IV, 441.
[151] Seh, IV, 485.
[152] Seh, IV, 442.
[153] Seh, IV, 444.

of Holy Baptism and admonishes both parents and sponsors to keep in mind their responsibilities to the confirmed children.[154] That the unusual emphasis on Baptism in the confirmation rite and its separation from the Lord's Supper do not reflect a Roman influence is clear throughout the church order and the agenda. Several references are made that the laying on of hands is merely symbolic of the imparting of the Spirit, who is invoked in the prayer. The congregation is to distinguish carefully between its ceremony and the "mumbo jumbo" of the Romanists with their chrism and *Backenschlag*.[155]

Only the agenda specifically states that the local pastor and the parents are to determine when first Communion is to take place. Nagel cites the jurist Augustin von Balthasar (1632—88) to show that such a separation actually took place. The jurist said that while the church order does not stipulate the age for confirmation, it does say that those who are confirmed may "soon go to the Lord's Supper." More specifically, Balthasar stated that the Greifswalder Ministerium set the age for confirmation at 14 for boys and 12 for girls but placed first Communion between the years 15 and 16 after prior instruction.[156]

An unusual aspect of this separation of confirmation from first Communion lies in that the separation was widely practiced in many areas of Pomerania till the beginning of the 19th century and in some parishes past the middle of that century, and this in the face of opposition from the Prussian government.[157] The Pomeranian confirmation did not deteriorate in the 19th century because of any inner weakness but because of the prevailing Rationalism and the pressure of the Prussian Union.[158]

[154] Seh, IV, 445.
[155] Seh, IV, 442, 443.
[156] Nagel, *Probleme*, p. 49.
[157] Hansen, pp. 206, 207, 290, 291, cites a number of 17th- and 18th-century cases in Schleswig-Holstein in which two to four years intervened between confirmation and first Communion, especially among those confirmed at 12 rather than the more usual age of 14 or later.
[158] For a more detailed history of the Pomeranian practice through the middle of the 19th century see Nagel, *Probleme*, pp. 149—151, and his "Die pommersche Confirmatio und ihre Beseitigung im 19. Jahrhundert," *Theologische Literaturzeitung*, LXXXV (Dec. 1960), 905—910.

The traditional form of confirmation with its separation of confirmation and first Communion is of more than historic interest. It has received renewed study in recent years by those who argue for a separation of confirmation and first Communion. This is true of both those who plead for an early first Communion followed by confirmation somewhat later and by those who favor confirmation first and participation of the Lord's Supper at some later period.

SUMMARY CONCLUSIONS

Some Generalizations

One of the most striking features of the 16th-century development of confirmation and preparation for first Communion is the almost total lack of uniformity. It is practically impossible to generalize, except in very broad terms, and say this is Lutheran. One of the few generalizations that may be made is that Lutherans universally rejected the Roman Catholic doctrine of confirmation as a sacrament. In fact, this rejection made a large segment of Lutherans very wary of accepting any substitute, even though cleansed of all Roman parts: the sacramental association with Baptism, the chrism, the light blow on the cheek, and administration of the rite solely by the bishop. In most instances even the practice of laying on hands was carefully guarded against a Roman interpretation. Though Melanchthon submitted to Roman Catholic pressures, his compromise did not hinder him in insisting that confirmation was not instituted by Christ or the apostles, that it is merely an adiaphoron.

A second generalization is that all Lutheran confirmation forms assumed and/or specified Christian instruction before the catechumen was presented for confirmation or first Communion. The home was considered primarily responsible for the instruction implied by Holy Baptism. The sponsors' obligations were to admonish and encourage parents to fulfill their responsibilities and, when necessary, personally to assume the duty of the parents. Instruction in the home was supplemented by the schools, wherever they existed, and by the church through *Cate-*

chismus, catechetical sermons, and sometimes through public reading from one of the catechisms. Preconfirmation instruction by the pastor was primarily a matter of review or a preparation for the questions required by the rite where it was observed. Often a period of six weeks was set aside for this purpose.[159] It was an opportunity for the pastor to assure himself that the catechumen could be presented for admission to the Lord's Supper.

A third broad generalization that may be made is that confirmation was directly associated with both sacraments, except in the case of the traditional type, which was not widely practiced. The pastor's instruction was to assure him that the obligation to instruct, which parents and sponsors had assumed with the child's baptism, had been met and that the catechumen was now ready for the second sacrament.

A fourth broad generalization is that the usual age of the catechumen who partook of his first Communion was quite early when compared to present-day practice. Indeed, age was not regarded an important criterion. The major criterion was the catechumen's readiness to partake of the Sacrament. Almost invariably the church orders used an expression such as "when the children have come of age." [160] According to German law, this was at age 12; according to Roman canon law, it could be interpreted variously as from 7 to 12.

Where a reference to confirmation age appears, the age is rarely higher than 12. Thus Hohenlohe, 1577,[161] and Ansbach, 1564,[162] specify 12. The same age is suggested by Allstedt, 1533,[163] and Lindow in Pomerania, 1571.[164] The former states that persons over 12 are to be subject to a personal tax, while

[159] Brandenburg-Ansbach-Kulmbach CO, 1556, in Seh, XI, 428.

[160] Liegnitz CO, 1535, in Seh, III, 436; Brandenburg CO, 1540, in Seh, III, 59; Wittenberg Reformation, 1545, in Seh, I, 1, 211; Württemberg CO, 1553, in Rich, II, 134; Saxony CO, 1557, in Seh. I, 1, 324; Lauenburg CO, 1585, in Seh, V, 458.

[161] Rich, II, 401.

[162] Pref. to Georg Karg's catechism, in ReuQ, I, 1, 580.

[163] Seh, I, 1, 511.

[164] Lindow Register, in Seh, IV, 517.

the latter requires 12-year-olds to contribute to the pastor's support. In both instances it may be assumed that the age was set at 12 because persons were normally confirmed or communicants by that time. Lower Austria, 1571, sets a range between 10 and 15.[165] Brandenburg-Ansbach-Kulmbach, 1556, indicates that the age for first Communion was to be 12 or over.[166] Braunschweig, 1542, suggests that the former custom of confirming at 10 or 11 be retained.[167] The Church Order of Sweden, drawn up by Laurentius Petri (1499—1573) in 1571, states that no child younger than 9, or 8 at the least, should attend the Lord's Supper. "For younger children can have little exact knowledge of the Sacrament." [168] During the 16th century the children in Denmark were often admitted to Communion when they were only 6 or 7.[169]

This seems to be the limit of verifiable generalizations concerning 16th-century Lutheran confirmation practice. Indeed, if confirmation is taken to mean primarily the ceremony, then as pointed out above, one can hardly generalize at all or speak of any uniformity, for in the 16th century the majority of Lutheran churches had no formal rite of any kind.

Essential Elements

In determining the essential elements for confirmation, one is again plagued with a definition of confirmation. The mixed concepts concerning confirmation in the Lutheran Church and the various tensions which played an important role behind the introduction or rejection of confirmation make it clear that history is of little help in determining what constitutes a Lutheran confirmation. If the catechetical form is accepted as a type of confirmation since its purpose was to confirm the catechumen's

---

[165] Kliefoth, III, 1, 102.

[166] Seh, XI, 1, 335.

[167] Seh, VI, 2, 841.

[168] "Church Order," in Eric E. Yelverton, *An Archbishop of the Reformation* (Minneapolis: Augsburg Publishing House, 1959), p. 122.

[169] Belfour, pp. 68, 69. In his *Institutio* (1536), IV, xix, 13, Calvin set the age at 10 for a ceremony similar to confirmation: "*Puer decennis ecclesiae se offeret, ad edendam fidei confessionem.*" CR, XXIX, 26.

faith and prepare him for his first Communion and even though it had no rite, then the essential elements may be said to be (a) the instruction, (b) the confession of the faith which is to be believed, and (c) the prayer of the congregation in behalf of the catechumen. If the ceremony is included as a necessary part of confirmation, then the essentials varied with the emphases. Additional features regarded essential by one form or another are a confession of the personal faith of the catechumen, a vow of some kind, and the laying on of hands. The vows were various, more than one often being present in the same rite: to remain loyal to the Christian faith, remain with the baptismal covenant, surrender to Christ, submit to church discipline, live the Christian life, or partake of the means of grace. The concept of renewing one's baptismal covenant was foreign to 16th-century Lutheranism. In the few instances where reference is made to a baptismal covenant in connection with confirmation, the children or parents were merely reminded of their covenant and urged to keep it.[170] Confirmation did not cease to develop with the close of the 16th century. New features were added while others were radically altered by succeeding generations.

The Date

The date for admission to the Lord's Supper or for confirmation varied greatly. Obviously, where there was no ceremony, almost any Sunday or even a weekday might be chosen. Where a closing ceremony was observed, its date varied greatly if the officiant had to be the superintendent or bishop, for the time was then dependent on his convenience. Where the ceremony was in the hands of the local pastor — this was usually the case — the dates became more fixed. Usually they were Easter (not Palm Sunday) and Pentecost. If confirmation was observed a third time during the year, it was usually at Christmas. Other

---

[170] Braunschweig-Wolfenbüttel CO, 1569, in Seh, VI, 1, 165; Mansfeld A, 1580, in Seh, I, 2, 234; Lauenburg CO, 1585, in Seh, V, 458; Saxony CO, 1580, in Seh, I, 1, 425. Wittenberg Reformation, 1545, in Seh, I, 1, 211, asks the children whether they intend to remain in their baptismal covenant.

fixed days were Maundy Thursday, the Sunday before St. Michael's Day, Quasimodogeniti, or the beginning of Lent.

The fact that a church order or agenda authorized confirmation was no assurance that the rite was actually observed. Often there was a lag of several years before the rite went beyond the paper stage. This became evident when church visitations were made. Sometimes the church order never went into effect, as in the case of the Cologne Reformation.[171] At other times the clergy resented the interference or accepted the church order with the reservation that their freedom not be limited thereby.[172] At still other times the civil authority soon changed, so that the church order was actually in effect for only a short time. The Braunschweig CO, 1542, lost much of its authority because the ruler turned Roman Catholic. Only the influence of the ruler's mother, who remained Lutheran, and the fortunes of war kept it from becoming invalid altogether.[173] The Hoya CO, 1581, became invalid within a year after Count Otto died without an heir and the land had to be divided. Since the neighboring church orders were quite similar, there was no drastic change in practice.

On the other hand, the situation was just the reverse in some instances; that is, a form for confirmation was set up years before the church order officially authorized it. For example, in Pomerania a synod at Greifswald established confirmation in 1545, but the church order did not authorize it till 1563.

[171] Caspari, p. 44; Diehl, p. 44.

[172] Synod at Greifswald in Pomerania, Balthasar, p. 17, Hansen, pp. 15, 16, points out that in Schleswig-Holstein many regulations concerning the instruction were dead letters because of apathy, passive resistance, or inability to enforce them.

[173] Seh, VI, 2, 704, 705.

CHAPTER II

THE DEVELOPMENT

OF CONFIRMATION IN EUROPE

The Period of Orthodoxy

The practice of confirmation continued to spread at a somewhat slower pace during the period of Orthodoxy, partly because of the ravages of the Thirty Years' War (1618–48), which demoralized a large section of the Lutheran Church. A great majority of the churches in Germany and Scandinavia continued to prepare children for their first Communion simply through the catechetical approach and without a rite.

There was a time when it was believed that confirmation had been practically wiped out during the Thirty Years' War and that it was not revived till the period of Pietism. While it is true that confirmation declined in some sections where it was theoretically still on the statute books,[1] it is equally true that confirmation continued with little interruption in other parts of Germany and was actually adopted in at least nine areas before the middle of the 17th century, in many cases in the midst of the war period.[2]

In addition to the public observance of confirmation, during this period some church regulations provided for private confirmation; for example, the Ratzeburg CO, 1614. At Ratzeburg,

[1] Graff, I, 317.

[2] Mecklenburg, 1602/1650, although it fell into disuse again for a time; Schaumberg-Lippe, 1614; Friedburg, before 1625; Falkenstein, 1628; Ostfriesland, 1631; Magdeburg-Land, 1639; Schleswig-Holstein, 1637 in places; Gotha, before 1645; Schwarzburg, before 1649. From Graff, I, 321, 322. Confirmation was officially introduced in Schleswig-Holstein in 1646. Emil Hansen, *Geschichte der Konfirmation in Schleswig-Holstein* (Kiel: n. pub., 1911), pp. 40, 41.

after the child had received sufficient instruction, he was asked whether he would continue in such knowledge, faith, and confession. Upon the child's consent the pastor placed his hand on the confirmand's head, prayed the confirmation prayer, and pronounced the blessing. On the following Sunday, when the child partook of his first Communion, there was a brief announcement of his confirmation and a prayer in his behalf by the congregation.[3]

In such areas as Braunschweig-Lüneburg, Pomerania, Nassau, and Hesse, public confirmation is known to have continued without interruption.[4] Wilhelm Diehl made an extensive study both of the reports of the church visitation authorized in 1628 by Landgrave George II (1605—61) for Hesse-Darmstadt and of the church records of the region during the war. The detailed questions asked on confirmation in the visitation indicate that confirmation was assumed to be in general use. The questions dealt with the registration of the names of those confirmed, the length of the instruction, whether persons were admitted to the Lord's Supper without confirmation, parental cooperation, and the like. The visitation showed that confirmation was widely practiced and well rooted in the life of the congregations. Even the church records were generally well kept.[5]

Although Hesse was officially neutral during the war, its neutrality was not respected. Plagues harassed the land, especially in 1635, when entire villages were threatened with extinction. A third hardship came for Hesse in 1647, when French troops invaded Darmstadt and put many villages to the torch. Nonetheless, the rite of confirmation was observed annually, sometimes even twice a year, as in Darmstadt. While confirmation was occasionally dropped for a year because there were no children, in practically every instance confirmation was resumed the following year.[6]

In Scandinavia the catechetical form continued to be the

[3] Graff, I, 314.

[4] Graff, I, 317.

[5] Diehl, *Zur Geschichte der Konfirmation: Beiträge aus der hessischen Kirchengeschichte* (Giessen: J. Ricker, 1897), pp. 53—60.

[6] Ibid., 76—81.

usual practice. In the latter half of the 17th century efforts were begun in Sweden to establish a ceremony to mark the cate- chumen's first Communion. Johannes Matthie (d. 1670) drew up a form which followed the pattern of the Bohemian Brethren and the Hessian church, but it was not found acceptable.[7] In 1663, Bishop Olaus Laurelius (1586–1670) suggested a simple rite which was to include a public examination, the laying on of hands, and a prayer by the congregation. It, too, failed. The orthodox leaders were simply not amenable to an increase in the number of ceremonies.[8] However, Laurelius was able to contribute to the improvement of instruction with a catechism called *Christelige spörsmål (A Christian Questionary)*, published about 1649.[9] His effort was supplemented in 1689 by an expla- nation of Luther's catechism written by Archbishop Olaus Svebilius (d. 1700) and authorized by the king. The manual was drawn up for the whole Swedish church and approved by the Ecclesiastical Estate of the *Riksdag*. Its importance may be seen in that it was the leading catechism until 1810, when a re- vised version drawn up by Archbishop Jacob Axelsson Lindblom (1746–1818) succeeded it.[10]

The Swedish church law of 1686 offered the possibility of separating the preparation of the children for first Communion from the normal catechizations required of all communicants. Thus both a form of confirmation instruction and a confirmation service were possible. But the Nordic wars were fatal to this development.[11] In Finland the very conservative pattern of Sweden was followed. Bishop Paavali Juusten (1516–76) di- rected the clergy to give more attention to the instruction of the laity. An encyclical of Ericus Ericis encouraged the clergy to require the entire family to come to confessional instruction

---

[7] Erkki Kansanaho, *Konfirmaatio: Liturgishistoriallinen tutkimus konfirmaa- tioaktista* (Helsinki: Suomalainen Teologinen Kirjallisuusseura, 1956), p. 284.

[8] Ibid., p. 285.

[9] Einar Lilja, *Den Svenska Katekestraditionen Mellan Svebilius och Lindblom*. Vol. 16 in *Acta Historico-Ecclesiastica Suecana*, ed. Hilding Pleijel (Stock- holm: Kyrkans Diakonistyrelses Bökforlag, 1947), p. 330.

[10] Ibid., p. 329.

[11] Kansanaho, p. 285.

so that all might be admonished to piety and learn the catechism.[12] To this end the orthodox bishops made a concerted effort to have pastors gather their congregations for confessional visits. By the middle of the 17th century more attention was being given to children. They were separated from adults and placed in special groups where greater demands were made of them. In time there developed the practice of having special confirmation instruction to prepare children for first Communion. However, this development was very slow, in most instances not appearing till the 18th century.[13]

A striking addition found its way into confirmation during the period of Orthodoxy. Some Lutheran territories were beginning to be disturbed by the effects of the Counter-Reformation, especially after Frederich August II (1670–1733), elector of Saxony, defected to the Roman Catholics. To meet this attack the confirmation rite for children from the nobility, especially from the ruling class, frequently included a solemn vow that the child remain true to the Lutheran Church.[14] Impressive ceremonies were in time introduced in connection with such confirmations. In the case of Princes Elizabeth Friderica Sophie von Bayreuth in 1748, the examination included questions even on the differences between Roman Catholicism and Lutheranism.[15]

The catechetical pattern, followed by the majority of the Lutheran churches in this century, fell far short of its goal, even though the church orders held parents responsible for the instruction of their children and required congregations to be deeply concerned that the parents fulfill this responsibility. Reading of the catechism from the pulpit frequently fell into disuse because it did not seem to have the desired effect.[16] Catechetical sermons no longer served their intended purpose. They had first

---

[12] Ibid., p. 284.

[13] Ibid., pp. 284—286.

[14] Walter Caspari, *Die evangelische Konfirmation, vornämlich in der lutherischen Kirche* (Erlangen, Leipzig: And. Deichert, 1890), pp. 96, 97.

[15] Lukas Vischer, *Die Geschichte der Konfirmation* (St. Gallen: Evangelischer Verlag AG., Zollikon, 1959), p. 80.

[16] Graff, I, 318.

been published during the early Reformation period to help out until conditions improved. What actually happened was that pastors continued to read them long after they had served their purpose. While some new sermon books appeared, the level on which they were written usually left much to be desired. The catechetical sermons of Aegidius Hunnius, for example, might have served well as university lectures, but they were unsuitable for the laity. Only a few authors were able to find the level of Johann Arndt's (1555—1621) sermons of 1620.[17] That the task of reading these sermons was often left to the *Küster* did not elevate them in the eyes of the people. Consequently the congregation generally did not respond, and the catechism services were poorly attended.[18]

The most serious weakness of the congregational instruction was the catechization itself. For practical reasons it was impossible to catechize all persons present, and so the questioning was soon limited to the children. Had there been several classes, at least one for noncommunicants and another for communicants, there might have been opportunity for some development. But continuous repetition at the most elementary level for young and adults was deadening. Although the need for variety had been pointed out by Andreas Hyperius in *De catechesi*, his suggestions went unheeded. Like the catechetical sermons, the catechizations frequently became the responsibility of the *Küster* because the pastors shied away from the routine of such teaching.[19]

When catechetical instruction was first introduced in the 16th century, conditions were such that the masses needed presenta-

[17] ReuC, p. 127.

[18] E[rnst] Chr[istian] Achelis, *Lehrbuch der Praktischen Theologie,* II, 3d ed. (Leipzig: J. C. Hinrich'sche Buchhandlung, 1911), p. 304.
The *Küster* was originally the pastor's helper who instructed the children in the catechism. In time he also taught reading, writing, and sometimes arithmetic. Thus the office developed, and the *Küster* became the first teacher in the German *Volksschule* of the 16th century. The church orders were very explicit in the qualifications of the *Küster*. Since the supply of qualified men was limited, many a *Küster* lacked the necessary qualifications. Georg Mertz, *Das Schulwesen der deutschen Reformation im 16. Jahrhundert* (Heidelberg: Carl Winter, 1902), pp. 405—407.

[19] Achelis, p. 304.

tions on an elementary level, for all were virtually children in their religious understanding. The people needed to become catechumens again every time they prepared for the Lord's Supper. After the level of general education had risen, however, the prevailing practice no longer sufficed. The churches failed to adjust to changing conditions also among the children. As long as they could not read because of the lack of schools, the catechism had to be taught by rote. This frequently led to a learning of words without appropriating their meaning. But when the same methods continued after the ability to read became more widespread, the effect was monotony that invited indifference. The decline of the catechizations should not be attributed so much to the war as to growing general disfavor because of the poor teaching methods that prevailed.[20]

Many of the catechisms that appeared during this period reflected much of the same formalism into which the church was gradually slipping. Few churchmen were interested in theories of education. It seemed more important to work into the catechisms as many theological ramifications as possible. A notable example is Conrad Dietrich's (1575–1639) *Institutiones catecheticae* (1613), written for Gymnasium students. While excellent for theological students and pastors, it was much too technical for the adolescent. Even the epitome, which was designed for elementary schools, was far too heavy for a period when many children had not yet acquired a simple reading ability. Naturally such a situation did not continue long without criticism; serious efforts were made to remedy the situation. There were frequent complaints that the average layman had little understanding of the Christian faith. One of the earliest of such critics was Andreas Hyperius, already referred to.[21] Justus Gesenius (1601–73), in *Vorrede zur kleine Catechismus Schule* (1634), deplored the fact that pastors as well as parents had God's Word but did not understand it. Therefore not even the spiritual leaders cared to explain the catechism. Gesenius complained that the pastors did not personally teach the cate-

20 Caspari, p. 74.
21 ReuQ, I, 2, 1, 419, 420.

chism in the villages, because of their difficulty in coming down to the level of the children and because of the sheer monotony of teaching the simple over and over again.[22] In 1622 Johann Valentin Andreae (1586–1654) wrote *Theophilus,* a scathing satire pointing up the painful results of parrotlike memorization.[23] In a catechism sermon, *Gedenke daran Hamburg,* Johann Balthasar Schuppius (1610–61) lamented that so many in his congregation did not know even the meaning of the Ten Commandments. To alleviate the situation somewhat, he suggested that the almoners, while making their rounds among the poor, also read — "that is," he said, "those who can read" — a section from Luther's catechism and pray the Lord's Prayer till something better can be supplied them.[24] Such criticism slowly brought about a change. Instead of discarding the catechism, as some had begun to do in despair, better catechisms began to appear. More attention was given to the importance of teaching children effectively. This was reflected in the *Zuchtbüchlein der Evangelischen Kirchen* of Johann Saubert (1638–88).[25]

Greater care began to be given to instruction. Some areas of Germany abandoned the catechetical approach to first Communion, adopted a public confirmation rite, and with it gave more attention to careful instruction of the catechumens.[26]

Unfortunately, efforts to reform the instruction of children were not limited to pedagogy; some unwittingly began to tamper with the theology. During the middle of the 17th century, Theophil Grossgebauer (1627–61) concluded that the sermon no longer seemed effective because of the unregenerate state of the people. This judgment prompted him to reexamine the relation of Holy Baptism and the Gospel to the conversion of the individual. In his *Wächterstimme* (1661), he stated that persons are baptized in infancy on condition that they later be converted through the Word of God and the Holy Spirit. Con-

---

[22] Caspari, p. 75.

[23] First printed in 1649; trans. from the Latin by V. Fr. Oehler in 1878.

[24] *Lehrreiche Schriften* (1663?), p. 187. Title page partly missing in the copy used.

[25] Printed in Nürnberg, 1633. Graff, I, 318.

[26] See above, p. 61.

version is brought about through the spoken Word, a power of God whereby the sinner, as a rational creature, is addressed, called, convinced, and stricken in his heart *(und zum Hertzen einen Stich bekombt).*[27] He asserted that personal conversion actually comes about through pastoral work with the individual. Conversion, he said, is the function of catechization, and therefore he attached great importance to confirmation. He appealed to Chemnitz as a proponent of confirmation and urged pastors to adopt it as a means for bringing about conversion and a "piercing of the heart." Philip Jacob Spener (1635–1705) was later greatly influenced by this understanding of conversion and adopted some of Grossgebauer's views on confirmation.[28]

In his efforts for reform, Justus Gesenius helped to encourage the concept that confirmation is a renewing of the baptismal covenant. Instead of speaking of remembering the covenant, he spoke of repeating it. It was not long till mention of a covenant renewal became more frequent in the literature, especially where confirmation began to take on a conversion emphasis. But a more radical change in the understanding of confirmation remained for Spener to bring about through his personal influence.

The Pietistic Type

With the rise of Pietism in the Lutheran Church, confirmation took on a different form. The new movement which spread over Lutheranism as a reaction against Orthodoxy used the rite as developed in Hesse, gave it a subjective emphasis, and shaped it for its own theological purposes. As Pietism became widely accepted, confirmation was introduced in areas where previously it had been unable to gain acceptance. So great was the influence of Pietism on confirmation, that the imprint of this fifth type may still be seen in many practices within present-day Lutheranism.

As stated above, some changes in catechetical instruction

[27] *Wächterstimme aus dem verwüsteten Zion* (Frankfort on the Main: Joachim Wildens, 1661), pp. 71, 72.

[28] Spener, *Theologisches Bedenken und andere Briefliche Antworten* (Halle: Verlegung des Wäysenhauses, 1715), III, 554; IV, 531, 579.

and in confirmation had already taken place before the rise of Pietism. As Philipp Spener became the movement's dominant figure, he lent the weight of his personal influence to popularize a new emphasis in confirmation and to accelerate its spread.

Spener was greatly concerned about the low spiritual conditions in the Lutheran Church of his day. The ravages of the Thirty Years' War and an intellectualism which frequently replaced personal faith had been major factors in the demoralization of the church. Spener was especially disturbed that most of the people partook of the Lord's Supper in such a casual and informal manner.[29] Like Grossgebauer, whom he admired, though not uncritically, Spener looked for some means by which he as pastor could deal with the individual to assure himself that his parishioner was truly converted. Using the expression ascribed to Mercurius von Helmut,[30] he wanted "to bring the head into the heart" *(den Kopf ins Herz zu bringen).*[31] Individuals thus affected should become an *ecclesiola,* that is, a group of "converted" persons within the church, whose influence he hoped would continue to affect an enlarging circle within the congregation.[32] Spener believed that confirmation could be utilized ideally to reach the individual and bring about his conversion. While he did not deny the regenerative power of Baptism, as did Grossgebauer, Spener did minimize its continuing power. It seemed to him that the faith created by the sacrament had in most instances died or at least become exceedingly weak during the ensuing years. For him the value of Baptism lay primarily in its covenant which the Christian needed to renew regularly. This thought he introduced into confirmation, and with it he gave the vow once introduced by Bucer a new meaning.

Spener had become acquainted with the Hessian type of confirmation while pastor near Frankfort on the Main.[33] He had

[29] Ibid., IV, 267.
[30] Achelis, p. 323.
[31] Spener, IV, 266.
[32] Martin Doerne, *Neubau der Konfirmation* (Gütersloh: C. Bertelsmann, 1936), p. 44.
[33] Spener, I, 636; IV, 259.

also learned to know the Hessian CO while pastor there.[34] Though confirmation was not practiced in Dresden, where Spener later became pastor, it was in vogue in Berlin when he arrived there in 1691. At the Nikolai Church, confirmation was observed semiannually and followed the pattern drawn up by Chemnitz.[35] In using confirmation to serve his "conversion theology," Spener seems to have been under the impression that he was following Chemnitz's approach to confirmation.

Like Bucer, Spener laid great stress on the vow, but with a purpose of his own. Instead of speaking about "remembering the baptismal covenant," he emphasized a "renewal of the covenant," to which he added a solemn promise. Spener maintained that since every Christian should in a sense daily renew his covenant, it is fitting that every catechumen be required to do this once solemnly and publicly in the presence of the congregation.[36]

Even greater emphasis was placed on the covenant when the confession of faith, which up to this time had been generally regarded simply as a confession of the faith of the church and as evidence that the catechumen understood the doctrine, was now understood to be a confession of the catechumen's personal faith. Confirmation became the occasion for the catechumen to ratify his baptismal covenant, to give witness of his personal faith or "conversion," and to accept the obligation to lead a Christian life.

Since the major importance of confirmation lay in the subjective element of covenant renewal and in the solemn vow, preconfirmation instruction was given a secondary position. This is not to say that Spener supposed instruction unimportant and did not seek to improve it. Spener and his followers showed great interest in such an improvement. They attempted to discard learning by rote or through stereotype questions and answers. Though no model catechist, Spener gave more emphasis

[34] Diehl, p. 91.
[35] Achelis, p. 323.
[36] Spener, IV, 257.

to analyzing questions.[37] He placed more stress on the ability to read so that rote memorization would be unnecessary. This additional requirement became one of the sources of irritation in Hesse, where the Pietists wanted all children to be able to read and write before their confirmation.[38] The Pietists also wanted to lengthen the period of instruction so that the pastor would have more time.[39] Furthermore, since the instruction was to have a pastoral approach, it was absolutely necessary for the pastor himself to be the instructor instead of delegating this as a chore to the *Küster*. If the pastor was to be certain that the individual was really a Christian, he himself must be concerned with teaching.

Up to this time admission to the Lord's Supper was chiefly a matter of congregational concern. This was especially true of Bucer's confirmation, of which the elders witnessed the examination and sometimes the final phases of the instruction. Since Spener placed the emphasis on conversion, admission to the Lord's Supper became more an individual matter. The view that the communicant became a part of the Communion-going congregation was lost. Spener attempted to permit only those who were converted to be confirmed and to attend the Lord's Supper.[40]

The subjective emphasis in confirmation gradually led to the use of individual *Einsegnungswünsche,* especially later during the period of Rationalism. These have come down to the present among Lutherans of German background as "memory verses" for the catechumen.

In spite of Spener's emphasis on public confirmation, which he regarded as an edifying experience for the congregation, he was able to observe it in private only.[41]

The disciples of Spener elaborated on the emphases he proposed. Trogillus Arnkiel (d. 1713), a contemporary in many

[37] ReuC, p. 135.
[38] Diehl, p. 85.
[39] Spener, IV, 267.
[40] Vischer, p. 78.
[41] Spener, I, 636; IV, 259.

71

ways sympathetic to Spener even though not a Pietist in the true sense of the word,[42] reflected the pietistic view of confirmation with an emphasis on renewal of the baptismal covenant, making the vow as binding as an oath.[43] Through his *De confirmatione* (1723), Christoph Matthäus Pfaff (1686–1760) was also instrumental in spreading the new view of confirmation. He encouraged an even greater degree of subjectivity by urging the catechist to make every effort to bring the children to "holy tears." [44] Going beyond Spener, he stated that Baptism needed to be completed and that the promise at confirmation served as the necessary complement.[45]

Another divergence was proposed by August Hermann Francke (1663–1727) of Halle. In the 16th century the confession of faith was usually in the words of the Apostles' Creed. A prescribed confession was too formal for Francke and other pietists. They believed that the child should be allowed to express his faith in his own words. Francke tried to follow through on his own proposal, but since this was expecting too much of the ordinary child with limited education, his suggestions became effective chiefly among the "cultured" classes, and the common children continued to use the catechism and the Creed.[46]

The altered concept of confirmation advocated by the Pietists was not accepted without serious opposition, even though it did gain a firm foothold in many places. The warnings of Flacius against a papal confirmation were not forgotton, so the promulgations of Arnkiel and Spener had to take such misgivings into

---

[42] Hansen, pp. 160, 161. Arnkiel was influential in putting the 1646 synodical resolution of Schleswig-Holstein into effect. Partly because of apathy the resolution had become a dead letter, but in spite of much opposition, Arnkiel's effective work resulted in the establishment or reestablishment of confirmation in many parishes after 1682. Ibid., pp. 147—150.

[43] Graff, I, 320; Hansen, p. 189. As Hansen points out, Arnkiel thought the renewal of the baptismal covenant necessary not because he believed it had been broken by the child, as did Spener, but as a consequence of the natural development when the Word of God is at work. Ibid., p. 191.

[44] Graff, I, 320.

[45] Doerne, p. 43.

[46] Theo[dor] Kliefoth, *Die Confirmation*, in *Liturgische Abhandlungen*, III, 1 (Schwerin: Stiller'schen Hof-Buchhandlung, 1856), 120.

consideration.[47] Where confirmation had been established for some time, as in Hesse, orthodox Lutherans rightly charged the Pietists with making radical changes.[48] So strong was resistance in Hesse that the agenda, revised in 1662 and in 1724, remained unchanged by pietistic influences.[49]

Not all opposition stemmed from tensions between orthodox pastors and those with pietistic leanings; both practiced confirmation. In many instances confirmation was opposed within congregations by the deacons, who saw in its introduction another pastoral threat to their office. One of the more important responsibilities of the deacons was to assist with confession, and the *Beichtgeld* was a major source of income. Since confirmation would determine admission to the Lord's Supper, it was feared that the first communicants would avoid the deacon and go to the pastor.[50] Opposition came also from the laymen, not merely because of the additional requirements for confirmation but because they sensed and feared the new direction. They were not adverse to private confirmation since it was similar to confession, but they vigorously resisted a public observance.[51]

Theologians with some pietistic leanings, like Johann Nicolaus Quistorp (1651–1715) of Rostock, favored confirmation. Quistorp regretted that confirmation was not generally practiced in Mecklenburg. Since he saw in it an instrument for better church discipline, he believed that if it were in use, the concerns about many parents and sponsors would be eased. Under existing circumstances they readily became negligent. If the practice were general, they would be pressured into it by public opinion.[52]

Valentin Ernst Löscher (1673–1749) was somewhat neutral on the subject. In a review of *Evangelische Firmung* (1713), by Christian Gerber (1660–1731), Löscher described confirmation

[47] Caspari, p. 91.

[48] Diehl, p. 85.

[49] Diehl, p. 95.

[50] Hansen, pp. 167—170. The laymen also feared that confirmation would increase the number of fees that they would be expected to pay.

[51] Caspari, p. 92.

[52] *Pia Desideria*, IX; *Variorum Auctorum Miscellanea Theologica*, ed. Johann Gottlob Pfeiffer (Leipzig: Impensis Lankisianorum Haeredum, 1736), p. 102.

as a praiseworthy and edifying ceremony but as one that could not be introduced in Saxony and that after all was not absolutely necessary.[53]

In spite of the opposition and cool reception in some places, the spread of confirmation accelerated, and by the middle of the 18th century it covered the greater part of Germany.[54]

After the Nordic War in 1736, confirmation gained entrance also into Norway and Denmark, largely through the influence of Pietism. From the catechetical form previously practiced, confirmation took on a liturgical form. The name confirmation was still avoided, and the rite was called "the renewing of the baptismal covenant," indicating its pietistic origin.[55] Confirmation was officially authorized by an ordinance of Jan. 13, 1736. The law required that the catechumen formally renew his baptismal vow before his first Communion, after he had been catechized in the presence of the congregation. The king assigned to the Danish bishop Eric Pontoppidan (1698—1764) the task of producing an explanation for Luther's Small Catechism. The pietistic leanings that he had acquired in Halle are apparent in his *Sandhed til gudfrygtighed (Truth unto Godliness)*, which was introduced in Norway and Denmark in 1737.[56] It became the chief text for confirmation instruction and was one of the most influential catechisms in the Lutheran Church. After confirmation was officially authorized in Norway, it gained entrance in Sweden particularly through the efforts of Jakob Serenius. Although he was not able to get any official recognition for confirmation, he was successful in improving the instruction of the catechumens for their first Communion.[57]

The first official and clear instruction for confirmation in the

---

[53] "Allerhand neue Bücher," *Unschuldige Nachrichten von Alten und Neuen Theologischen Sachen*, IV (Leipzig: Johann Friedrich Braun, 1713), 694, 695.

[54] Compare Graff, I, 321, 322, and R-G, 643, for lists of dates when confirmation was permitted in various territories of Germany. See also Johann Fr. Bachmann, *Die Confirmation der Catechumenen in der evangelischen Kirche* (Berlin: Wilhelm Schultze, 1852), pp. 145—180, for churches outside Germany.

[55] Kansanaho, p. 285. Confirmation was introduced also in Iceland in 1736. Bachmann, pp. 164, 165.

[56] ReuK, pp. 285, 286.

[57] Kansanaho, p. 285.

kingdom of Sweden originated in Finland when in 1740 Bishop Jonas Fahlenius issued an encyclical urging the establishment of confirmation. Soon similar encyclicals were issued by other bishops. The criticism of the Pietists forced the conservative element to review its requirements for admission to the Lord's Supper. Many pastors feared to increase the requirements lest they add to their work. While practical considerations sometimes gave meaning to their fears, this was not always the case.[58] Nevertheless the bishops continued to make many recommendations. They urged that there be a public examination, a confession of faith, a vow, and a prayer in behalf of the catechumen, but an actual ceremony was not pressed.[59] There was little hope of gaining official recognition for confirmation in Sweden during the 18th century.

The principal effect of Pietism on confirmation was not that the rite became more widely accepted in the Lutheran Church but rather that it came to be introduced in a form so foreign to its earlier history. Confirmation's subjective element became its chief characteristic. No longer were children asked merely to remember their baptismal covenant. Instead a renewal of the covenant became part of nearly every agenda.[60]

Because the catechumen was expected to examine himself to determine whether he was truly a Christian, whether he understood the Christian doctrine and was able to apply it to himself, and not merely to "discern" the body and blood of the Lord in the Sacrament, it became necessary that he be somewhat older than formerly. Before Pietism the catechumen was rarely older than 12 and usually a year or two younger. Under the influence of Pietism the church orders gradually required the catechumen to be older. The Lüneburg CO, 1689, set the age at 15, and the Schleswig-Holstein order required boys to be 16. Generally, however, the age was nearer 14.[61]

During the 16th century the rubrics for confirmation usually

[58] Ibid., p. 286.
[59] Ibid., p. 287.
[60] Instead of "renewal," similar words might be used: ratify, repeat, or confirm. Kliefoth, III, 1, 122.
[61] Graff, I, 326. Arnkiel advocated age 16 for all. Hansen, p. 209.

called for *Komm, Heiliger Geist* ("Come, Holy Ghost") or a hymn of praise. Later hymnals included under a special rubric songs originally written for other occasions. In Hesse-Darmstadt the *Grosse Cantionale oder Kirchengesangbuch* (1687) had under the rubric "At the Confirmation of Children" the hymn *Herr Gott, du bist von Ewigkeit.*[62] It was written by Ludwig Helmbod and first appeared in 1575 (1572?) as a song of prayer and praise for a children's festival.[63] The Hessian *Mentzer'sche Gesangbuch,* 3d ed. (1724), added a second hymn, *Schaffe in mir Gott ein reines hertze.* Neither hymn seems to have been suitable for children, though both may have been suitable for adults who were reminded of their own confirmation.[64]

The first hymn written specifically for confirmation appeared during the period of Pietism. It was *Mein Schöpfer, steh mir bei* ("My Maker, Be Thou Nigh," 1729), by Johann Jakob Rambach (1693–1735). It was accepted in the *Hannoverisches Gesang Buch* (1740), the first hymnal to include a hymn written specifically for confirmation.[65]

Reu's remarks on the Pietistic emphases of confirmation are worthy of note. The Pietists regarded

> confirmation as a renewal, on the part of *God* and man, of the baptismal covenant, as a result, the instruction of confirmands, completely overshadowed all other forms of religious instruction; moreover, the catechist was expected to lead the catechumens through the several stages of the way of salvation in such a manner that they actually experienced conversion and regeneration, and on the basis of their experience vowed henceforth to be God's own.[66]

The Rationalistic Type

A sixth major influence on the practice of confirmation came from the Rationalists, who were peculiarly attracted to it. Once the Pietists had undermined the importance of the Word and

---

[62] Diehl, p. 102.

[63] Philipp Wackernagel, *Das deutsche Kirchenlied* (Leipzig: B. G. Teubner, 1874), IV, 637.

[64] Diehl, p. 102.

[65] Graff, II, 256.

[66] ReuC, p. 136.

sacraments and shifted the emphasis to Christian experience, it was only a matter of time before the intellect replaced both the emotions and the Word and Rationalism began to take over.

Under the influence of Rationalism, confirmation grew in importance as Holy Baptism was minimized. The sacramental emphasis of the 16th century now came into full bloom in a strange manner. The late Pietist Georg Friedrich Seiler (1733 to 1807), who was already affected by Rationalism, stated that confirmation was a substitute for Baptism. For adults, confirmation was the formal completion of the baptismal covenant. Almost all objections made against infant baptism, Seiler advanced, could be met when one showed that in confirmation the instructed children of Christians now publicly declared their own convictions.[67] Friedrich Daniel Ernst Schleiermacher (1768 to 1834) went a step farther by sharply attacking the validity of Baptism. He considered confirmation the second half of Baptism — in fact, the more important half.[68] Th. Ludolph Parisius, in *Über die Konfirmation der Kinder* (1810), pointed out that Baptism first receives its greater meaning with confirmation, for in it Baptism achieves its real purpose. If one separates confirmation from Baptism, it is an empty ceremony with little purpose.[69]

The theological implications of confirmation were further confused in reference to the doctrine of the church. The dogmaticians of the day maintained that while in Holy Baptism the child becomes a member of the Christian fellowship, confirmation determines his affiliation with a particular religious party or congregation. Karl Gottlieb Bretschneider (1776–1848) affirmed that with confirmation the young Christian assumes the duties of a member in the congregation and thus receives certain rights and at the same time submits himself to its regulations. Since this can take place only in an existing congregation or denomination, the confirmand must join one. The con-

[67] Graff, II, 244.
[68] *Der christliche Glaube nach den Grundsäzen der evangelischen Kirche,* 4th ed. (Berlin: G. Reimer, 1843), II (138, 2), 386, 387.
[69] I, 26, quoted by Caspari, p. 106; Graff, II, 244.

gregational rights and duties begin not with Baptism but with confirmation. Baptism is in the name and faith of the Father, Son, and Holy Spirit and in the doctrine of Christianity, not in the distinctive doctrine of either the Roman Catholic or the Evangelical Church.[70]

With such an exalted and distorted view of confirmation, extravagant statements naturally followed. In contrast to the casual practice of the 16th century, confirmation became "the great festival of youth," *die Kinderweihe,* "the festival of human nature," "the most important day of a child's life," "the festival that cannot be made solemn enough." "Know this day is really your first true baptismal day," said J. F. Schlez. Chr. W. Oemler asserted that confirmation can not be sufficiently recommended, for it is an institution which is never too important for a real servant of Christ. The confirmation day must be like another birthday for children, a holy festival for the congregation, and the beginning of a new spiritual harvest for the teacher. Georg Seiler referred to the confirmands in his prayer as "new cocitizens of the kingdom of God." [71]

Obviously, if these extravagances were to be taken seriously, the practices associated with confirmation should measure up to them. The address became the most important part of the observance. From the confirmation sermons of the day one receives a clear picture of the exalted place the ceremony had been given.

The importance given to the sermon is seen even in the extraordinary length of some of the addresses. Graff cites the example of a printed sermon by H. Ph. Sextro, 1809, which had been preached in the castle church in Hannover. It was 53 pages long! Another by B. Chr. L. Natorp, 1805, ran on for 28 pages after the examination. These were, no doubt, extreme cases, but long sermons were common enough for pastors to complain about them. Others, like Johann Caspar Velthusen (1740—1814), followed the prescribed address in the agenda.[72]

---

[70] *Handbuch der Dogmatik der evangelisch-lutherischen Kirche,* 2d rev. ed. (Reutlingen: J. J. Maecken'schen Buchhandlung, 1823), II, 579, 580. So also G. Benj. Eisenschmid. Graff, II, 244.

[71] Graff, II, 244, 245.

[72] Graff, II, 250.

in the Lutheran Church

As with the addresses, so the examinations were extended. In fact, they became so long that the practice of separating the examination from the confirmation ceremony became prevalent during this period. This was particularly true in larger congregations, as in Bremen-Verden, 1785, and in Saxony, 1812. On the other hand, there were those who believed that the examination should continue to be short. They argued that an extensive examination tires the children unduly and is not appreciated by the congregation because the answers are often inaudible. This is reflected in the Schleswig-Holstein Agenda of 1797, which prescribed that the examination should last only about half an hour.[73]

A confession of faith was usually required in the rite. In some instances the confession was written by the confirmands themselves. As would be expected, the questions usually reflected the Rationalism of the times. In Württemberg, 1809, three questions were asked, each requiring an affirmative answer: (1) Do you confess with your mouth and heart the doctrine of Jesus Christ? (2) Do you renounce all unbelief? (3) Do you obligate yourselves to be eternally loyal to God, Father, and Son?[74] The Schleswig-Holstein A of 1797 provided three sets of questions, giving the pastor the choice of one set of three brief questions or another covering three and a half pages and allowing individuals and the group to answer alternately.[75]

The rendering of the vow in connection with the confession of faith became a dramatic moment. Although there were some protests, the vow was frequently referred to as an oath. A *Religionseid* Christoph Timotheus Seidel (d. 1758) called it in his *Pastoraltheologie* of 1749.[76] Some of the theatrical extravagances may be seen in one of Karl Georg Sonntag's addresses. He told his confirmands: "You have sworn! God has heard it! He will judge you not only in the far-off eternity but now already, here

[73] *Schleswig-Holsteinsche Kirchen Agenda* (Schleswig: Joh. Gottl. Roehss, 1797), p. 12.
[74] Graff, II, 251, 252.
[75] *Schleswig-Holsteinsche Kirchen Agenda*, pp. 187—192.
[76] Pp. 145 ff., cited by Caspari, p. 104.

already. . . . Oh, hold fast, hold fast what you have vowed for your welfare in time and eternity." [77]

Caspari describes a form for a *Bibelschwur* from Heinrich Stephani:

> The pastor says: You are to give your oath not to man but to God Himself. Here at this holy place where you were once baptized lies the Holy Book which is to receive from you the oath of eternal loyalty. Approach it individually now in all earnestness and with solemn reverence. (It is best to have a small table which can readily be placed in front of the altar. It is to be covered with a white cloth on which a black Bible with gold letters has been placed. If one wishes, a crucifix may also be placed on it. If the number of children is not very large, each one can make his own vow individually; otherwise groups of five shall place their right hand on the Bible and say . . .[78]

Those who feared that unnecessary difficulties were invited by exalting the vow into an oath regarded the handclasp sufficient, the latter having by this time become standard practice.

After the vow was given, the pastor consecrated the confirmand with a special Bible passage, hymn stanza, or folk saying. Many of these *Einsegnungswünsche,* as they were called, were suggested in the agenda. The Schleswig-Holstein A, 1797, listed 33 from various sources, including Bible passages as well as such moralistic sayings as "Love Virtue; she is the soul's eternal fortune" and "Tremble at the first step, for with it the succeeding steps are accomplished for an early fall." [79] From sentences of this type the practice of giving individual memory verses to the confirmands spread rapidly in the Lutheran Church, especially in Germany.

Since the authority of the church orders had broken down under the impact of Rationalism, every pastor had opportunity to manipulate the liturgy to suit his fancy. In the spirit of the day, sentimentalism was given free rein. Some of these illustrations have already been given. The dramatic moment sketched

[77] Cited from his *Formulare, Reden und Ansichten bey Amtshandlungen,* II, 132, by Graff, II, 253.

[78] From [Heinrich] Stephani's *Winke [zur Vervollkommung des Confirmanden-Unterrichts,* 1805], p. 294, as cited by Caspari, p. 108.

[79] *Schleswig-Holsteinsche Kirchen Agenda,* pp. 192, 195.

in the sermon was heightened when the children, after their consecration, left the chancel to go to their parents and ask their forgiveness and blessing.[80]

Many other external customs became associated with the day to make it more significant: antiphonal songs between the children and the congregation or between the confirmands and the school children, floral wreaths and foliage decorating the church, dramatic ringing of the bells at the proper moment, and special clothes for the event. Like Baptism and marriage, confirmation became an occasion for great family festivity.[81]

Since confirmation lost much of its original significance, it is not surprising that totally unrelated acts became attached to it by law. As the rite was introduced in all parts of Germany, the regulations became systematized within the different territories. A certain amount of education became a prerequisite for confirmation. It was used to enforce schooling. No child was to be confirmed unless he had attended school regularly during the past two years, at least one year of which had been spent in the upper classes. Confirmation was thus tied to Germany's school system. For the majority of children, confirmation meant the end of schooling.[82] Confirmation became even more important to the average person because only the confirmed could attend the Lord's Supper, give an oath, be married in the church, or become sponsors.

As life became more regulated, confirmation was associated even with civic and economic privileges. Unless a person was confirmed, he was not permitted to leave the parish, go to work, join a guild, attend a state school, or go off to boarding schoool.[83] While the regulations were not at all uniform even in the German states, there and elsewhere certain extraneous conditions were commonly associated with confirmation. In Russia (Mitau CO, 1808) the children were expected to give solemn promise to live up to their duties as citizens. Hence confirmation included

[80] Graff, II, 250.
[81] Graff, II, 253—259.
[82] Kliefoth, III, 1, 139—142.
[83] Ibid., III, 1, 142—145.

instruction in civic duties.[84] Elsewhere health education was part of the curriculum.[85] In some places even evidence of successful vaccination was a prerequisite.[86] Because confirmation was sometimes associated with their debut in society, girls of the upper classes frequently postponed the rite a few years.[87] Since confirmation became so closely coupled with school, the minimum age of the confirmands was usually about 14,[88] though in some areas 15 and 16 were preferred.[89] The association of confirmation with school soon helped to determine not only the age but also the time of year when confirmation was customarily held. While the dates still varied according to locality, there was a tendency for them to cluster around Holy Week,[90] for many of the schools closed for spring planting about that season or with Easter. In time Palm Sunday or Maundy Thursday came to be designated by law,[91] and greater uniformity in the closing of the school year then followed.

From all this it is evident that confirmation became part of the structure of the Lutheran churches of Germany during the period of Rationalism. The last of the great Lutheran centers surrendered to social and civic pressure and introduced confirmation. Even Hesse, which had retained its original type of confirmation during Pietism, succumbed to the effects of Rationalism. A strong tie was created between the church and the people through confirmation, as well as through marriage and burial, but this gain was at the expense of serious losses. Con-

[84] Graff, II, 253. Mitau is the present-day Yelgava in Latvia, U. S. S. R.

[85] Hansen, p. 284.

[86] E. g., Schleswig-Holstein. Hansen, p. 296.

[87] Kliefoth, III, 1, 216. A law of 1805 outlined the liturgical structure for confirmation, requiring a vow of Christian morality. Bachmann, p. 301.

[88] Kliefoth, III, 1, 140; Bachmann, p. 294, for Bavaria. In Schleswig-Holstein the normal minimum age for boys was 15. Hansen, p. 293.

[89] Claus Harms warned against an earlier age because it meant sending children out into the world too early and against a later age because the children might neglect confirmation altogether when they were on their own. *Pastoral-Theologie in Reden an Theologiestudirende*, II (Stuttgart: Christian Hausmann, 1834), 192.

[90] Graff, II, 247.

[91] Kliefoth, III, 1, 139.

firmation became more and more a part of the cultus rather than a part of the spiritual life of German Lutherans.

Rationalism reached Norway and Sweden about 1770, having come to Denmark somewhat earlier. In Sweden it came in the form of Wolffianism.[92] Although the Scandinavian countries were affected by Rationalism, there confirmation did not undergo the same dramatic changes that took place in Germany. One reason was that in Sweden confirmation had not yet developed as far; in fact, it had not yet been adopted officially. However, Rationalism did affect the catechisms used in instruction there. One of the first so to be influenced was the *Lärobok för ungdomen* (*Book of Instruction for the Youth*, 1771) of Anton Friedrich Buesching (1724–93).[93] Another was G. F. Seiler's *Lärobok för barn (Book of Instruction for Children)*, which appeared in 1779.[94]

In reaction to catechisms of this type, orthodox pastors were able to have the use of Svebilius' catechism, which had appeared in 1689, made mandatory in 1773. The effort proved to be a failure. Both the Pietists and the Rationalists demanded catechism reforms because of a growing aversion to Luther's catechism. In response to much agitation, some official steps were finally taken in 1793. Archbishop J. A. Lindblom was authorized to prepare a revised catechism, the final version of which was not sanctioned till 1810. His catechism was in the main quite conservative, though it showed some pietistic and rationalistic influences.[95]

After all this, confirmation was still not accepted in Sweden. Not till 1811, with the revision of the agenda, was confirmation officially sanctioned.[96] The ceremony was called "the rite for the admission to the Lord's Supper." It included eight promises with emphasis chiefly on renewal of the baptismal vow. The rubrics

[92] After Christian Freiherr von Wolff (1679—1754), one-time professor of mathematics and philosophy at Halle.

[93] Lilja, p. 120.

[94] Lilja, p. 123.

[95] Lilja, pp. 340, 341.

[96] Kansanaho, p. 287.

called for an address to the confirmands and a prayer but did not permit the laying on of hands. The influence of Pietism and Rationalism was unmistakable. This Swedish agenda was translated into Finnish in 1817.[97]

Through its church order of 1808 the Lutheran Church in Russia reflected the influence of Rationalism. The order was drawn up by Georg Friedrich Sahlfeld and published in Mitau.[98] According to it, confirmation conferred church majority rights on the confirmand. For a short time this church order had some influence in eastern Finland through the Finnish A of 1808, which the consistorium of Hamina produced and which reflected certain Russian views. Both the Russian and the Finnish efforts were short-lived.[99]

The 19th Century

The harmful effects of weaving confirmation into the social fabric were not long in coming to the surface. As education became compulsory among the Germans, even in the villages, confirmation likewise became compulsory. Unfortunately, this was happening during the very time that the German people were becoming estranged from the church. The drift of the discontent away from the church was evident soon after 1848 and particularly in the 1850s.

There were many causes — economic and political as well as social — for the growing estrangement of the people from the church. The expanding industrialization of the German states contributed to the rapid growth of cities, which in turn destroyed old parish roots and produced a new type of freedom. The churches were not prepared for this onrush and found themselves unable to cope with the changes. As a result, intimate relationships between pastors and people broke down. Especially in the cities the parishes became what Doerne calls "phantom congregations" (*Scheingemeinden*).[100] Rationalism had already weakened the spiritual fiber of the masses and now contributed even

97 Ibid., pp. 287, 288.
98 Graff, II, 23.
99 Kansanaho, pp. 147, 288.
100 Doerne, pp. 49, 50.

more to the breakdown of the church's prestige. The conservative stand the church usually took on the political issues that kept Germany in ferment only fostered the estrangement of the more aggressive people. In a few instances drastic changes in church life prompted structural reorganization of the church orders, as in Bavaria. But by and large no major reorganization took place, because the Germans did not wish to surrender the ties of their churches with the state.[101]

The state of the church under compulsory Baptism and confirmation made it more and more apparent that changing conditions would force a review of the manner in which the church recruited and extended itself. It was obvious to some leaders that annual reception into the church of people who did not know and cared less about its essence and task would soon dilute the strength of the church.[102] Since the majority of the people understood confirmation as acceptance into membership in the congregation, it was apparent that particularly this rite needed critical study if it was to be more than "an artificial melodrama" *(ein unwahres Rührakt).*[103]

One of the earlier critics of confirmation in the 19th century was Claus Harms (1788–1855), who in his vehement opposition to Rationalism also questioned some of the practices surrounding confirmation, particularly the rite itself. Of it he said, "Don't make too much of this ceremony."[104] He redirected emphasis on confirmation instruction, which he preferred to call "preparation." Speaking to prospective pastors, he declared:

> We are to teach, but not so much to teach, to instruct, for this the school is to do without exception . . . We are to edify as distinguished from teaching; we are to prepare, cleanse (in the ancient church the catechist was the exorcist), consecrate, awaken the extant gift of the Spirit, ordain to the royal priesthood . . . bring the head to the heart, baptize with the Holy Spirit and with fire, help in the process of regeneration . . . But is not this the task of confirmation itself? Answer: He

[101] Ibid., p. 51.
[102] Ibid., pp. 51—53.
[103] Ibid., p. 45.
[104] Harms, II, 200.

who is not confirmed before he is confirmed will hardly be confirmed when he is confirmed.[105]

Harms's unique observation on the function of the "preparation" did not imply a denial of the power of Holy Baptism. It did mean, however, that he saw little sign of spiritual life among the children coming from homes and schools deeply affected by Rationalism.

The advice which Harms gave his students reveals much about the prevailing practices and his concerns.

> With respect to the [confirmation] sermon I caution you against six mistakes. 1. Do not speak as though you did it all, the parents and teachers did nothing; 2. To picture the children as holy angels; 3. and the others, the world, as black and thus frighten the children; 4. To overemphasize the vow, to make it an oath; 5. To speak disparagingly about Baptism, as though it were incomplete, needed to be supplemented, had become obsolete, or needed to be renewed; 6. To permit the Christian element to be completely absorbed by the human which, of course, is much more emotional.

Concerning the last mistake, Harms noted that it was easy for preachers to move people to tears and so be regarded as great orators.[106]

Harms was critical also of the renewal of the baptismal covenant, which he said should not be renewed: "It must not become old." Similarly he disapproved of the idea that one joins the church with confirmation. "The confirmed had not withdrawn," he pointed out.[107]

As opposed as Harms was to many of the practices, he could not completely dissociate himself from the spiritual climate in which he lived. In 1828 he produced a new hymnal. Some of the hymns which he included for confirmation reflect the very mistakes against which he warned and betrayed his own pietistic leanings.[108]

As early as 1841 Johann Hinrich Wichern (1808—81) ex-

---

[105] Harms, I, 169.
[106] Harms, II, 202.
[107] From his *Leitfaden* (1821), quoted by Hansen, p. 302.
[108] Ibid., pp. 304—306.

pressed his misgivings about the practice of confirmation, declaring that thereby the church was plotting its own destruction.[109] He, with other critics, saw that at the heart of any reform must lie an attempt to restore truthfulness to what was taking place at confirmation. If from the start it was a foregone conclusion that in spite of their solemn promises the majority of the children — estimated as high as 80 percent — would never again partake of the Lord's Supper, it was obvious that some major changes must take place.[110] Ernst Christian Achelis (1838 to 1912) described the existing practice as interference in the prerogative of God, because children were required by law to make a vow to God at a stated time. This, Achelis contended, created an impossible situation. Man cannot bring children to faith through artificial means. Only through instruction in the Word can true faith be created. Requiring a confession of faith of all children, as was then done, was making hypocrites of most of them.[111] Marx, speaking as an educator, felt that children are in danger of having their concept of the truth seriously damaged when they are required to make a confession and a vow which for many is beyond their understanding.[112] Adolf Stöcker (1835 to 1909) agreed, believing that it was psychologically unsound to demand a vow of all children at the early age of 14.[113]

Because most of the critics were interested in reform and not in revolution, few went as far as Sören Aabye Kierkegaard (1813 to 1855), who in his *Attack upon "Christendom"* (1854–55) in a typical overstatement caustically referred to confirmation as "a Christian comedy — or something worse":

> "The tender infant," says "Christendom," "cannot personally take the baptismal vow, for which a real *person* is requisite." And so (is this genius or ingenious?) they have chosen the period from fourteen to fifteen years of age, the age of boyhood. This real person — there can be no objection, he's man enough

---

[109] Heinrich Rendtorff, *Konfirmation und Kirche* (Dresden: C. Ludwig Ungelenk, 1928), p. 9.

[110] Achelis, p. 328.

[111] Ibid., p. 335.

[112] Doerne, p. 94.

[113] Ibid., p. 92.

87

to undertake to perform the baptismal vows made in behalf of the tender infant.

A boy of fifteen! In case it were a question of ten dollars, the father would say, "No, my boy, that can't be left to your discretion, you're not yet dry behind the ears." But as for his eternal blessedness, and when a real personality must concentrate the seriousness of personality upon what in a deeper sense could not be called seriousness, namely, that a tender infant is bound by a vow — for that the age of fifteen years is the most appropriate.

.   .   .   .

Confirmation then is easily seen to be far deeper nonsense than infant baptism, precisely because confirmation claims to supply what was lacking in infant baptism: a real personality which can consciously assume responsibility for a vow which has to do with the decision of an eternal blessedness. On the other hand, this nonsense is in another sense shrewd enough, ministering to the egoism of the priesthood, which understands very well that, if the decision with regard to religion is postponed to the mature age of man (the only Christian and the only sensible thing), many would perhaps have character enough not to want to be feignedly Christian. Hence the priest seeks to take possession of people in young and tender years, so that in maturer years they might have the difficulty of breaking a "sacred" obligation, imposed to be sure in boyhood, but which many perhaps may feel superstitious about breaking. Therefore the priesthood takes possession of the child, the boy, receives from him sacred vows, etc. And what the "priest," this man of God, proposes to do is surely a godly undertaking.[114]

Many proposals to reform confirmation were introduced during the decades following. Accepting the fact that confirmation was obligatory for all, most critics either sought a way in which confirmation might be separated from first Communion and the attainment of majority or devised some type of minor ceremony to mark the end of formal Christian education and then reserved confirmation for a later age. In this way the reformers hoped that a large majority of children who at the age of 14 did not intend to become active church members would be screened out

[114] As translated by Walter Lowrie in *A Kierkegaard Anthology*, ed. Robert [Walter] Bretall (Princeton, N. J.: Princeton University Press, 1946), pp. 453, 454.

and that only those prepared for and willing to assume responsible membership would continue on to the second step. In effect this created two types of church membership, active and inactive, since all were still expected to be baptized in the church. Yet only those who of their own free will wanted to assume responsibilities were expected to make a confession of faith and assume some type of vow.

Some of the more vigorous proposals for reform came from the Erlangen school of theologians: Johann Wilhelm Friedrich Höfling (1802–53), Johann Christian Konrad Von Hofmann (1810–77), Theodosius Harnack (1817–89), and Carl Adolf Gerhard Von Zezschwitz (1825–86). Höfling was greatly disturbed by a church membership forced on the individual by law. Communicant membership must be separated from responsible voting membership *(Gemeinebürgerrecht)*. Under existing conditions both privileges were conferred on the catechumen through confirmation, and this, Höfling believed, was untenable. The two privileges should be conferred in separate acts. In the first the youth should be taken into communicant membership as required by the ordinances. This would not be confirmation. Höfling proposed that the goal of confirmation be the preparation for an active membership in which the confirmand voluntarily assumes his responsibilities as a Christian. Confirmation should be a sort of ordination of the laity. Thus Höfling separated confirmation from first Communion and gave confirmation a hierarchical or disciplinary emphasis.[115]

Von Hofmann, in turn, wanted to reserve the Lord's Supper for a congregation established in the confirmation rite through the laying on of hands. He proposed what he termed a "Biblical confirmation," which revolved about the apostolic laying on of hands. Only this act, he affirmed, elevates confirmation to an act which is more than a termination of religious instruction. Only a "correct confirmation" is able to produce a "correct congregation." Confirmation with the laying on of hands is related to Holy Baptism in this, that with the latter the child is received

115 Joh. Wilh. Friedrich Höfling, *Das Sakrament der Taufe*, II (Erlangen: Palm'schen Verlagsbuchhandlung, 1848), 430—434.

into fellowship with God and with the former he voluntarily becomes an active member. The one deals with participation in the peace of God, the other with participation in the work of God's church on earth. Von Hofmann maintained that the obligatory elementary instruction then a part of confirmation should be divorced from the entire rite and be terminated with a simple ceremony. Confirmation itself should follow some years later, if and when the candidate wants to take this second step.[116]

While Von Hofmann did not posit the idea that a special gift of the Spirit was bestowed through the laying on of hands, August Friedrich Christian Vilmar (1800–68) did make a sacramental act of confirmation and declared that it should not be omitted by the Christian. To Vilmar the laying on of hands was a communication of the Spirit for strengthening the life which the child had received in Holy Baptism. Vilmar took Bucer's formula, "Receive ye the Holy Ghost," to mean an actual imparting of the Spirit.[117] Wilhelm Rohnert concurred with Vilmar in accepting this sacramental view of confirmation in addition to the catechetical and disciplinary aspects of the Hessian church orders.[118] Through Von Hofmann and especially through Vilmar the sacramental emphases of the 16th century were given new life and injected into the debate evoked by study of the confirmation problem.

Theodosius Harnack, like Von Hofmann, did not wish to separate confirmation and first Communion. He identified the *Abendmahlsgemeinde* with the *Bekenntnissgemeinde*.[119] He suggested that religious instruction be given in two stages. The first should be required of all baptized persons during their school years and be concluded with a private ceremony and public intercession in their behalf. This ceremony was not to be called confirmation. The second step was to be taken voluntarily. Additional instruction was to prepare the catechumen for a confirma-

[116] Johann Chr. K. von Hofmann, *Encyclopädie der Theologie*, ed. H. J. Bestmann (Nördlingen: C. H. Beck, 1879), p. 293.

[117] Doerne, pp. 68, 69.

[118] *Die Dogmatik der evangelisch-lutherischen Kirche* (Braunschweig: Hellmuth Wollermann, 1902), p. 435.

[119] *Die freie lutherische Volkskirche* (Erlangen: A. Deichert, 1870), p. 126.

tion admitting him to communicant membership. The rite was to be observed with a solemn service in which the catechumen made a confession of faith and a vow. The rite included the laying on of hands and intercessory prayers. If the confirmand was old enough, he assumed voting rights; if not, he continued in part as a catechumen until he was of age. Thus the voting privileges and rights associated with majority were not automatically given with confirmation.[120]

Von Zezschwitz' suggestion was quite similar to Harnack's. He, too, believed that the normal goal of confirmation is participation in the Lord's Supper. All Christian education in the church extends between the two sacramental poles. Holy Baptism is the beginning and admission to the Lord's Supper the end. Von Zezschwitz distinguished between two types or stages of membership, a sort of embryonic *(keimgemässig)* membership bestowed in Holy Baptism and a full *(vollentfaltete)* membership received with first Communion. The Lord's Supper, he stressed, is the particular sacrament for gathering and uniting the congregation of the Lord as such.[121] But Von Zezschwitz did not believe that this full membership, including the right to partake of the Lord's Supper, should permit the 14-year-old to assume the final step, that is, majority membership and full responsibility in the work of the church. Such active participation he reserved for a later period when the young Christian might personally apply for it. Then a vow was to be exacted. Thereupon the youth should be equipped for Christian witness by the laying on of hands, that is, confirmation.

Many others not associated with the Erlangen school participated in the lively discussion about confirmation. In 1869 Johann Wichern also suggested a division in the practice of confirmation. The first step was to be a simple *Einsegnung* including an examination, an admonition to the children and their parents, and a public intercession. The confession of faith, the vow, and the admission to the Lord's Supper were to be reserved for

120 Ibid., p. 127.
121 Carl Adolph Gerhard v[on] Zezschwitz, *System der christlich kirchlichen Katechetik*, I (Leipzig: Dörffling und Francke, 1863), 627—636.

a later rite. This should be a voluntary step by the youth. Before the second step could be taken, the congregation, through its established authorities, was to review the youth's application.[122] This plan was quite similar to Von Hofmann's but dropped his concern for the laying on of hands.

Soon after the turn of the century, Ernst Christian Achelis (1838–1912) suggested a revision of confirmation by proposing steps leading to confirmation but not to first Communion. He maintained that the first step in any reform should be the separation of confirmation, which was obligatory, from first Communion, which should never be regulated by law. Confirmation should retain the objective element of Christian instruction. The subjective elements, such as the confession of faith, participation in the Lord's Supper, the vow, and the assumption of responsible church membership, should be kept separate and reserved for the time when the catechumen is ready and willing to assume them. Achelis outlined three steps leading to confirmation which, he said, rested on Holy Baptism *(Tauferziehung):* (1) parental instruction, (2) the *Kindergottesdienst* of the congregation during the years of the child's elementary schooling till about age 12, and (3) extended instruction for about two years, leading to confirmation. After completing the third step, the confirmand was acknowledged to have sufficient religious understanding to be a fully qualified member. Because of his youth it was understood that he was still in need of the guidance and care of the pastor and congregation.[123]

In spite of these and other proposals, no important changes were made in Germany. Confirmation had become so deeply rooted in the social life of the people that no major modification was possible. As long as confirmation was enforced by law and had so many extraneous privileges associated with it, it seemed next to impossible to correct what had become a serious situation within the Lutheran Church.

The suggested revisions made in Germany seemed to have had some influence in the Scandinavian countries in that the con-

---

[122] Rendtorff, p. 9.
[123] Achelis, pp. 338—344.

firmation formula became more objective and that some of the pietistic influences were gradually deleted. A case in point was the change adopted in Finland in 1913, two years after confirmation was no longer obligatory on all. The vows were given an emphasis of intent rather than of firm promise. Instead of a reference to the baptismal covenant and a confession of faith, the formula stressed growth in Christian knowledge and life.[124]

The value of the specific proposals for a new type of confirmation lay chiefly in the pioneer thinking which they provided against the time when a major change would have to be made if the church was to survive a confirmation which Adolf Stöcker had characterized as "the organized destruction of the church." [125] Meanwhile the church wrestled with the problem of assimilating the various types of confirmation in trying to meet the rapidly changing conditions in which it found itself — but without finding a satisfactory solution.

[124] Kansanaho, pp. 291, 292.

[125] Achelis, p. 328. The statement was made before the Berlin Pastoral Conference, June 12 and 13, 1895.

CHAPTER III

CONFIRMATION

IN THE UNITED STATES

The Colonial and Early National Period

Lutheran immigrants seeking a new home in America naturally brought with them the type of confirmation to which they had been accustomed. That some of the old customs were inappropriate in their new environment did not seem evident to them. It was not unusual, therefore, that they held on to many of the customs from mere habit or out of a mistaken loyalty to what they conceived to be a part of their Lutheran heritage.

The removal to the American colonies, later the United States, had religious advantages which the Lutheran settlers had probably not foreseen. The Lutheran Church in America was singularly free from Rationalism. Most of the Rationalistic element that had continued to cling to the church in Europe found it more convenient to make a clean break after they arrived in the new country, relieved that they were no longer forced by law to conform to a religion that they did not accept. The form of Rationalism that did trouble some of the eastern synods at the beginning of the 19th century came not so much through the channels of the church in Europe as from the deism prevalent in the young country.[1] However, European Rationalism did

---

[1] Frederick Henry Quitman (1760—1832), president of the New York Ministerium (1807—25), was an outstanding proponent of Rationalism. His *Evangelical Catechism* (1814), though often cited as an example of the sad state of Lutheranism in the United States during this period, exerted little influence. The original ed., about 1,000 copies, sold slowly. Ten years later over 200 copies were still unsold, and the synod was asked to take them over. This it declined to do. Although the catechism stated it was printed "with consent and approbation of the Synod," a record of approval does not appear in the minutes. The synod did not meet in 1812 and 1814 because of the war. J[ohann] Nicum, *Geschichte des Evangelisch-Lutherischen Ministeriums vom Staate New York und angrenzenden Staaten und Ländern* (New York: Verlag des New York Ministeriums, 1888), p. 97.

affect some of the practices accompanying confirmation, as will become apparent below.

A second major advantage that Lutherans enjoyed in America was that the church was no longer tied to the state. While independence from the state was at first an economic hardship, the church was able to grow much stronger from within once it was established. It was spared in large measure some of the confirmation problems that plagued the Lutheran Church in Europe. Those who were baptized and confirmed were not pressured into the church by law. To be sure, many continued to remain in the church out of habit, but sooner or later they, too, were confronted with a decision. For the most part those who continued did so voluntarily; hence many of the reforms proposed in Europe during the 19th century were not relevant for the Lutheran Church in America.

This is not to say that in America there were no problems in connection with confirmation. One of the major handicaps was the ordinary catechumen's lack of Christian education. While in Europe the child usually received much preliminary instruction before being presented to the pastor for confirmation, in America the child usually approached confirmation age with little or no previous religious instruction. Most pioneer parents were so deeply involved in the struggle for existence that they had little time and energy to teach their children. Lutheran schools were nonexistent, except where congregations were able to support them. Most parishes were much too small to maintain schools. Very often families were so isolated from one another that they could do little more than serve as preaching stations for traveling missionaries. The few schools that did exist were more likely to be Calvinistic, Quaker, or Anglican. Later, when public schools were established, a Calvinistic influence was evident in the curriculum, except where Unitarian interests debased it to a bland morality with a Protestant image.

In colonial days and for some time thereafter the strongest single influence evident in the practice of confirmation as observed in America was Pietism. In time Pietism combined with elements of Methodism and Arminianism to produce a strange mixture called "American Lutheranism." The Pietism that first came to the colonies came mainly by way of Halle through Heinrich Melchior Mühlenberg (1711–87), the father of Lutheranism in America. This outstanding pioneer and missionary, more than anyone else, was responsible for the organization of the first Lutheran synod in this country and for giving it a strong Lutheran character. Colonial Lutheranism strongly reflected the influence of Mühlenberg's theology, and he himself was a product of Pietism. This was apparent especially in his practice of confirmation. In his journal for 1764 he recorded a summary of his views as he had expressed them in a confirmation address. From the summary it is evident that confirmation was criticized severely by his English neighbors and perhaps even more so by some of the German sects in Pennsylvania. Under June 24 he wrote:

> Our children . . . have been intrusted to us . . . in Holy Baptism in the presence of witnesses and sponsors. However, these children lose this unction very early in life, and the sponsors are lost and scattered.

The question is asked,

> how old or how young should the baptized children be, or how long should we wait before they are called back and prepared to renew their baptismal covenant?

To this Mühlenberg answered that in the first seven years the spiritual powers of human life are developed to know right from wrong. This power is doubled during the next seven years. "So it follows naturally that young people must be recalled early and taught to renew their broken baptismal covenant, and that their newly recovered faith should be strengthened by the Lord's Supper." [2]

Mühlenberg often expressed his satisfaction that the confirmands were "awakened" with their confirmation, for this, he believed, was the purpose of the instruction and the ceremony concluding it. With him "the renewing of the baptismal covenant" meant just that.

[2] *The Journals of Henry Melchior Muhlenberg*, trans. Theodore G. Tappert and John W. Doberstein (Philadelphia: Muhlenberg Press, 1942—58), II, 92.

Confirmation

Mühlenberg has left us several graphic pictures of his confirmation services. One of these services took place on May 29, 1763, and was recorded in his journal:

The confirmands marched by two's from the schoolhouse to the church, the deacons in front and we preachers behind. We sang the second stanza of *"Komm Heiliger Geist, Herre Gott, erfülle mit deiner,"* etc. I acted as deacon and baptized a child. Sang *"Dreyeinigkeit, der Gottheit wahrer Spiegel."* Mr. Handschuh preached on the Gospel, John 3: On Regeneration.

After the sermon

I commenced with the examination of the confirmands, but first delivered a brief address on the manner of instruction and confirmation in Germany and here. I had the confirmands read three of the penitential Psalms. Then there followed:

1) The recitation of the five chief parts of the Catechism without the explanations.

2) Questioned them on the gist of the chief parts, in order, from the first to the fifth.

3) Went through the *Glaubens-Lied, cursorie,* with them.

4) Had them recite a number of *dicta probantia.*

5) The Order of Salvation by articles.

6) Had them answer questions concerning the steps from natural theology, (a) Of the creation of the universe, (b) Of Man in particular, his state of innocence, fall into sin, guilt, etc., (c) Of redemption through Christ, (d) Of sanctification, (e) Of the means of sanctification, namely the Word of God, Old and New Testaments, and the two Sacraments.

7) Finally I had them kneel and renew their baptismal covenant and pledge their faithfulness; then prayed and commended them to their faithful Chief Shepherd, Jesus Christ.

8) After this I had the boys kneel around the altar and laid hands upon them for the blessing during the singing of the hymn, *"Komm Heil. Geist, Herre Gott,"* and then the girls, in all about eighty in number.

9) Thereupon Mr. Handschuh consecrated and both of us administered the Communion. We were through about two o'clock.[3]

[3] Ibid., I, 632, 633.

Under pioneer conditions uniformity of practice could hardly be expected. Persons were confirmed when the pastor could get them ready, regardless of the time of year. The age range was usually quite broad because it might often be years before the colonists would be near a pastor. The struggle for survival and loosened ties with the church made many parents negligent, so that they delayed the instruction necessary for confirmation. Age ranges from 13 to 32 were not unusual.[4]

Sometimes the ages represented in the group were more like those of an adult class. Pastor Arnold Roschen of Rowan County, N. C., reported in 1789 that he had men and women in his class up to the age of 30, though there were some young people between 16 and 20. The married couples brought their children, and it was not unusual for a young mother to quiet her infant by nursing it as she continued to listen attentively. It is not surprising that under such circumstances the pastor sometimes made excursions in his catechizations and attempted to apply some "practical theology." Roschen, for instance, told unmarried members of the group not to marry the Irish or the English. The former were slovenly, lazy, and poor. As for the English, their blood did not mix well with the Germans', and weak children were produced from such unions. Furthermore,

---

[4] Ibid., I, 505, 506. The records of Mühlenberg's congregation at Trappe, Pa., which include those of preaching stations at Providence, Pikestown (Chester Co.), and Oley Mountains, Pa., and New Germantown, N. J., show that 431 persons were confirmed June 16, 1745, to June 21, 1778. No age is given for 101 of the confirmands. The age range of the other 330 was from 12 to 63, though only 4 were older than 24. The median age was 16, with the mode at 15. "The Trappe Records," *The Pennsylvania-German Society*, III (1896), 509—523.

The church records of the New Hanover, Pa., congregation indicate the age of the confirmands for the first time in 1748. The class of 19 had an age range from 12 to 22, most of them 14 (7) and 15 (6). J. J. Kline, "The Lutheran Church in New Hanover, Montgomery County (Falckner Swamp)," *The Pennsylvania-German Society*, XX (1911), 347. In 1767 the class of 46 had an age range from 13 to 20, with the bulk of the class from 15 to 17. Ibid., p. 359. A similar mode was recorded for the 1768 class of 33 (ibid., p. 359) and a few years later for a class of 61 Ibid., p. 380. A similar mode was found in the first recorded list of confirmands of the Lebanon church for 1782. Pastor William Kurtz (d. 1799) confirmed 13 children ranging from 14 to 17, with almost half age 16 (6). Theodore E. Schmauk, *Old Salem in Lebanon* (Lebanon: Press of Report Publishing Co., 1898), p. 121.

such marriages resulted in strife. The English were unchurched and forbade their children to be baptized and go to school.[5] The amount of instruction varied with the circumstances. Roschen taught his class for seven weeks, three days each week.[6] Mühlenberg was very conscientious in his effort to give the young people a sound background. His *Journals* reveal a great concern for giving the confirmands more than mere head knowledge. He earnestly tried to reach their hearts and lives with the Gospel.

One of the serious problems which faced the colonial pastors was how to provide the children with catechisms. As soon as it was practical, efforts were made to produce catechisms suitable to the American scene. The first catechisms sponsored by Lutheran pastors were printed in Philadelphia in 1749, one in English and the other in German. The German catechism was written by Peter Brunnholz (d. 1757) and printed by Benjamin Franklin and J. Boehm. The English catechism, a translation prepared by author Brunnholz with the assistance of Peter Kock (Koch; d. 1749), a prominent Swedish Lutheran layman of Philadelphia, was printed by J. Behm (sic).[7] Frequent reprints of Brunnholz' catechisms, often with some changes, served the Lutherans in America for more than a century. Nevertheless, even after American catechisms began to appear, pastors were

---

[5] Johann C. Velthusen, *Nordcarolinische Kirchennachrichten* (Leipzig: Siegfried Lebrecht Crusius, 1790), I, 31, 32. The same report, somewhat abbreviated, is found in G[otthardt] D. Bernheim, *History of the German Settlements and of the Lutheran Church in North and South Carolina* (Philadelphia: The Lutheran Book Store, 1872), 330—334.

[6] Velthusen, I, 32.

[7] ReuK, pp. 228, 233. The German copy bears No. 1139 in Cha[rle]s R. Hildeburn, *Issues of the Press in Pennsylvania, 1685—1784* (Philadelphia: Matlack and Harvey, 1885). The English copy bears No. 4626. The eds. which soon followed appeared in 1752 in German (Historical Society of Pennsylvania; Hildeburn, No. 1264), 1761 in English (Hildeburn, No. 4642), and 1765 in German (Hildeburn, No. 2111). *Der kleine Darmstädtische Catechismus,* printed by Chr. Sauer in 1759 (Concordia Seminary Library, St. Louis), appeared in another ed. in 1763 (Hildeburn, No. 1884). In 1774 Count Nicolaus Ludwig von Zinzendorf (1700—60) issued a catechism of Luther with explanation (Hildeburn, No. 885), but it was not acceptable to the Lutherans. The *Grondlycke Onderricht* of Justus Falckner (1672—1723), from the W. Bradfordt [sic] press (1708), was intended for adults. Copies of both catechisms are in the library of the Historical Society of Pennsylvania.

still bothered with the many different versions, representing various territorial churches of Europe, in the hands of the confirmands.[8]

A milestone in the development of confirmation in America was reached in 1786, when the Pennsylvania Ministerium produced its first printed agenda. The agenda included a confirmation formula based on one published in Württemberg.[9] Before this the ministerium operated with only a written copy of the agenda which had been adopted in 1748 but which did not include a formula for confirmation.[10]

Because no form for confirmation had been agreed on prior to this, existing practices varied greatly. Therefore, when the Pennsylvania Ministerium gave its final approval of the agenda in 1787, it agreed to allow liberty "in the rite of Confirmation to conform more to the former usage, if the congregations were otherwise accustomed." [11]

The 1786 formula is important not only because it served as a model for Lutherans in the New World but also because it showed how deeply they had been affected by Pietism. Confirmation was divided into three steps: the instruction, the examination, and the rite itself. For the first step the rubrics repeatedly emphasized that the pastor must be concerned with more than giving the catechumen head knowledge. The pastor must make it a point of conscience that "the hearts of the children were improved" and that he point out to them that the sole purpose of the Christian religion is to make them happy here and for eternity. Without this religion "it would be im-

8 Mühlenberg, I, 98. The problem persisted past the middle of the 19th century. Olaus Fredrik Duus (1824—93) lamented the same situation among his Norwegian frontiersmen in Wisconsin in 1858. Letter dated Jan. 27, 1858, from Waupaca Co., Wis., *Frontier Parsonage: The Letters of Olaus Fredrik Duus, Norwegian Pastor in Wisconsin, 1855—1858,* trans. Verdandi Study Club of Minneapolis, ed. Theodore C. Blegen (Northfield, Minn.: The Norwegian-American Historical Association, 1947), pp. 97, 98.

9 *Documentary History of the Evangelical Lutheran Ministerium of Pennsylvania and Adjacent States* (Philadelphia: Board of Publications of the General Council of the Evangelical Lutheran Church in North America, 1898), p. 183. The New York Ministerium adopted it in 1796. Nicum, p. 74.

10 *Documentary History,* pp. 13—18.

11 Ibid., p. 216.

possible to be happy; for a true Christian, especially a pious child, is the happiest creature of God." The pastor must furthermore show the child how to pray from the heart and also point to the dangers "as they now go out into the wide world." A particular effort should be made to show as clearly as possible what the renewal of the baptismal covenant means. The rubrics strongly emphasized that the pastor's instruction should be prepared carefully and display his patience and personal concern for each catechumen.

The examination, the second step in confirmation, was to be held separately if at all possible, in order not to detract from the rite, which was the solemn climax. Where possible, the examination was to last no longer than an hour and a half.

The final step, the rite itself, was to be observed in two stages. Since confirmation was "one of the most solemn rites" which the pastor experienced in his office, every effort was to be made to reach the hearts of the children and the congregation. The influence of Pietism came fully to the fore in the rite. The first stage was optional but was intended to add to the solemnity of the occasion when observed. The rubrics suggested that there be a sort of preconfirmation service held privately with eligible catechumens and lasting several hours. Here in solemn and fervent manner the pastor was to impress on each candidate the importance of confirmation. He must clearly point out to the child that his becoming a member of a congregation is of least importance at confirmation. The primary purpose of confirmation is to impress on him that from then on he become a true and faithful child of God who surrenders everything that saddens God. Confirmation marks the catechumen's transfer from the kingdom of sin to the kingdom of Jesus and His fellowship. Further to impress on him the seriousness of the step he was taking and the gravity of the occasion, each candidate was to repeat the vow which he would make publicly at confirmation. Thereupon, with the laying on of hands, the pastor was to pray "briefly, fervently, and forcefully." [12]

[12] This optional preconfirmation was omitted in the 1818 revision and in the subsequent agendas.

At the public confirmation, the second stage, four questions were addressed to the confirmands. The first question asked whether they renounce the devil and all his nature; the second, whether they confess their faith in the Triune God as prescribed in their catechism; the third, whether they solemnly renew their baptismal covenant and would "cross over from the kingdom of Satan, the world, and the dominion of sin into the fellowship of God and to the blessed freedom of a true disciple of Jesus"; and the fourth, whether they intend to remain faithful unto death in the acknowledged and solemnly confessed truth of the Evangelical Lutheran Church and especially in the beautiful confession of Jesus Christ.

In this form of 1786 the full effect of the pietistic concept of the renewal of the baptismal covenant and the conversion theology may be seen. Such was the view commonly shared by Lutherans during this period and for some decades to come. "Conversion," the "awakening of the heart," and that God would "touch their hearts" are expressions that were used in connection with confirmation instruction or the rite itself.[13]

Even when confirmation began to decline, the effect of Pietism continued.[14] In some sections, especially outside the

[13] The General Synod A, 1847, declared the main object to be to lead the catechumens "to repentance and true conversion." Mrs. Sarah Harkey is said to have been "converted" while attending catechetical instruction in 1809. Simon W. Harkey, James H. Harkey, and Sidney L. Harkey, "A Tribute Of Affection To The Memory Of Our Departed Mother, Mrs. Sarah Harkey," *The Lutheran and Missionary*, I (Nov. 28, 1861), 18. In his autobiography, John Stauch (1767—1845), a pioneer pastor and later one of the founders of the Ohio Synod, said of the period shortly before 1800 that three individuals had been converted directly "by my catechetical instruction and the fourth while I was in the act of confirming him." C[larence] V[alentine] Sheatsley, *History of the Evangelical Lutheran Joint Synod of Ohio and Other States* (Columbus, Ohio: Lutheran Book Concern, 1919), p. 22. See also "Instruction of Children and Confirmation," *The Evangelical Lutheran Intelligencer*, IV (Nov. 28, 1861), 145; C. B. T., "On the Rite of Confirmation," *The Lutheran Observer*, I (Jan. 2, 1832), 163; and Benjamin Kurtz, *Why Are You A Lutheran? or A Series of Dissertations* (Baltimore: Evangelical Lutheran Church, 1843), p. 184.

[14] Independent of the pietistic confirmation rite in the Pennsylvania A, 1786, which was commonly used in the congregations of the New York Ministerium, is the rite published by Rev. Ralph Williston for his congregation, English Lutheran Church Zion in New York, in 1806. The rite is found in his *A Choice Selection of Evangelical Hymns from Various Authors for the Use of the English Evangelical Lutheran Church in New York* (New York: J. C. Totten, 1806),

103

Pennsylvania and New York ministeria, confirmation was dropped entirely in favor of the "new measures," as the revivals were called.[15] Thus the conversion theology of Pietism completed its natural course. Where confirmation was continued, it was weakened through further loss of its distinctively confessional character, by omission of the name Lutheran from the rite. While the 1786 agenda pledged the catechumen to "The Evangelical Lutheran Church," the 1818 agenda changed it to "The Evangelical Church" and the 1842 agenda to "our Evangelical Church."[16] Without any reference to the Lutheran Church or

which contained a liturgy as a supplement. The book had the approval of John Christoph Kunze, president of the New York Ministerium and pastor of The United German Lutheran Churches in New York.

Williston, formerly a Methodist, was accepted as a Lutheran pastor in 1805. Unfortunately, he and his congregation left the Lutheran Church to go over to the Episcopalians in 1810. Harry Kreider, *History of the United Lutheran Synod of New York and New England,* I (Philadelphia: Muhlenberg Press, 1954), 37. Although Williston's rite showed little pietistic influence, it contained nothing distinctively Lutheran. The unusually brief rite was approximately one page long. It included three questions, a prayer, and several rubrics for the officiant. Noteworthy is that it distinguished between the baptismal vow and the baptismal covenant. In the first question the catechumen was asked to "renew the solemn vow and promise, made at your baptism." In the third question an interesting association was made with the Lord's Supper, which was to follow immediately after the rite of confirmation: "Is it your sincere desire and intention, now in the Last Supper of our Lord, to renew your baptismal vow and covenant?

15 *Ibid.,* I, 163, 164. The defenders of "new measures" received zealous support from Benjamin Kurtz (1795—1865), ed. of *The Lutheran Observer* (1833—61). This important periodical often criticized confirmation as encouraging a formal religion without life.

16 An alternate set of questions in the 1818 A and the 1842 A, which pledged the confirmands to profess their faith merely "in the doctrine and the church *(Gemeinde)* of Jesus," was adopted also by the New York Ministerium and the Joint Synod of Ohio. The General Synod A, 1847, deviated here from the Pennsylvania A, 1842. Although the former suggested two sets of questions, neither set referred to a distinct confession or church except to say "the doctrines of Christ."

The New York Ministerium reflected the same loss of confessionalism in its English agendas of 1814, 1817, and 1834. The rubrics in these eds. state that the catechumens were to have "been previously instructed in a regular series of lectures concerning the doctrines and duties of the Christian religion." Rationalistic influence is seen throughout, not only in omissions, but also in references which speak of Christianity as a "practical religion," in the petition that the catechumens "find by their own happy experience that Religion's ways are ways of pleasantness, and that in all her paths are paths of peace," and in the statement that it may be the catechumen's "great aim to secure thy [God's] friendship."

or to a specific catechism, the English agenda of Ohio, 1830, pledged children simply to confess "the doctrine (you were taught in your Catechisms) as declared in the sacred writings of God."

During and after the thirties, new waves of German immigrants began to arrive in this country, bringing with them more confessional convictions and stronger consciousness of the importance of confirmation. Consequently the practice of confirmation was slowly reintroduced in the older Lutheran areas where the immigrants settled and was observed from the very start in the newer regions. Among the older synods, Pennsylvania, New York, and Ohio were affected most.

When the issues between "American Lutheranism" and a confessional Lutheranism were drawn in the forties and after the defeat of the former in the fifties, the agendas became more confessional in nature. As a consequence, confirmation was gradually introduced even in the synods which had never before practiced it. In 1842 the Allegheny Synod resolved to admit no one without catechetical instruction.[17] The president of the Hartwick Synod, William N. Scholl, reported in 1861 that increased attention was given to catechetical instruction in his body.[18] The Wittenberg Synod, which had been aligned with "American Lutheranism" and had seldom used the catechism for teaching the children, marked a new era in 1864, when pastors were urged to get parents to cooperate by sending children to catechism instruction.[19] Thus confirmation slowly replaced the revivals, while less emphasis was placed on the Sunday schools, which had been assigned the major task of teaching.

The *Lutheran Standard* of the Ohio Synod strongly urged its English-speaking congregations to introduce confirmation. Unfortunately, many of the earlier articles in this periodical were

[17] Dr. Erskine, "Catechising," *Lutheran Standard*, I (Dec. 7, 1842), 2.

[18] "Timely and Sensible," *The Lutheran and Missionary*, I (Nov. 21, 1861), 13.

[19] C. S. Ernsberger, *A History of the Wittenberg Synod of the General Synod of the Evangelical Lutheran Church, 1847—1916* (Columbus, Ohio: Lutheran Book Concern, 1917), p. 108.

exchanges written by Episcopalians who in their praise of confirmation gave it a sacramental emphasis.[20] However, their influence seems not to have had an adverse effect, because little of the sacramental emphasis appeared in the synod's practices.

The stronger Lutheran confessional emphasis became evident also in the formulas for confirmation. The Tennessee A, 1843, asked for a confession of the "truths of the Evangelical Lutheran Church." [21]

The Americanization of the Lutheran Church

With the rapid growth of Lutheranism in the United States after 1830, chiefly through immigration from Germany and later from the Scandinavian countries, confirmation became normal and generally accepted. But even though the rite was accepted, actual confirmation practice varied greatly among and often within the various bodies. Lutherans in America struggled with many of the questions raised by Pietism and Rationalism, questions they had faced already in the Old World. Even antagonism against confirmation, evident in the early period of Lutheranism, was reflected in some of the agendas. Thus the Swedish agendas never spoke of the rite as a confirmation but rather as a preparation of the children for first Communion. When Lutherans from different territorial churches of Europe settled in the same congregation, the existing differences were all the more obvious because often troublesome. Unfortunately, many of the problems of varying or conflicting confirmation practices and attitudes have never yet been solved. Shifting emphases within synods betray uneasiness in the absence of wholly satisfactory solutions. Since most of the variant practices and interpretations were not drawn along synodical lines, it is necessary to study the continued development of confirmation according to the different problems which arose in connection with the practice.

[20] "Catechization," I (Oct. 26, 1842), 2; "Confirmation," II (April 6, 1844), 2; Bishop Kaye, Lincoln, England, "History of the Rite of Confirmation," V (Aug. 4, 1847), 2.

[21] The Pennsylvania A, 1855, specifically stated that the catechumens were to be instructed in Luther's Small Catechism.

in the Lutheran Church

The Baptismal Covenant

One of the foremost problems was that of relating Baptism to confirmation. It was generally agreed that Holy Baptism obligates the parents and the church to teach and that Baptism is one of the sacramental poles about which confirmation revolves. Only rarely did anyone state that confirmation completes Baptism. Even where a conversion theology was taught, it was not necessarily denied that faith is created in Holy Baptism but rather affirmed that this faith in most instances has died and needs to be revived through instruction. Some believed that the communion with God which Holy Baptism brought about in a general way needs to become a matter of personal conviction or experience through instruction.[22]

The kind of emphasis placed on the baptismal covenant indicates some confusion and the continued influence of Pietism. The Pennsylvania A, 1855, referred to confirmation as a "sacred covenant observance" *(eine heilige Bundesfeier)*. What is the nature of this covenant? Is it a covenant of *grace* made unilaterally by God with the child in the sacrament? If so, then as the 16th-century Lutherans said, the child should *remember* the covenant in his confirmation. Few seem to have expressed the view of Ludwig Fuerbringer (1864–1947) that the baptismal covenant is made by God and is lasting, needing neither renewal nor confirmation.[23] More frequently a bilateral covenant was pictured in which there is reciprocal obligation between two parties — God in grace accepting the child in Holy Baptism and giving him the merits of Christ, whereupon the child, through his sponsor or parent, obligates himself to die to sin and live a new life. In such a covenant, God does not change; only man changes.[24] But man's failure to live up to his part of

[22] P. Bergstresser, "Catechisations and Confirmation in the Lutheran Church," *The Lutheran Quarterly*, XXI (Oct. 1891), 518, 519.

[23] "Zur kirchlichen Chronik: Die Konfirmation," *Der Lutheraner*, LXIII (March 12, 1907), 86.

[24] Schneider, Ino., "Auszug aus Kollege [B. F.] Zismers Katechese über die Konfirmation," *Evangelisch-Lutherisches Schulblatt*, XXVI (July 1891), 202. Zismer's catechization was presented and discussed in sessions of the North Ohio teachers conference in Cleveland in Dec. 1890. Schneider was secretary.

107

the covenant apparently nullifies or breaks it, and therefore the covenant needs to be renewed and confirmed. What happens to a bilateral covenant when one party breaks it? Is it canceled also by God? Most of the agendas were silent on this. Löhe's agenda of 1844 said that because of our sins we merit God's cancellation, but that He is faithful and merciful. The catechumen who has been instructed concerning his sin and God's faithfulness is invited to renew the covenant. The English agendas of the Missouri Synod, which used the word covenant in two different ways, similarly stressed that God keeps His covenant and that the Christian should remain faithful.[25] The Ohio A, 1864, with one exception, was singularly free of any reference to the baptismal covenant. The only reference was in the address to the children immediately after the rite; in the address the pastor admonished the children not to follow the example of such who deliberately transgress and leave their baptismal covenant. Regrettably, later agendas followed the more customary references to a renewal of the covenant.[26] The agendas of several Lutheran church bodies — such as the Norwegian Evangelical Synod, 1891; the United Norwegian Lutheran Church of America, 1915; the Evangelical Lutheran Church, 1952; the Lutheran Free Church, 1948, and the *Service Book and Hymnal of the Lutheran Church in America,* 1958 — all pledge the catechumen simply to continue steadfast "in this covenant of thy baptism."

More frequently the promises made by the sponsors or the parents on behalf of the child were referred to as the baptismal covenant without any mention or reference to a covenant of grace. In such cases the covenant could be understood as the human part of the bilateral covenant or simply as a vow without any direct reference to the covenant of grace. The sponsors or parents made this kind of covenant at Baptism because the children could not make it themselves. At confirmation, after

[25] 1917, 1921, 1936, and the Synodical Conference A, 1949.

[26] Ohio's Selection of Forms, 1870, spoke of both a covenant of grace and a renewal of the covenant.

he had been instructed, the catechumen was asked to confirm,[27] ratify,[28] or renew it,[29] or to "pledge anew." [30]

The Wisconsin A, 1896, which followed closely the German Missouri A, 1890, made a significant change. Where the Missouri A spoke of renewing the baptismal covenant, Wisconsin changed it to "confess the baptismal covenant with your own mouth" and omitted the first question, in which the catechumen was asked publicly to renew the covenant made in his behalf by the sponsors. The questions in the German agenda of Missouri, 1922, were reworded to read "vow" instead of "covenant," the noun that had appeared in all editions from 1856 till then. However, the first English edition, 1917, did not make the change, nor did subsequent revisions. That the vow and the baptismal covenant were considered interchangeable is clearly indicated in the General Synod A, 1881. Striking is the fact that every reference to the baptismal covenant was omitted in the General Council A, 1891; the Augustana A, 1928; and the United Lutheran Church A, 1918 and thereafter.

The Vows

The promises or vows made by the catechumens reflected, as a rule, the promises made or implied in Holy Baptism. Now that the catechumen had been instructed, he was able to make the promises on his own. However, there were some, like Carl Ferdinand W. Walther (1811–87), who emphasized that the implication was not that this was the first time that such a promise was made by the catechumen.[31] The editor of the *Lutheran Standard,* Walter E. Schuette, said: "Nothing is done at confirmation which should not be done every day." [32]

27 General Synod A, 1881: Synodical Conference A, 1949; and General Council A, 1891.

28 Pennsylvania A, 1860; General Synod A, 1881; United Synod in the South A, 1888; and General Council A, 1891.

29 Ohio A, 1909; Missouri English A, 1917, 1921, and 1936; and Tennessee A, 1843, which speaks also of a "return to your covenant."

30 Missouri English A, 1917, 1921, and 1936.

31 *Americanisch-Lutherische Pastoraltheologie* (St. Louis: Druckerei der Synode von Missouri, Ohio u. a. Staaten, 1872), p. 266; hereafter referred to as *Pastoraltheologie.*

32 LXXII (April 4, 1914), 213.

109

Some of the promises exacted indicate a lack of confessional stamp; the lack was characteristic in the early part of the 19th century. Thus the Ohio A, 1830, was quite vague: "Will you, by the help of God, ever adhere to those doctrines [declared in the sacred writings of God]; live in obedience to the order of the Christian Church, and continue faithful thereunto until death?" But as the confessional character of the Lutheran Church in America was strengthened, the confirmation promises came to be less general and more explicitly confessional.

The content and the number of vows varied greatly. The catechumens were pledged to loyalty to the Evangelical Lutheran Church [33] and to remain members of it till their end.[34] The Löhe A was unique in that it pledged the catechumens to the "one, holy, Christian Church which in this world bears the name Evangelical Lutheran." [35] The catechumens were asked to adhere to the doctrine of Jesus Christ,[36] to the Creed,[37] to the teachings of the Christian Church,[38] or more specifically, to remain with the teachings of the Lutheran Church.[39] The confirmands further promised to live a Christian life,[40] to shun all

[33] Tennessee A, 1843; and United Lutheran Church A, 1918.

[34] Löhe A, 1844; Ohio A, 1909; Missouri German A, 1922, and the English A after 1917; and the Synodical Conference A, 1949.

[35] The Löhe agenda was prepared for Lutherans in America and became in time the official agenda of the Iowa Synod. It was used by Missouri Synod pastors and congregations till their own was published in 1856. *Der Lutheraner,* V (Nov. 14, 1848), 45; *Briefe von C. F. W. Walther an seine Freunde, Synodalgenossen und Familienglieder,* ed. L[udwig] Fürbringer, I (St. Louis: Concordia Publishing House, 1915), 51. It was officially adopted by the Frankenmuth and Frankentrost congregations in Michigan. "Kirchenordnung, 1848," X, 77, in Chr. Otto Kraushaar, *Verfassungsformen der Lutherischen Kirche Amerikas* (Gütersloh: C. Bertelsmann, 1911), p. 124. In the 2d ed. of the agenda, 1859, Löhe changed the pledge to "the true church, called here on earth the Evangelical Lutheran Church."

[36] Tennessee A, 1843.

[37] United Lutheran Church A, 1918; and *SBH,* 1958.

[38] Lutheran Free Church A, 1948.

[39] Pennsylvania A, 1860; Ohio A, 1864; General Council A, 1891; all the Missouri A and the Synodical Conference A, 1949; Wisconsin A, 1896; and Augustana Swedish A, 1895, and English A, 1898 and 1928.

[40] All the Missouri A; Wisconsin A, 1896; Synodical Conference A, 1949; and Augustana Swedish A, 1895, and English A, 1898 and 1928.

false doctrines,[41] and faithfully to use the means of grace.[42] The children were also asked to assume the promises made at their baptism [43] or to continue in their baptismal covenant.[44] The number of promises to be pledged varied from one, as with the Norwegian synods (except the Lutheran Free Church) and the National Lutheran Council, to four, as with the Synodical Conference A, 1949. Some were broad in nature, having no specific reference to the Lutheran Church; others were very specific, as was the Missouri Synod A. But all the agendas published in the 20th century made it very clear, either in the formula or in the rubrics, that loyalty to the doctrine of the Lutheran Church was implied.

The binding nature of the vow was frequently discussed. The effect of the 18th century was not lost in this respect either. The German A of the Missouri Synod at first went all the way by referring to the vow as a "solemn oath," though this expression was omitted in the 1922 edition of the German and in the 1917 edition of the English.[45] The unconditional and binding character of the vow pledging the catechumen to the Lutheran Church brought criticism not only from non-Lutherans [46] but also from Lutheran pastors and laymen, especially when by inter-

41 Buffalo A, 1888, and Augustana A, 1928.

42 United Lutheran Church A, 1918; and Augustana Swedish A, 1895, and English A, 1898 and 1928.

43 Ohio A, 1830 and 1864.

44 Buffalo A, 1888, and Lutheran Free Church A, 1948. An interesting addition to the variety of promises exacted is the one by a pastor who required all catechumens to sign a pledge that they would attend the high school Bible class for four years. O. B. Anderson, "Three Approaches to the Post-Confirmation Problem," reprinted from *Lutheran Herald* in *The American Lutheran*, XXV (Jan. 1942), 18, 19.

45 C[arl A.] Abbetmeyer's ed., 1904, had already omitted the sentence as found in the 1881 ed. Even after changes in the agenda, some of the literature referred to the vow as an oath in dramatizing the importance of the day. Cf. *Kehre Wieder! Worte der Liebe an einen früheren Konfirmanden von seinem lutherischen Pastor* (St. Louis: Luth. Concordia Verlag, 1883), p. 16; C. F. W. Walther, *Festklänge: Predigten über Festtexte des Kirchenjahrs*, comp. C. L. Janzow (St. Louis: Concordia Publishing House, 1892), p. 189; "Confirmation," *The Lutheran Witness*, XXXIV (March 23, 1915), 94; Daniel F. Goerss, "Fight the Good Fight of Faith," *The Concordia Pulpit for 1947*, XVIII (St. Louis: Concordia Publishing House, 1946), 363.

46 *Lutheran Standard*, LXXXVIII (March 27, 1920), 193.

pretation the vow was restricted to a specific synod.[47] Martin T. Ringstrom discussed the nature of the vow required in the Augustana A. He, too, questioned whether it was fair to bind the adolescent to a lasting vow; later as an adult it might become a matter of conscience for him to make a change. He also questioned the right of the church to exact more than the Scriptural requirements of Baptism, repentance, and a confession of faith. Many pastors of his synod believed the vow to be irrevocable. His analysis of the wording in the agenda led him to believe that the formula was ambiguous and allowed the interpretation which he urged, that the vow was binding in the sense that it expressed the desire and intent of the catechumen to continue in the faith which he professed.[48]

In a reminder that the importance of confirmation should not be overemphasized and that the entire rite could be omitted as was customarily done with unbaptized adults, one writer stated that the confirmation vow was only a repetition of the baptismal vow, something which the Christian should be ready to make every day.[49] This had been similarly stated somewhat earlier by another anonymous contributor who had said that the confirmation vow is a renewal of the baptismal vow only as every prayer is a renewal of that vow.[50] In the folk theology of the Lutheran Church, however, the confirmation vow had much greater significance.

[47] *The Lutheran Layman*, XXVI (June 1, 1955), 5; *The Northwestern Lutheran*, XLIV (Feb. 17, 1957), 53.

[48] "The Significance of the Confirmation Vows," *Augustana Quarterly*, XVII (Jan. 1938), 59—66. Variations of this specific promise may be seen in the following. Augustana A, 1928: "Will you also shun all false doctrines and be faithful to the Word of God according to our Evangelical Lutheran Confessions?" United Synod in the South A, 1888: "Will you remain faithful to the doctrines of our Lord Jesus, according to the Confession of our Evangelical Lutheran Church, and will you render a conscientious obedience there until death?" Synodical Conference A, 1949: "Do you also, as a member of the Evangelical Lutheran Church, intend to continue steadfast in the confession of this Church, and suffer all, even death, rather than fall away from it?" *SBH*, 1958: "Do you promise to abide in this Faith and in the covenant of your baptism, and as a member of the Church to be diligent in the use of the Means of Grace and in prayer?"

[49] A. F., *"Ihr habt einen andern Geist!"* Part II, *Der Lutheraner*, LXVIII (Feb. 6, 1912), 35.

[50] W, "Confirmation," *The Lutheran Witness*, XVIII (Feb. 7, 1900), 130, 131.

The Confession of Faith

One of the oldest elements of a Lutheran confirmation is the confession of faith. It was an essential element from the start. It seems that originally the confession was objective, that is, a confession in which the catechumen made it clear that he understood the doctrine of the Lutheran Church and was now able to examine himself in preparation for his first Communion. In time, however, this confession was interpreted to mean a confession of one's personal faith, and as such it was generally accepted. Johann Michael Reu (1869–1943) believed that the objective confession is the only one permissible in the rite. Since the working of faith is exclusively the operation of the Holy Spirit, no one in the church should require the catechumen to make a personal confession. "The Word of God, which the teacher of religious truth employs, is indeed efficacious; but it does not always unfold its power at the time when it is proclaimed." [51]

Furthermore, Reu asked, how can "we now expect at the time of confirmation from all catechized children alike the confession of their saving faith, the faith of their hearts, and require all to go to Holy Communion? Should we not, in that case, do violence to our own better judgment and put a falsehood upon the lips of those children in whom saving faith has not been aroused as yet?" [52] Reu recognized that the European state churches had a more serious problem, but even in the free churches of America "we have no absolute assurance that all the children instructed by us are in a state of saving faith at the end of the period of instruction." [53]

Generally speaking, the confession of faith was understood to be subjective. The examination was considered the objective phase of the confession, and the answers to the specific questions required by the rite were thought to be the subjective element. Such interpretations exaggerated the subjective during the pietistic period in the United States, but since then this overem-

[51] ReuC, p. 278.
[52] ReuC, p. 631.
[53] ReuC, p. 631.

Confirmation

phasis has decreased somewhat. Yet the current emphasis on functional instruction incurs the danger of a return to pietism. This danger is evident in a suggestion that the pastor should try to establish "whether that change has really taken place which the Bible calls the new birth, whether the confirmand's personal acceptance of Jesus Christ as Lord and Master is real and earnest." [54]

The Lutheran confessional imprint on confirmation has become clearer with each generation. No longer is there such laxity as in the Pennsylvania A, 1818 and 1842, which gave the pastor the option of two series of questions, depending on his or his congregation's confessional consciousness. In every instance after 1850, and frequently before that, the confession of faith established in the various orders of confirmation was clearly Lutheran, though in some agendas more unmistakably than in others.

Since the examination was regarded as the most important phase of the confession of faith, the questions varied according to the emphases. Usually the vow supplemented the confessional content of the statement of faith. The churches with a Norwegian heritage usually followed the Norwegian *Alterbog* and simply asked the children to confess their faith in God the Father, Son, and Holy Ghost.[55] Others limited the confession to the Apostles' Creed, the ancient baptismal creed.[56] In addition to the Apostles' Creed, the Wisconsin and the Missouri A asked the children to confess their acceptance of all the canonical books of the Bible as the inspired Word of God and of the doctrine of the Lutheran Church, drawn from the Bible, as taught in Luther's Small Catechism.

[54] O[swald] A. Waech, "Advancing in Evangelism: Confirmation," *Advance,* II (March 1955), 22. A similar thought was expressed in the General Synod A, 1847, where the pastor was instructed to admit to confirmation those "who afford satisfactory evidence to the pastor and the church-council that they are determined, and sincerely striving, to serve the Lord."

[55] Norwegian A, 1891; Evangelical Lutheran Church A, 1952; Norwegian Evangelical Lutheran Synod A, 1901; and Lutheran Free Church A, 1948.

[56] Löhe A, 1844; General Synod A, 1881; General Council A, 1891; Ohio A, 1909; all Augustana Swedish and English A; United Lutheran Church A, 1918; and *SBH,* 1958.

Church Membership

Does confirmation change the catechumen's relation to the church or to the congregation? This question seems to have been as much a source of confusion in the development of confirmation in the United States as it was in Europe. While Lutherans have generally tried to avoid every sacramental implication in confirmation, they have had difficulty in reconciling the fact that the child had become a member of the holy Christian church by Baptism and through it ordinarily also of a specific congregation. Since the sacrament was administered in Christ's name, usually by a called servant of the Word, a pastor of the church at a given place and through it a member of the denomination to which his congregation professed adherence, Baptism made the child a member also of the congregation where he was baptized. Nevertheless, the Old World problems of church membership haunted all the Lutheran synods.

Theodore Graebner (1876–1950) wrote in the *Lutheran Witness:* "Confirmation is a rite by which Christians are received into communion with the visible church of Christ on earth." [57] Similarly, another writer declared that by confirmation "These souls have been added to the church visible, and many, let us hope, to the church invisible." [58] Löhe had the pastor receive the confirmands in the name of the Lord Jesus Christ and in the stead of the holy Christian church into the fellowship of the grace and favor of God, the fellowship of the blood of Jesus, and the fellowship of the comfort and light of the Holy Spirit. In the 1859 agenda this was omitted. Löhe explained that he

[57] XXXVII (March 5, 1918), 67, 68. In a booklet prepared for the newly confirmed, Graebner wrote: "While you were preparing for confirmation, you were proceeding steadily towards a certain goal: admission to membership in a local Christian congregation. While a member of Christ's invisible church since the day of your Baptism, you are now, through your public confession on the day of your confirmation, to be granted membership in a congregation of believers, which has raised up in its midst, according to the Lord's command, the sacred office of the ministry, of the gospel, and which gathers at stated seasons in its house of worship, to hear the Word of Life." *Our Faith Victorious* (New York: Ernst Kaufmann, n. d.), p. 23.

[58] G. H. S., "Care of the Confirmed," *Lutheran Standard*, XLIII (April 4, 1885), 108.

had been influenced by Höfling but had come to believe that such a wording depreciated Baptism. He regretted that he could find no proper way of expressing the confirmand's reception into communicant membership.[59] The Ohio A, 1830, received the confirmands as "members of the Church of Christ." [60] More often the word "church" is spoken of without a closer definition. One of the most common statements found in periodicals and church bulletins each spring is that on a certain confirmation day a specified number of "members have been added to the church."

As in Europe the idea that confirmation makes one a member of a specific denomination persistently appears in the literature. "The *act* of confirmation may be defined to be that solemn ceremony, by which a baptized person, formally and voluntarily joins the christian church, and in it, a special portion or denomination of which latter he becomes a member." [61] The same was succinctly stated by Friedrich Kuegele (1846–1916) in a confirmation sermon when he told the children: ". . . you are to be members of the Evangelical Lutheran Church." [62]

It is not surprising that the Pennsylvania A, 1786, in accord with its Pietistic emphasis, spoke of a reception into the Lutheran Church. What does surprise is that the German A of the Missouri Synod, before the 1922 revision, asked the catechumen whether he desired to be a member of the Evangelical Lutheran Church. The import of the question was not changed when the pastor finally acknowledged him to be a member who may partake of the Lord's Supper. The 1922 revision changed the question to read: "Do you desire to remain . . . ?" The Synodical Conference A of 1949, strangely enough, followed the original formula of Missouri, asking the children to become members. The Wisconsin A, 1896, had asked the same question.

[59] Löhe A, 1859, pp. 54, 55.

[60] So also the General Synod A, 1847, which stated that the members were to receive the confirmands "as members of the household of faith." But the Ohio agendas corrected this from 1864 on.

[61] C. F. S., "Confirmation," *Lutheran Observer*, I (May 15, 1832), 308. The confirmation certificates printed in this period reflected the same view.

[62] "Confirmation Sermon," *The Lutheran Witness*, XVI (June 21, 1897), 10.

Even more specific than confirmation conferrals of member-ship in a denomination are statements that at confirmation the catechumen becomes a member of the local congregation. Par-ticularly in regions of early Lutheran settlement in America the confirmation orders assumed association of confirmation with congregational membership. Examples are the New York A, 1814 and later editions, and the Pennsylvania A, 1842, which received the children into "this congregation." The General Synod A, 1881, was similar. The agenda of the United Lutheran Church, 1918 and thereafter, which specifically stated that Holy Baptism made one a member of Christ's church, nevertheless had the pastor say to each catechumen individually, "I hereby declare thee a member of this Congregation." [63]

In spite of this confusion concerning membership in the church, there were those who spoke of the catechumens becom-ing "confirmed members" [64] or communicant members.[65]

The term "full member" was also imported into the literature, and the catechumen was then invited to become a full member with all spiritual rights and privileges.[66] The agenda writers usually used the term in the sense of communicant membership and sometimes mentioned specifically the right to be a sponsor.[67] The rubrics of the United Lutheran Church make it plain that participation in the temporal affairs of the local congregation is governed by its constitution.

Because confirmation does not change the catechumen's mem-bership in the holy Christian church or in the local congregation even though it invites him to participate in the Lord's Supper,

[63] Similarly the Pennsylvania A, 1860, and the United Synod in the South A, 1888.

[64] Ohio A, 1864; Selection of Forms, 1870; and A, 1909.

[65] "You are entering your majority; you then become also communicant members . . ." Fr[iedrich] B[ente], "Eine katechetische Besprechung des Konfir-mationsgelübdes mit der Konfirmandenklasse," *Magazin für Ev.-luth. Homiletik und Pastoraltheologie*, XXXVII (Feb. 1913), 90.

[66] Buffalo A, 1888. Variants of this are "full communion in the Church of Christ," Bergstresser, p. 515; and "in full connection with the church," *Lutheran Standard*, I (March 22, 1843), 2.

[67] General Council A, 1891, 1892 (German), and 1908.

some agendas omit all references to membership in the church [68] or, when speaking of the vow, refer to continuing in membership.[69]

Since so much of the literature is freighted with accretions of 18th-century Pietism and Rationalism, we need not be surprised that many Lutheran catechumens believe that in confirmation they are "joining the church."

The Laying On of Hands

The laying on of hands is a prominent feature of confirmation as observed in America. The agendas generally prescribe the act, though the Augustana agendas make it optional. In several agendas the laying on of hands is described as an ancient custom and passages are cited to show its Biblical origin.[70] With J. K. Wilhelm Löhe (1808—72) and the later editions of the Iowa Synod, before the solemn act the confirmands say in unison: "God be gracious to us and bless us. May He make His face to shine upon us. Selah — That we may know here on earth His way and among all heathen His salvation. — May God, our God, bless us; may He bless us and all the world fear Him."[71] The Ohio A, 1864, which avoided the usual pietistic references to the baptismal covenant and church membership and reflected a sound Lutheran confirmation, nevertheless gave unusual emphasis to the laying on of hands. Not only did it suggest the prayer "Receive the Holy Spirit" at this point, but it also gave the rite additional emphasis by reminding in the address to the congregation that the confirmands, by the laying on of hands and prayer, "had been committed anew to the goodness and grace of God."[72] However, great care was usually taken to avoid the implication that the Holy Spirit was actually imparted. It is

[68] General Council A, 1891; Norwegian Evangelical Lutheran Synod A, 1891; Evangelical Lutheran Church A, 1929 and 1952; all Augustana A, Swedish and English; and Lutheran Free Church A, 1948.

[69] Tennessee A, 1843.

[70] Wisconsin A, 1896, and Missouri German A before 1922.

[71] Löhe A, 1844 and 1859; Löhe-Deinzer A, 1884; and Iowa A, 1919.

[72] The Selection of Forms, 1870, which quite generally followed the Ohio A of 1864 in translation, omitted the reference in the address; the A, 1909, omitted also the prayer, though it otherwise followed Löhe in many respects.

clear that the act was generally regarded as symbolic of the Spirit's coming, though at times the agendas were ambiguous and could permit a sacramental emphasis. The Tennessee A, 1843, petitioned: ". . . we therefore beseech thee to grant unto these our young friends, by the imposition of our hands in thy name, thy grace and the Holy Spirit, the Spirit of all power . . ." Yet the actual prayers which accompanied the imposition were addressed not to the Spirit but to the Lord Jesus. One of the suggested prayers asked Jesus to "grant unto *him* the aid of thy Holy Spirit, that *he* may continue faithful in thy service, until death."

Similarly Löhe had an alternate section in one of the prayers. The rubrics suggested: "Grant these Thy children, upon whom we now in Thy name lay hands and thereby assure them of Thy gracious, fatherly hand and the power and help of Thy Holy Spirit unto a true Christian life . . ." Here, too, the context implied that the laying on of hands was a symbolic act.

The number and types of "prayers of blessing" *(Segenswünsche)* which usually accompanied the laying on of hands varied. Many formulas call for only one, while the Ohio A, 1909, had seventeen. The growing feeling that more prayers were needed is illustrated in the Pennsylvania A. It started out in 1786 with one. In 1818 there were five; in 1842, twelve, including the controversial *Nimm hin* of Bucer, though in an altered form. In 1855 a thirteenth prayer was added.[73] The Bucer prayer was one of five in the Löhe A, 1844.[74] It was generally omitted, even in the agendas which borrowed heavily from Löhe.

The statement "By the laying on of hands the church, through the pastor, confirms these young confessors in this new privilege [of partaking of the Lord's Supper]" is representative of the view held by many in the Lutheran Church.[75]

[73] The Pennsylvania A, 1860, an English trans. of the 1855 A, included the original Bucer version in addition to the altered one in the 1855 A.

[74] Löhe omitted it in his 1859 ed. because it implied more than a prayer. Compare also pp. 21 f., esp. his n. 91 a. The Buffalo A, 1888, had only one such blessing, that of Bucer.

[75] "Confirmation," *The American Lutheran*, XXVIII (Feb. 1945), 45.

Church Discipline

While the Lutheran church was singularly free from the hierarchical emphases of Bucer, his influence was still in evidence. The United Synod in the South A, 1888, required its confirmands to submit themselves to the rules of government and discipline of "this Christian Church." The Wisconsin A, 1896, spoke of confirmation as a custom in which the catechumens surrender themselves to the discipline of God and His church. Missouri pursued the same thought in its German editions before 1922, the English translation of 1881, and in the Abbetmeyer edition of 1904. Beginning with that of 1917, the official English agendas omitted these references. Peculiarly enough, the Synodical Conference A, 1949, asked members transferring in from other Lutheran congregations: "Do you intend to submit to the government and discipline of this congregation, administered according to its established form and order?" [76]

The Examination

The examination of the confirmands was considered, though not exclusively, an essential part of confirmation, because it was interpreted as primarily a confession of faith. The simple and brief catechization of the 16th century, which was intended to serve only as a confession of faith, no longer served as the pattern. Exceptions to the usually broadened interpretations are found in synods with a Scandinavian background. In them the examination was held on the same day as the confirmation itself and was intended as the confession of faith, instead of the concise confession usually made later in the formal act.[77]

In the majority of the Lutheran churches the more extensive examination of the 18th century was also to demonstrate that even the weakest could examine himself in preparation for first Communion.[78]

[76] P. 32.

[77] Norwegian Evangelical Lutheran Synod A, 1891; Evangelical Lutheran Church A, 1929 and 1952; Lutheran Free Church A, 1948; and Augustana A, 1928 and 1951.

[78] Ohio A, 1909; all Missouri A; and Synodical Conference A, 1949.

In some instances the examination was to show that the confession of faith to be made later in the confirmation rite was thoroughly understood by all the confirmands. The examination was thus more pedagogical than confessional and might be quite extensive.[79] When repentance and conversion were the chief objectives of confirmation, the examination was to give evidence that these objectives had been achieved.[80]

When the examination was held separate from the remainder of the rite, it was held either in a morning, afternoon, or evening service on a preceding Sunday[81] or in a vesper service sometime during the week.[82] The parents, sponsors, and congregation were expected to be present,[83] though the church council might represent the congregation.[84] While it was usually the local pastor who examined the children, Löhe made a unique suggestion to avoid any charge of partiality. He proposed that a neighboring pastor, perhaps an official, be invited as examiner. In accord with some early church orders of Europe, Löhe believed that the examination should also serve to screen out those children not yet ready for first Communion. Accordingly, the children should be informed of the results of the examination as soon as it was completed, so that they might know in advance whether or not they were to partake of the Lord's Supper. Löhe also suggested that the examination be held in conjunction with the usual *Kinderlehre* during the week so that the visiting pastor need not miss a Sunday service.[85]

Separation of the examination from the rest of the ceremony allowed the pastor more time. Most agendas did not suggest

[79] Earlier agendas of the Missouri Synod did not suggest examination on a separate day. This was first suggested in the Synodical Conference A, 1949, but the custom was long established in the Missouri Synod prior to this date.

[80] General Synod A, 1847, as was also the case in the early agendas of the Pennsylvania Ministerium.

[81] Buffalo A, 1888.

[82] Synodical Conference A, 1949.

[83] Wisconsin A, 1896; Ohio A, 1909; Buffalo A, 1888; all Missouri A; and Synodical Conference A, 1949.

[84] Pennsylvania A, 1842; General Council A, 1891; United Lutheran Church A, 1918.

[85] 1844, 1859, and 1884 eds., but dropped in Iowa A, 1919. Found also in Pennsylvania A, 1786.

the hour and a half of the Pennsylvania A, 1786, but limited the length to about an hour. The examination was not to be hurried; if more time was needed, it would be better to break up the examination into service periods. This was Löhe's suggestion. Occasionally his advice was followed. Rev. Karl August Wilhelm Röbbelen (1817–66) of Frankenmuth, Mich., had a five-day examination before the congregation, three hours in the mornings and two hours in the afternoons, in which time the entire catechism was carefully reviewed so that the congregation would be assured that the confirmands really knew their doctrine.[86] However, this was hardly typical.[87] Under such circumstances the examination was sure to be much more pedagogical than confessional and to go far beyond the original intent of confirmation examination.

That the examination was on a day separate from the rest of the ceremony or was not even regarded a part of the confirmation rite served to give it a different emphasis. This was recognized in the Buffalo A, 1888; in addition to a lengthy examination on a different day, it suggested a token examination for the confirmation service proper, thus tying the two together more closely.

The formula for the examination was quite simple. The sermon was usually omitted.[88] Sometimes the rubrics suggested that the pastor give a free address for the occasion,[69] but more often a prescribed address was part of the ritual. The order of service for the usual catechizations was suggested by Löhe. Otherwise a simple opening and closing was outlined, including prayers, hymns, and the benediction.

[86] E[mmanuel] A. Mayer, *Geschichte der evangelisch-lutherischen St. Lorenz-Gemeinde U. A. C. zu Frankenmuth, Mich.* (St. Louis: Concordia Publishing House, 1895), p. 63.

[87] Other isolated instances reported are, for example, a congregation in Hooper, Nebr., where the confirmation classes were examined six times orally and seven times in writing, the last by the circuit visitor. *The Lutheran Witness,* XVI (May 18, 1937), 171. Rev. Carl A. Abbetmeyer (1867—1929), Baltimore, had six such public examinations, one for each of the six chief parts of the catechism. *The Lutheran Witness,* XVII (May 7, 1899), 180, 181.

[88] Ohio A, 1909.

[89] Ibid.

Additional Traditions Associated with the Rite

The many embellishments which had arisen in Europe during the period of Pietism and Rationalism to dramatize and emotionalize confirmation continued to cling to the rite in America. The handclasp was commonly used to ratify the privileges extended in confirmation or to confirm the vows made by the catechumen. The Löhe A, the General Council A, 1891, and the agendas of churches with Swedish backgrounds are among the few that did not include the handclasp.[90]

The use of a specially selected memory verse for each confirmand was continued in a few of the synods. References to this custom are found especially where there was a strong German background, though Löhe made no reference to the custom.[91] The manner in which the memory verses were used varied. Sometimes the pastor selected the passage with great care and discussed it with the respective catechumen before his confirmation. The memory verse was then written into the certificate by the pastor. The catechumen might be expected to memorize and recite it on the day of his confirmation or at some later occasion, as at a class reunion. Insead of painstakingly writing the passage into each certificate, the pastor might purchase a supply of stock certificates, each already imprinted with one or another from a large selection of suitable passages. Very often the pastor merely read the memory verse while the catechumen knelt at the altar for the imposition.

A special song by the confirmands was suggested in only a few agendas, indicating that this custom was not general, though it was observed in some congregations even when the rubrics did not indicate it.[92] Reprints of the confirmation vow were usually

[90] All Augustana A, Swedish and English. The Norwegian Evangelical Lutheran Synod A, 1891; United Norwegian Church A, 1915; Evangelical Lutheran Church A, 1952; and the Lutheran Free Church A, 1948 include the handclasp. While the Iowa, 1919, followed Löhe in omitting the handclasp, it stated that confirmation conferred the privileges of attending the Lord's Supper, being sponsors, and participating in all the rights and privileges "of our Christian congregation."

[91] Wisconsin A, 1896; all Missouri A; Synodical Conference A, 1949; Buffalo A, 1888; Ohio A, 1909; and United Lutheran Church A, 1918.

[92] Ohio A, 1909, and the German A of Missouri, including the 1881 trans. and the Abbetmeyer ed., 1904.

provided for the catechumens in the Missouri Synod. These reprints suggested a hymn that might be sung.[93]

Most of the hymnals presently used include a special section for confirmation, though the hymns collected in the section may not have been written for such an occasion or use. Some agendas suggested appropriate hymns, usually the traditional "Come, Holy Spirit" and perhaps "Lord, Keep Us Steadfast in Thy Word" or "Let Me Be Thine Forever." The Tennessee A, 1843, printed out two hymns for the occasion: "O Jesus, Faithful Shepherd, Lord!" and "The Grace of God Be with You Hence."

The highly exaggerated language of the 18th century was not lost in the sermons or even in the agendas, even after the extreme forms of Pietism of the colonial days were no longer in use. Especially the Germans who came to this country during the middle and latter half of the 19th century enjoyed the literary extravagances of Europe. Thus the early agenda of Missouri addressed the children in this dramatic form: "The blessed moment has now arrived, my most precious dearly beloved children *(meine herzinniggeliebten theuren Kinder)*, in which you now publicly, with your own lips, dedicate yourselves to the Lord your God, in body and soul, for time and for eternity, and will confirm this with a solemn oath."

The solemnity of the occasion was heightened by the toll of the bell during the confirmation questions or as the children were individually addressed and "confirmed." Löhe suggested that all bells be rung during the laying on of hands.[94]

That confirmation was thus dramatized was not lost on the congregation. The solemn drama naturally invited further extraneous traditions within the family circle. Special clothes, white dresses for the girls and dark suits, usually navy-blue serge, for the boys; floral bouquets especially for the girls; gifts in the form of jewelry, Bibles, prayer books, and hymnals; and a festive family dinner were part of the important occasion. It was quite

[93] "Baptized into Thy Name Most Holy," "Let Me Be Thine Forever," and "My Maker, Be Thou Nigh" were commonly suggested.

[94] In at least two congregations in the St. Louis area the vow was dramatized by having the choir solemnly sing a triple "So help you God" after each of the promises made by the confirmands.

natural that, in spite of the pastor's admonitions and much editorializing in church periodicals, in the minds of the people confirmation day assumed greater importance than either Holy Baptism or first Communion.

The Age for Confirmation

The question of the proper age of the catechumen is one of the most debated in confirmation practice. In the early days of the Lutheran Church in America it was customary, because of the physical difficulties associated with pioneer life, for the catechumens to be older than was the case in Europe. The strong influences of Pietism, with its emphasis on conversion, also naturally encouraged that the catechumen be somewhat older. As late as 1855 the Pennsylvania A put the minimum age at 14 and the actual age was usually higher. Benjamin Kurtz (1795–1865) stated in 1843 that the great majority of those confirmed in the United States were 15 to 20 years old.[95]

Where the chief emphasis remained on preparation for first Communion, the actual age of confirmation was considerably lower.

Löhe wrote in his agenda:

When children have arrived at an understanding of the catechism that they can examine themselves according to the command of the holy apostle, 1 Cor. 11:28, then they should no longer be restrained from partaking of the Holy Supper. Not knowledge attained at school but an understanding of the catechism shall be decisive. This does not mean that a high degree of knowledge of the catechism is essential, but rather the minimum essentials necessary for self-examination.

Löhe continued:

Admission to the examination should not be determined by a specified age. In fact few will be mature enough before ten or eleven. One should therefore keep in mind children of this age and older. But this should not eliminate a younger child whom the pastor or parents regard as sufficiently mature, so

[95] Op. cit., p. 202. The General Synod A, 1847, a trans. of the Pennsylvania A, 1842, deviated at this point by stating that confirmation should in no case "be delayed beyond the age of fourteen years."

125

that he is not turned back simply because of his age . . .
Not age but the required ability of 1 Cor. 11:28 to examine
oneself is to be decisive in every case.[96]

In commenting on the stipulation of age 13 or 14, Löhe referred to it in 1858 as a "comfortable church ordinance." Such an ordinance makes it unnecessary to determine when the individual child is actually mature enough; then the average becomes the norm. "One is free of all exceptions, and there are no embarrassments." But, he added, to make exceptions would be more fruitful of blessings.[97] Walther believed that the completion of the twelfth year should be the minimum in most cases.[98]

Since confirmation instruction proved to be more than simply a preparation for first Communion and became an opportunity to concentrate on the catechumen's general religious instruction with confirmation as a sort of a terminal point, the tendency to advance the age to 13 and 14 prevailed. This was especially true when confirmation instruction was associated with the close of school, as had been the case in Europe. Congregations that conducted parish schools, especially in the rural areas, followed the European pattern of closing the school term at Easter. A child's confirmation therefore coincided with his graduation from grammar school. Formerly most children did not continue with education beyond grammar schools, and the parents were sometimes inclined to have them confirmed before 14 so that they could then help on the farm or get a job in town. Therefore it became customary for congregations to insist that children be 14 before confirmation, to keep them from leaving home or being put to work.[99]

The majority of pastors did not agree with Löhe in requiring only the minimum understanding for admission to the Lord's Supper. Eating worthily was for them more than repentance

[96] Found also in the 2d (1859) and the 3d (1884) ed., but dropped in Iowa's 4th ed. (1919).

[97] "Neuendettelsauer Briefe, 1858," 3 in *Gesammelte Werke*, III, 1 (Neuendettelsau: Freimund Verlag, 1951), 227.

[98] *Pastoraltheologie*, p. 265.

[99] L. F[ürbringer], "Ein Schlusswort an die Eltern unserer Confirmanden," *Der Lutheraner*, LIV (April 19, 1898), 68; LX (April 12, 1904), 118, 119.

and a recognition of our Lord's real presence in the Sacrament. For them it included the attainment of a higher level of intellectual accomplishment that could ordinarily not be reached much before age 14. In his *Chronica* Pastor Leberecht Friedrich Ehregott Krause of Freistadt, Wis., recorded that in his congregation no child was permitted to be confirmed before 14.

> We remain with God's Word that he who can examine himself before the Lord and proclaim His death, that is, he who has the knowledge in his heart and sincerely holds to the way to eternal life, he may receive the Lord's Supper. Children whom we admit to the Holy Supper are permitted to come only after they know from memory, without a flaw, the chief parts of the holy catechism of Dr. M. Luther, the Table of Duties, and the eight sections of the Order of Salvation. We desire with the help of God that they also have this in their heart, although we reject all fanatical torture and are satisfied with their confession that they believe it, God will it, or not. They also learn hymns from our genuinely Lutheran hymn books that we have . . . John Hübner's pure *Biblische Historie* as well as the Gospels and Epistles are also carefully studied by us.[100]

When preparation for church membership as well as a comprehensive course of study was associated with confirmation, arguments in favor of an early confirmation could not be sustained. One pastor deplored the fact that some confirmed children at 12. "They may be mentally sufficiently bright to keep pace with the class in the memory work [sic], but they are too immature to assume the duties and privileges of church-mem-

---

[100] "Chronica der evangelisch lutherischen Kirche in Town Nine Washington County, Territory of Wisconsin, Nord Amerika, deutscher Zunge zur Freystatt" (1848), p. 22. The original is in the archives of Trinity Lutheran Church, Freistadt, Wis. (Mequon, 3 W).

The Iowa A, 1919, dropped the references to an early age for the confirmand as suggested by Löhe and added the following for the congregation. "Christian confirmation is observed in the church in order that the precious youth may be instructed in their Christianity, be examined in the catechism, and be prevented from partaking the Blessed Sacrament in ignorance to their harm and with offence. But rather when they have learned the catechism that we pray over them together with the entire congregation, implore God with the laying on of hands, and bless them. In doing this they will be confirmed in their Christian faith and life, be given a testimony of their Baptism so that they may be strengthened in their Baptism against Satan, and be reminded that they are to live in the true faith, in holiness and righteousness in the presence of God as is pleasing to Him."

bership." [101] When the keeping of the vows, especially the solemn oath to remain loyal to the Lutheran Church till death, became an added obligation of the confirmand and when these vows were argued in determining the age of the catechumen, one can well understand the complaint that children at 12 or 13 were "too immature to comply with the demands implied in confirmation." [102] Yet it is difficult to picture the age of 14 as much more suitable for this serious obligation.

As more and more Lutheran children continued to go on to high school, the age level was stabilized at approximately 14, though there were still many exceptions. Where the junior high school system was in vogue, some congregations tended to lower the age to 12 and 13 and a few raised the age requirement to 15, the ninth-grade level. An interesting carry-over from the period of Rationalism, when confirmation was delayed, has been experienced by some pastors since World War II. Lutheran immigrants from Latvia usually insist that their children be at least 16 or even older before they permit them to be confirmed.

In Europe, where confirmation was closely associated with the school system, confirmation was customarily held on Palm Sunday or during Holy Week, since Easter usually marked the end of the school term. Immigrants from Europe after the 1830s generally favored the same time of year for confirmation in the United States. Before then it was practically impossible to confirm with any degree of seasonal regularity or uniformity, for the pastors usually served more than one parish. Nor were the rigors of pioneer life conducive to consistency in such matters. Before 1850 confirmation was therefore likely to be observed on almost any Sunday and sometimes on a weekday. Through suggestions of suitable days the agendas helped to encourage some uniformity as this became possible. The Pennsylvania A, 1786, suggested Maundy Thursday or Good Friday. Löhe proposed that confirmation be held together with the examination during the week or on a special day, either Good Friday afternoon or

[101] Quoted by [Theodore] G[raebner], "Touching a Sore Spot," *The Lutheran Witness*, XLII (Oct 23, 1923), 339.

[102] "Early Confirmation," *The Lutheran Witness*, XIV (Jan. 21, 1896), 121, 122.

in a vesper service the Friday before Pentecost. Thus the confirmands might attend first Communion on Quasimodogeniti or on the Feast of the Holy Trinity.[103] Walther suggested either Palm Sunday or Quasimodogeniti, but he spoke against confirmation on one of the high festivals or even on the second day of Pentecost, for he feared that observance then would detract from the commemoration of the mighty acts of God.[104]

Nevertheless, many congregations continued to confirm on Easter,[105] the Feast of Pentecost,[106] Exaudi,[107] or after a summer of instruction on some Sunday in the fall of the year.[108] These days were chosen in addition to Palm Sunday, which was rapidly becoming more popular as the number of immigrants increased. Some, like the editor of the *Lutheran Standard*, were concerned about the lack of uniformity and urged the congregations to come to some general agreement. In time Palm Sunday became the favorite day, though some favored the Feast of Pentecost because it gave pastors more time and fitted better with the church year. Those who hesitated to observe confirmation on Pentecost suggested Exaudi because it allowed the confirmand to attend his first Communion on the following Sunday and at the same time encouraged congregations to continue their schools until June, which was more in harmony with the public school calendar.[109] Currently either Palm Sunday or the Feast of Pentecost is the usual day set for confirmation, although adults are confirmed on practically any Sunday of the year.

The Instruction

The lack of uniformity in the observance of the confirmation rite was minor when compared to the great divergences in in-

103 So in all three eds., 1844, 1859, and 1884. This direction was dropped in Iowa A, 1919.

104 *Pastoraltheologie*, pp. 265, 266.

105 *The Lutheran Witness*, X (May 21, 1892), 191; IX (Jan. 7, 1891), 113.

106 A[dolf] T. H[anser], "Der Tag der Konfirmation," *Der Lutheraner*, LXIX (March 4, 1913), 70, 71.

107 *Der Lutheraner*, LXIX (March 4, 1913), 1.

108 *Lutheran Standard*, LXVII (April 10, 1909), 226

109 H[anser], pp. 70, 71.

129

struction preceding the ceremony. Practically all pastors were agreed on two things: (1) that the instruction was the real confirmation and the ceremony merely the public recognition that the catechumen had the knowledge necessary for his first Communion and (2) that the instruction was to be based primarily on Luther's Small Catechism. Here the consensus ended. Even in these points of agreement there were various interpretations of the implications involved. In Europe, it will be recalled, the Lutheran Church relied heavily on the Christian home and the school for the child's initial instruction in religion. Confirmation instruction was therefore mainly a review to round out the catechumen's understanding. In transplanting confirmation to American soil the church found both of these recourses much weaker. The Lutheran home, especially in the cities, was surrounded by homes that were not simply Lutheran, Roman Catholic, or perhaps Reformed, but homes that represented the scores of sects so peculiar to this country. Moreover, there were also those who had "emancipated" themselves from all forms of religion. What little religious context still existed was likely to be Calvinistic or some hybrid "American Protestant moralism." All this had a tendency to dull the Lutheran consciousness, especially if "Lutheran" was equated with "foreigner" and became an obstacle for those desiring to Americanize.

The second disturbing factor was that the public school could not prepare children for confirmation instruction. The responsibility for formal religious instruction fell to the Sunday school unless the congregation had the foresight and resources to establish its own parish school. If there was no school of any type in the parish or if parents did not avail themselves of the meager facilities available, the problems that faced the pastors were almost overwhelming. Some of this was reflected in the early agendas of Pennsylvania (1786, 1818, and 1842, as well as the Ohio A, 1830), which stated: "The children should necessarily all be able to read; but since the pastors in this country must unfortunately accept for instruction such who cannot read, yes, can hardly spell, it is all the more necessary to work toward the end that they grasp at least the basic fundamental truths of our holy religion and with it are earnestly encouraged also to learn to read where possible." [110]

The great variations in instruction were due in part to differing objectives for confirmation. The goals varied from simply preparing children for their first Communion, or for conversion, to being an important if not the major instructional agency within the congregation. When the latter was the case, confirmation became terminal by the very nature of the emphasis. This, in turn, made it seem important to include in the curriculum some materials besides Luther's Small Catechism. Enlarged catechisms setting forth detailed theological explanations were popular. Bible stories and hymnals were used as supplementary material. Since some expected the children to be able to defend the position of the Lutheran Church, in 1849 a Chicago pastoral conference of the Missouri Synod resolved that a book be prepared to point out the major errors taught by the many American denominations and to supply the children with the Biblical basis for refuting such teachings. [111]

It is difficult to estimate the length of time which was given to confirmation instruction because the number of months reported could mean months of weekly, semiweekly, or daily instruction. In 1843 Kurtz stated that the instruction began with one class a week and was subsequently increased to two or three a week for two or three months and sometimes longer. [112] Three or four months were quite common, with the instruction frequently beginning with the new year and closing with Palm Sunday or Easter Day. [113] Some pastors utilized the summer months, when the children were not in school. [114] In its first

[110] Similarly the General Synod A, 1847. All these agendas urged the pastor to be zealous and conscientious in his instruction and to keep the catechumens in mind in his prayers.

[111] *Vierter Synodal-Bericht: Verhandlungen der deutschen evangelisch-lutherischen Synode von Missouri, Ohio und anderen Staaten, 1850* (St. Louis: M. Niedner, 1851), p. 27.

[112] Op. cit., pp. 186, 187.

[113] *Lutheran Standard*, XXVI (Jan. 1, 1866), 8; "The Catechetical Class," *The Lutheran and Missionary*, V (Jan. 18, 1866), 50.

[114] *Lutheran Standard*, LXVII (April 10, 1909), 226. Some of the Tennessee Synod congregations in the mountain country conducted "catechising schools" for the preparation of the confirmands. As late as 1914, Pastor Martin F. Kuegele

constitution the Missouri Synod set 100 hours of instruction as the goal.[115] Since a large number of congregations of the synod had parish schools, this relatively high standard was possible. A writer in the *Lutheran Standard* urged congregations without a parish school to have catechetical classes all the year round for several years, meeting twice a week, preparatory to confirmation instruction, which then could be of shorter duration.[116]

By the turn of the century most congregations seem to have had at least six months of instruction, beginning soon after the opening of the schools and no later than the first week of October. In more recent years the tendency to require two years of instruction has been gaining, though it is not yet the trend in all synods. A survey made in 1954 indicated that the majority of the pastors interviewed required two or more years of confirmation instruction. Listed according to the major Lutheran bodies, the results were as follows: American Lutheran Church, 88%; The United Evangelical Lutheran Church, 80%; the Evangelical Lutheran Church, 90%; The United Lutheran Church, 65%; and the Augustana Lutheran Church, 44%.[117]

The pastors generally reported holding classes once a week for nine or more months a year. A similar survey, conducted in 1938 in the Missouri Synod, showed that 81% of the children were required to go two years where there was no parish school and 68% where there was a parochial school. In congregations having a parish school the seventh and eighth grades in religion were often regarded as the confirmation class.[118]

conducted such schools in the four parishes he served in North Carolina. In a note to the author he wrote, "In the Catechising School the minister would stay with them a week or two and lecture all day on the Catechism. Everybody came, men and women, boys and girls, babies and grandparents. This was a preparation for church membership. It had the advantage of being a review for the members and also gave outside visitors an insight into the Lutheran teaching."

[115] Article V, 17, *Concordia Historical Institute Quarterly*, XVI (April 1943), 13, 14.

[116] *Lutheran Standard*, XXVII (April 1, 1867), 60, 61.

[117] "Report on the Results of the Intersynodical Questionnaire on Catechetical Instruction" as found in "The Report to the Seminar on Confirmation and Confirmation Instruction, August 24—27, 1954," Racine, Wis., p. 1.

[118] A[rnold] C. Mueller, "Report on Confirmation Instruction, May 13, 1941," p. 2.

Catechisms

The number of explanations of Luther's Small Catechism designed for confirmation instruction in the United States exceeded several scores; only a few of the more widely used can be mentioned. For more than a century the catechism originally prepared by Peter Brunnholtz in 1749 was used by early Lutherans. It was printed in scores of editions and with frequent changes even after 1860. It included, besides an explanation of Luther's catechism, several orders of salvation. Already the early editions added *Das Würtembergische Kurze Kinder-Examen* ("A Short Examination of Catechumens") and *Eine Zergliederung des Catechismus* ("Analysis of the Catechism").

Philip Friedrich Mayer (1781–1858) translated Luther's catechism and published it together with his explanation, *Instruction in the Principles and Duties of the Christian Religion for Children and Youth* (1816). Mayer's catechism is important because his translation became basic for many later revisions, e. g., those of Gruber and May (1825), David Henkel (1829), and John Gottlieb Morris (1844). Probably of greater importance was the fact that it appeared in the New York Ministerium as a quiet protest against Frederick Quitman's rationalistic attempt, *The Evangelical Catechism* (1814).[119] A catechism of extensive influence was the one composed by the Danish pietist Erik Pontoppidan, *Truth unto Godliness (Sandhed til gudfrygtighed)* which appeared in 1737 and was first used in Denmark and Norway and later in Sweden. Through the efforts of Elling Eielsen (1804–83) an American edition of the epitome appeared in 1842, the first Norwegian book to be printed in America. "Anxious that no change should be made in the text of his beloved Pontopiddan's Explanation, Eielsen walked the whole distance from Rock County, Wisconsin, to New York City in search of a printer who had precisely the same kinds of types as those used in Eielsen's copy." [120] Pontoppidan's catechism appeared in all the Scandinavian languages and was translated at various

119 Nicum, p. 99.
120 J. Magnus Rohne, *Norwegian American Lutheranism up to 1872* (New York: Macmillan Co., 1926), p. 41.

times into English. Among the better known translations is the one by Edmund Belfour (1877).

A derived edition of Pontoppidan was made by H. U. Sverdrup of the Church of Norway and authorized in 1865. It appeared in this country both in Norwegian and in English.[121] Another important catechism used by the Norwegians was the Dietrich, while the Swedish pastors used also the Lindblom revision of the old Svebelius catechism.

A catechism which had its roots in the period of Orthodoxy and was widely used in this country was Conrad Dietrich's exposition, originally issued in 1613 and shortened in 1627. The epitome was the basis of the first official catechism of the Missouri Synod. It was expanded with material from the *Dresdener-Kreuz Catechismus* (1688) and the Book of Concord. This revised Dietrich was still very detailed in its theological explanations and went far beyond the basic materials of Luther. It lacked much of the warmth of Pontoppidan and lent itself to an intellectual approach to teaching. The Missouri Synod edition was received with some misgivings when it appeared in 1858;[122] yet it served for some time even after it was officially replaced by the Schwan edition in 1896.

In 1863, William Julius Mann (1819–92) and Gottlob Friedrich Krotel (1826–1907) published a 154-page exposition of Luther's catechism, based largely on H. Caspari's explanation (1856). It became the standard for some time in the Pennsylvania Ministerium and replaced the many forms of the Brunnholtz explanation.

Another catechism that had its roots in the orthodox period was J. E. Stohlmann's reprint, which was authorized by the New York Ministerium and appeared in 1873. It was Albert Lührs' revision (1862) of a 1651 catechism by Michael Walther (1593 to 1662) and was generally known as the Hannover catechism.

In 1896 the Missouri Synod replaced the Dietrich catechism

[121] Trans. Emil G. Lund (1903) and Hans A. Urseth (1910).

[122] *Der Lutheraner*, XV (Nov. 30, 1858), 57, 58; "The Missouri Synod and Dietrich's Catechism," *Theological Quarterly*, X (July 1906), 129—152; Richard G. Maassel, "A History of the Early Catechisms of the Missouri Synod," unpub. master's thesis (Concordia Seminary, St. Louis, 1957).

with a new explanation by Heinrich Christian Schwan (1819 to 1905), though he was not the final editor. Schwan attempted to simplify the Dietrich edition but was not as successful as he had hoped; the editorial committee reworked his manuscript and "rescued much of Dietrich."[123] When the catechism appeared, Schwan did not wish to have his name associated with it, but it came to be popularly known as the Schwan catechism. With minor additions and revisions it was used till 1943.

J. Michael Reu's outstanding explanation of Luther's catechism appeared in 1904 for use in the Iowa Synod. It differed from many previous catechisms in that it followed the expository principles of Wilhelm Löhe. In the preface Reu pointed out that his catechism adhered to the principle that "an explanation should be no more than an introduction into the fullness of religious truth, as contained in the *words* of Luther's Catechism." Accordingly, he omitted every addition from dogmatics and sacred history, as well as every attempt to convert Luther's five parts into a system by means of transitions.[124]

Reu differed from other catechists also in the form of his book. Instead of using questions and answers, he used the thetic form, which permitted the teacher to begin and conclude where he chose, since he was not bound "to the progress and connection of the questions and answers of the explanation, which have been deliberately put."[125]

In 1907 Joseph Stump (1866–1935), educator and author, prepared a catechism for the General Council. Like Reu, Stump followed the thetical form. However, he did add a "fuller explanation of the *text* of the catechism than that which Luther gives" and supplemented "its contents with such additional matter as the needs of our catechumens require."[126]

---

[123] Letter, F[rederick] Lindemann (1851—1907) to Heinrich G. Sauer, Jan. 5, 1896. Photocopy in the possession of the author.

[124] J. M[ichael] Reu, *Explanation of Dr. Martin Luther's Small Catechism* (Chicago: Wartburg Publishing House, 1904), p. v.

[125] Ibid., pp. v, vi.

[126] *An Explanation of Luther's Small Catechism* (Philadelphia: United Lutheran Publication House, 1907), p. iii.

Confirmation

Efforts to improve catechetical instruction were constantly being made. The work of Carl Adolf Gerhard von Zezschwitz (1825–86) and Theodor Kaftan (1847–1932) in Germany did not go unnoticed. Kaftan's ideas were given widespread attention through John Winebrenner Horine's *The Catechist's Handbook* (1909). *The Lutheran Catechist* (1910), by George Henry Gerberding (1847–1927), was a favorite text. The monumental work was, of course, J. Michael Reu's *Catechetics,* which first appeared in German in 1915. Reu was undoubtedly the outstanding authority on Luther's catechism. The *Schulpraxis* of Johann Christoph Wilhelm Lindemann (1827–79) was widely used in the Missouri Synod, especially in the training of parish school teachers.

Among the commentaries on Luther's catechism the following should be mentioned: John W. Horine, *The Catechist's Handbook* (1909), Henry Jacob Schuh (1851–1934), *Catechizations* (1914), and George Mezger (1857–1931), *Entwürfe zu Katechesen über Luthers Kleinen Katechismus* (3d ed., 1916). In addition to many other American works, European texts were freely used and became standard helps for Lutheran pastors.

What Is Confirmation?

The many movements which had their impact on the development of confirmation in this country made diversity rather than uniformity quite general. The two pages allotted to confirmation in the 1891 *Church Liturgy* of the Norwegian Evangelical Lutheran Synod are in sharp contrast to the twelve pages in the Ohio A of 1909. While most congregations now observe the examination, the rite, and first Communion in three separate services, fortunately some still combine all three in a single service.

Even the question "What is confirmed?" has not been uniformly answered. While all seem to agree that the catechumen's faith is confirmed through instruction in God's Word, many place equal importance on the confirmation of the promises, vows, or covenant. Who confirms? More than one answer has been given:

God through His means of grace; the pastor as God's servant.[127]
Yet some say it is the catechumen because he confirms his sponsor's vows; others, the congregation as it confirms the catechumen
"in the profession of church privileges." [128]

[127] In his revision of the Löhe A, 1859, Deinzer added the following to the
1884 A: "The pastor signs each child on the forehead with the sign of the cross,
lays his hands upon him and says, 'I sign thee with the sign of the holy cross †
and confirm thee in the Name of the Father and the Son and the Holy Spirit.
Amen.'" This was omitted in the Iowa A, 1919.

[128] *Lutheran Standard,* XLV (Sept. 17, 1887), 298.

CHAPTER IV

RECENT DEVELOPMENTS

Developments in Europe

Despite the many 19th-century proposals for major changes in the practice of confirmation, little or nothing happened. The roots of the confirmation tradition had tapped too deeply the soil of European culture. What few changes did take place came through the loosening of ties between church and state after World War I, but these did not materially improve conditions. While many of the people were able by law to sever their ties with the church, the great majority continued to maintain some connections. One association with the church was through confirmation, even though there was little feeling of personal responsibility among the parents or the youth. The complaint was still heard in Germany that confirmation was more an *Aussegnung* than an *Einsegnung.* In 1926 Helmuth Schreiner of Hamburg lamented in his *Geist und Gestalt* that year after year at Easter the youth of the church were crowding the altars, where the church publicly declared them to have reached majority and permitted them to assume responsibilities as "full members," and this seven years before they were accepted as such for their civic duties. True, for the average German boy or girl, confirmation was not the end but the beginning. But what kind of beginning, Schreiner asked.

> For the first time the girl wears the new fashions at the altar; for the first time her hair is bobbed; at this celebration, for the first time, a black or dark sleeveless dress is permitted, and for the first time the boy can smoke a cigarette without reproof and breathe in "the life of freedom," released from church and school and eager for whatever new thing may come. For the first time the daughter is permitted to go on a date; for the

first time the newly confirmed are permitted to mingle with members of the other sex.[1]

This was the meaning that confirmation had for a great majority of the church's youth.

The manner in which the church presently bridges the generations with confirmation serves only to becloud the Gospel. The current observance of confirmation signifies a continuous suicide by the church, for it denies therein the essence and efficacy of the Gospel.[2]

A few years before World War II, Martin Doerne made a major contribution to the study of confirmation in *Neubau der Konfirmation*. Among other things, he noted that the existing practice of confirmation violated a number of Biblical principles and therefore worked against its own success. By allowing confirmation at age 14 to become terminal for the formal religious instruction of the children the church was failing to keep before the mind of its youth and adults the fact that Christian education, in its broader aspects, has no terminal point. Education, he said, must be continuous throughout life, for God desires continually to sanctify His own more fully. Furthermore, Baptism assumes a lifetime of contrition and repentance, and for this the Holy Spirit is to teach the Christian throughout his life.[3] The church must therefore have an aggressive educational program for its youth for a long time after they have been confirmed.

Doerne's stress on the importance of continuous instruction is based on a view that Christian education has a threefold task. First, witness to the revelation of God in Christ must be regarded as the church's only task. Such witness receives its reality in history; hence the church has the Word and the catechism. Second, this witness must become part of the life of every individual Christian. His faith is not something that he

[1] *Geist und Gestalt* (Schwerin: F. Bahn, 1926), pp. 22ff., as quoted in Heinrich Rendtorff, *Konfirmation und Kirche* (Leipzig: C. Ludwig Ungelenk, 1928), p. 7.

[2] H[ermann] Schafft, *Vom Kampf gegen die Kirche für die Kirche* (Habertshof, 1925), pp. 79f., cited by Rendtorff, p. 8.

[3] Martin Doerne, *Neubau der Konfirmation* (Gütersloh: C. Bertelsmann, 1936), pp. 120—122.

maintains in a vacuum. It is to permeate his total existence. Third, the Christian must grow into the membership of the body of Christ, into the people of God. He has to partake of, or listen to, the "great cloud of witnesses" and himself become a witness to others. Once it is recognized that this is the church's God-given task, then instruction takes on both greater depth and broader scope. Confirmation marks that period of the young Christian's life when the church is assured that the catechumen has an understanding of the implications of the church's task and acknowledges his willingness and readiness to be a Christian in earnest and when the church, in turn, invests him with privileges and obligations appropriate to this responsibility.[4]

If with confirmation the church is expected to give assurance that the child is ready in attitudes and understanding to fulfill all responsibilities of mature church membership and if the church is then expected to grant the child the privileges of such membership, confirmation at 14 is obviously premature. Hence Doerne proposed a number of steps leading to later confirmation. The first step would be to utilize the present period of instruction as an elementary, or baptismal, catechumenate. It would be terminated with a brief service, and every resemblance to confirmation would be omitted. There would be no confession of faith, no vow, no examination, not even the laying on of hands — simply a prayer and a blessing. The sermon would emphasize that the children have not yet reached their majority and that a new stage is now to follow. In this way the pastor might emphasize that the act is not terminal.[5]

Doerne divided the second step into two periods, from 14 to 17 and from 18 to 21. Ordinarily the terminal age would be 21, though there should be no hard and fast rule. Nineteen might be the minimum. During the second step the instruction would necessarily be less formal. Doerne said that the pastor's concern should be fourfold: (1) to help the youth answer his doubts and meet attacks and temptations from without; (2) to assist the youth in acquiring a personal and functional "at homeness"

4 Ibid., pp. 124—130.
5 Ibid., pp. 169—175.

in the Bible; (3) to offer pastoral services for the youth's spiritual welfare; and (4) to help make the church become a reality for the youth.[6]

To accomplish this, Doerne suggested two series of Bible evenings a year, each lasting about two months. In addition there should be monthly periods for discussion of questions related to the needs and concerns of young people. These occasions should be utilized to acquaint them with the life and work of the church as well as with its worship.

At 17 there would be several examinations, somewhat like the early church's scrutinies. The examinations would be closed with a formal service at which the young people are reminded that the final period now lies before them, at the end of which they become active members of the church and are permitted to participate in the privileges of communicant memberhip.

During this last period there would be intensive preparation for the catechumen's first Communion and final equipment for personal, active membership in the church. The second step would be concluded with the rite of confirmation in a public service, the rite to include a confession of faith based on the Apostles' Creed and a vow. In the vow the candidate would declare his loyalty to the church as a fellowship of the means of grace and promise submission to the church's ordinances.[7]

Doerne's suggestions aroused considerable discussion, but the tragedy of World War II as well as the events leading up to it deflected energies elsewhere.

Since World War II the questions revolving about confirmation have again been discussed with renewed vigor. Many of the critics have been concerned with making confirmation more meaningful in the life of the church. Instead of placing the major emphasis on the liturgical and theological aspects of the ceremony as had been done in the previous century, some have urged that more emphasis be given to study of the instructional obligation associated with confirmation. Such an emphasis Alfred Niebergall believed necessary for Germany if the church was to

[6] Ibid., pp. 176—183.
[7] Ibid., pp. 190—200.

meet the threat of the communists, who had substituted a *Jugendweihe* ("youth consecration") for confirmation in their determination to win the youth. Such an emphasis was essential if confirmation was to become a necessary stabilizing factor after the dissolution of the *Volkskirche*.[8] Among the many proposals for reconstructing confirmation, some of the more important plans have been offered by Karl Hauschildt,[9] Georg Gründler and Ernst Klessmann,[10] William Nagel,[11] and Lukas Vischer.[12]

Among the severest critics of confirmation are Karl Barth and Johannes Hamel, though for widely different reasons. Because Karl Barth rejects infant baptism, he finds no place for confirmation. Barth, like many others, thinks of confirmation as "the ratification of the baptismal covenant." This, he supposes, is evidence that Baptism requires an act to complete or supplement it.

> But what is baptism in itself and as such, if it has no reference to the conscious acknowledgement of regeneration and faith, to the complete divine-human reality, which is portrayed within it; if it cannot be in a really intelligible sense the confirming and binding in allegiance of the second of the chief actors, the one baptized; if it cannot be a matter of decision and confession at all? Is it in this case a full baptism? Is it not rather, and notoriously, half-baptism? And, on the other hand, what right have we to attribute to confirmation the significance of a half-sacrament? Can it be more than admission to the Lord's Supper, the climax of the instruction given by the Church? [13]

[8] "Das Unbehagen an der Konfirmation," *Evangelische Welt*, XII (Nov. 16, 1958), 657, 658.

[9] *Konfirmation ganz anders* (Kiel: Evangelischer Presseverband Schleswig-Holstein, 1958).

[10] *Reformation der Konfirmation* (Göttingen: Vandenhoeck & Ruprecht, 1960).

[11] *Probleme der Konfirmation* (Berlin: Evangelische Verlagsanstalt, 1959).

[12] *Die Geschichte der Konfirmation* (St. Gallen: Evangelischer Verlag AG., Zollikon, 1958).

For a brief overview of a number of reform proposals and some of the literature see Karl Hauschildt, "Zur Geschichte und Diskussion der Konfirmationsfrage vom Pietismus bis zum 20. Jahrhundert," *Confirmatio: Forschungen zur Geschichte und Praxis der Konfirmation,* ed. Kurt Frör (Munich: Evang[elischer] Presseverband für Bayern, 1959).

[13] *The Teachings of the Church Regarding Baptism,* trans. Ernest A. Payne (London: S. C. M. Press, 1948), pp. 47, 48.

143

Largely because of his experience in East Germany, Johannes Hamel is very critical of confirmation. He regrets that the church there made *Jugendweihe* and confirmation the issue on which it drew the battle line against communism. While *Jugendweihe* and confirmation are in fact irreconcilable, parents for the most part confirm their children primarily as a means of preserving a part of their cultural heritage. Their decision to permit the religious act to be performed is not, according to Hamel, an expression of their religious convictions. As a result, both parents and children are often as indifferent after confirmation as they were before they resolved to oppose the state's determination to win their children through *Jugendweihe*. It would have been far better to have raised the issue with communism on the basis of the First Commandment. Then the church would have been on firm ground. Now it is attempting to preserve a questionable custom which God may at this time wish to take away from the church.[14]

Presently there are in Germany three camps represented in the confirmation debate. The conservatives, a first camp, believe that except for a moderation of the vow, there should be no major changes. They contend that there is no proof that any change will actually remedy the situation. The suggestions which have been made are so varied and so contradictory that no single person is in a position to determine what is best. Confirmation has developed and changed with the times, and any radical change might easily eliminate one of its major essential elements.

The liberals, a second camp, believe that confirmation should be divided into several steps. They propose early Communion after brief instruction on the Lord's Supper, perhaps sometime between 8 and 12. A second step, to coincide with the completion of grammar school, would mark the end of formal instruction and signify the close of the baptismal instruction. For this there should be an *Einsegnung*. A third step, at about age 18, would be acceptance of the youth into the congregation and the granting of majority rights. Critics have raised the question: Which

14 *Christ in der DDR* (Berlin: A. Seydal, 1957), pp. 12—17.

of the three steps would really be "confirmation"? Would the church, in the end, lose everything? What would happen to those who would not continue through all the steps? Would the result be a two-class system of membership?

The radicals, a third camp, urge the abolishment of confirmation. Children should be permitted to go to their first Communion when accompanied by their parents or, in the event of their death, by their sponsors or guardians but without participating in a ceremony. The pastor would merely question the children at this time to avoid any abuses. The children would attend the Lord's Supper with their parents until a year after their graduation from elementary school. Then, upon examination by the pastor, the children would be allowed to partake of the Sacrament without accompaniment by parent or guardian. Proponents of this plan point out that it allows for individual response and places greater responsibility on the family. Opponents say that in time some kind of form would be called for. In fact, they ask, would not the pastor of a large congregation wait till a number of children have announced their intention to undergo pastoral examination for communing without parental or other sponsorship? Would not this give additional significance to the occasion and eventually produce a formal ceremony similar to confirmation? [15]

In 1952 a revised formula for confirmation was adopted for the agenda of the United Evangelical Lutheran Church of Germany (VELKD). The formula keeps the examination and the actual confirmation separate, as had been the custom. The new rite has been stripped of all controversial elements and kept very simple. After the opening of the service and following the sermon the children are addressed by the pastor. They are reminded of the benefits which they received in Holy Baptism and of their instruction in the Word according to the Lutheran Confessions. Having already given account of their faith in the public examination, they are now called on to make the same Christian confession which the sponsors made at their Baptism.

[15] Richard Eckstein, "Um die Neuordnung der Konfirmation," *Evangelisch-Lutherische Kirchenzeitung*, XIII (Feb. 15, 1959), pp. 50, 51.

Confirmation

Thereupon the children confess the Apostles' Creed, after which they are asked: "Do you, by the grace of God, intend to remain and grow in this faith which you have professed, then declare this by saying, Yes." Upon this confession and promise the congregation is bidden to ask God to continue the work which He has begun in the children. After a suitable prayer the catechumens are blessed with an appropriate Bible passage. The laying on of hands is accompanied by a prayer that God would give them His gracious protection. The children may partake of their first Communion at this service or in a later service.

There is no reference to a baptismal covenant in this rite, nor to a promise of submission to the church. The rite is unique in its emphasis that the right to partake of the Lord's Supper is given in Holy Baptism. The essential elements are instruction, the confession of faith, the expression of the children's desire to remain loyal, and the prayers of the congregation.

Similar far-reaching changes have been made in Sweden and Norway. The problems have not been as acute in Finland, though the territorial synod resolved in 1953 to study the theological, educational, and psychological questions involved in confirmation.[16]

Since the discussion of confirmation is so widespread, several important committees are presently making comprehensive studies. The Evangelical Church in Germany (EKiD) and the United Evangelical Lutheran Church of Germany (VELKD) have appointed committees for this purpose. What promises to be one of the most far-reaching studies on confirmation is being conducted by the Commission on Education of the Lutheran World Federation, which conducted an international seminar in Loccum, Germany, April 18–21, 1961.[17]

[16] Erkki Kansanaho, *Konfirmaatio: Liturgishistoriallinen tutkimus konfirmaatioaktista* (Helsinki: Suomalainen Teologinen Kirjallisuusseura, 1956), pp. 293, 294.

[17] During October 1957 a meeting of educators and theologians was conducted in Hofgeismar, Germany, in preparation for the international seminar. Frör's *Confirmatio* is a collection of the papers delivered at that conference. Among the 40 participants at the international seminar were representatives from Germany, Norway, Sweden, Finland, the United States, the minority churches, and churches in Africa and Asia. For a report of the meeting see Kurt Frör, "Confirmation: A Lutheran World Federation Seminar," *Lutheran World,* VIII

in the Lutheran Church

Developments in the United States

Confirmation has not caused the heated discussion in the United States that it has in Europe. American churches are not faced with the tremendous losses after confirmation, because they are essentially "free churches" whose members for the most part intend to remain loyal to the church. Those who have no intention of continuing membership in the Lutheran Church usually feel little social pressure to prevent them from withdrawing. When American parents send their children to confirmation instruction, it is normally with the intent that the children continue with the Lutheran Church. Nor are the American churches forced to contend with a political ideology that seeks to win the youth over for itself. This is not to say the church in the United States is free from pressures. The emergence of an "American religion" is seen by some as the rise of a strong competitor of the Christian church. Others, especially in small towns and in the rural areas, believe that as the American school system broadens its educational base, it is gradually preempting the time and effort of the youth, even after normal school hours. Yet such competition seems to be a threat more for the future than for the present.

Because the Lutheran Church has thus been relatively free in the United States, it has not had to face problems as far reaching as those in Europe. However, two questions are being asked with great persistence; both revolve about the age of the catechumen. A fairly large number of pastors are beginning to favor, at least in theory, a more advanced age for the catechumen. Since confirmation has become more than mere preparation for first Communion and is in fact the major teaching opportunity

(Sept. 1961), 174—181. An English trans. of most of the lectures has been prepared in mimeograph form by the Commission on Education of the Lutheran World Federation. Most of the papers have appeared in German under the title *Zur Geschichte und Ordnung der Konfirmation in den lutherischen Kirchen,* ed. Kurt Frör (Munich: Claudius Verlag, 1962). The Commision on Education of the L. W. F. presented its report to the Fourth Assembly, July 30—Aug. 11, 1963, at Helsinki. The report was prepared by Dr. Joachim Heubach and presented by the chairman of the commission, Bjarne Hareide. It is known as Document No. 16. The document includes a valuable bibliography on confirmation prepared by Dr. Karl Hauschildt.

of the church and since this has greatly expanded the scope of confirmation instruction, a more mature catechumen seems to be warranted. To insure that the implications of the vow are taken seriously is an additional reason for urging that confirmation be held no earlier than 15 and preferably later. With the church reaching out more and more among the unchurched, a large number of the catechumens have had little or no previous instruction in Christianity. In spite of these considerations, most pastors have not made any changes, because of the practical problems connected with advancing the age of the catechumen. The threat of possible losses before a later confirmation has been an important factor in preventing a change.[18]

The second question, which has troubled a relatively small number, is whether the church has any right to withhold the sacrament of the Lord's Supper until the catechumen is 14 or older. A vocal minority has been urging that the age be lowered, possibly to 9 or 10. This group has argued that the church has no warrant to interpret 1 Corinthians 11:28, 29 by its practice to mean more than the passage actually says or to go beyond the Lutheran tradition of the 16th century. They argue further that the present custom implies that the criterion is intellectual achievement in religion rather than repentance and faith and the ability to distinguish the bread and wine in the Sacrament from the bread and wine used otherwise.[19] They point out also that since Christian education is not to be terminal at age 8, 14, or even 18, the church should not make confirmation terminal, even unwittingly, with a "last chance" emphasis in its curriculum.

As in Europe, official commissions of several Lutheran synods are studying the problems of confirmation in the United States and Canada. One of these was a joint commission of the individual bodies which formed the Lutheran Church in America

[18] "Report on the Results of the Intersynodical Questionnaire on Catechetical Instruction," in "The Report to the Seminar on Confirmation and Confirmation Instruction, August 24—27, 1954," Racine, Wis., pp. 1, 2.

[19] William D. Streng, "The Age for First Communion," *The Lutheran Quarterly*, X (Aug. 1958), 255—262; Berthold von Schenk, "Confirmation and First Communion," *Una Sancta*, XIV (Pentecost 1957), 3—7; Carl W. Sodergren, "Christian Nurture Continuous . . . Confirmation at What Age?" *The Lutheran Companion*, CV (April 29, 1959), 8.

in June 1962. The commission, after a three-year study, reported the following theses at the constituting convention of the Lutheran Church in America. The report was strongly reminiscent of the traditional type of confirmation in the 16th century and reflected some of the discussions among the European liberals: [20]

1) that baptized children be admitted to holy communion at the age of ten years, provided
   a) that they have been instructed in the meaning of the sacrament,
   b) that they have an adult communicant sponsor, and
   c) that they participate in the context of the whole congregation; and

2) that the present practice of catechetical instruction and confirmation upon its completion remain unchanged except that such instruction and confirmation be no longer regarded as necessary for admission to holy communion, and that the age for confirmation be raised to the completion of grade eleven.[21]

When the matter was presented on the floor, the chairman of the commission "urged prompt approval of the report." Two commission members dissented. After considerable discussion it was agreed that no unilateral steps should be taken. The delegates urged that the American Lutheran Church and the Missouri Synod be brought into the discussion of the subject and that the commission's report "be transmitted 'as information' to the new study group." [22]

Besides questions of this nature, the major discussions of confirmation in the United States have explored its more practical elements, for example, the improvement of instruction, more suitable curricular material, and ways of keeping the newly confirmed with the church.

[20] See above, pp. 44—55 and 144, 145.

[21] Unsigned, "Communion Before Confirmation?" *The Lutheran*, XLIV (July 11, 1962), 19.

[22] Unsigned, "Report from Detroit," *The Lutheran*, XLIV (July 11, 1962), 7. Reasons against a separation of first Communion and confirmation as well as against an early first Communion are ably set forth by Martin J. Heinecken, "Confirmation in Relation to the Lord's Supper," *The Lutheran Quarterly*, XV (Feb. 1963), 22—28; Lloyd E. Sheneman. "Instruction and Admission to Communion in Our Time," *The Lutheran Quarterly*, XV (Nov. 1963), 291—307.

Surveys within various Lutheran bodies in the United States and Canada have directed the attention of many to the deficiencies in the practical elements of confirmation. From the surveys it is crystal clear that there are not merely wide differences of practice within the Lutheran church but also much that is unhealthy and needs to be corrected. The surveys have further served to emphasize that confirmation means many things to many different people even within the same synodical body.[23]

Efforts at improving the instruction have been directed largely at making it more relevant to the youth for their life in the church and in the world of today. To this end, certain aspects of the Christian life which do not seem to be stressed sufficiently in Luther's catechism have been added or given more emphasis. Greater care has also been given to the use of proper vocabulary and to the thought structure of the learning material.

Not all attempts at improving the curricular materials have been equally successful. The catechism explanation issued by the Missouri Synod in 1943 made some important physical changes but retains much of the content and format of the Schwan catechism, though it is somewhat more personal in its approach.[24] More far-reaching are the changes in the junior catechism *Growing in Christ* (St. Louis: Concordia Publishing House, 1953). It allows the teacher greater leeway in organizing the teaching units and gives him more assistance in keeping the lessons within the capacities and needs of the learner. Some of the other catechism explanations which have appeared in recent years are those by Henry P. Grimsby,[25] Jacob Tanner,[26] Philip R.

[23] "Report on the Results of the Intersynodical Questionnaire . . ." (see above, n. 18), pp. 1, 2; A. C. Mueller, "Report on Confirmation Instruction, May 13, 1941"; Robert T. Koehler, "A Survey of the Confirmation Instruction of the Children Within a Pastoral Conference," unpub. B. D. thesis (Concordia Seminary, St. Louis, 1948); Paul K. Koepchen, "A Survey of Confirmation Instruction for Children," unpub. B. D. thesis (Concordia Seminary, St. Louis, 1952).

[24] *A Short Explanation of Dr. Martin Luther's Small Catechism: A Handbook of Christian Doctrine* (St. Louis: Concordia Publishing House, 1943).

[25] *An Explanation of the Catechism* (Minneapolis, Minn.: Augsburg Publishing House, 1941).

[26] *The Junior Confirmation Book* (1943) and *The Senior Confirmation Book* (Minneapolis, Minn.: Augsburg Publishing House, 1941).

in the Lutheran Church

Hoh,[27] and the revision prepared by the Augustana Church.[28] This revision uses the Revised Standard Version throughout, except in the Lord's Prayer, "where the language of the liturgy is preserved." The revision attempts to clarify both the language and the doctrine of the earlier explanations. Sections on war and Christian stewardship were added.

One of the most important tasks nearing completion is a new translation of Luther's Small Catechism, drawn up under the auspices of the boards of parish education of the major church bodies in America. "The translation is based on the 1531 edition of Luther's text and attempts to render into simple, contemporary English the intended rather than a literal meaning of the original." [29]

In the production of new catechisms greater emphasis is naturally being placed on the use of modern educational theories and methods. This is not without its problems. As Gustav K. Wiencke points out, it "reveals an unresolved tension. How can the authoritative form of the catechism fit into modern educational methods?" [30] Otto Frederick Nolde attempts to resolve the problem to some extent in *A Guide to Catechetical Instruction*. In his preliminary remarks to pastors he states that he has attempted to apply the experience-centered approach in educa-

[27] *Called to Be Christian* (Philadelphia: Muhlenberg Press, 1961).

[28] *Dr. Martin Luther's Small Catechism with Explanation* (Rock Island, Ill.: Augustana Press, 1957).

An important study now under way is A Long-Range Program, begun in 1957 and planned for 1964, under the auspices of the boards of parish education of the various synods now constituting the Lutheran Church in America. The study is intended for all levels of parish education, including a three-year period in which confirmation instruction is generally given (Grades 7—9). The material is being prepared under the general editorship of W. Kent Gilbert.

The Lutheran Church — Missouri Synod has authorized its Board of Parish Education to prepare a series of three graded catechisms for Grades 3—9 and seven primary readers for Grades 1 and 2. Suitable workbooks and teacher's manuals are being prepared for all levels. Dr. Walter M. Wangerin has been appointed general ed. for the series.

[29] Unsigned, "The Small Catechism by Martin Luther: A New Translation: A Handbook of Basic Christian Instruction for the Family and the Congregation," *Interaction*, III (Jan. 1963), 10. The tentative text is given on pp. 11—14.

[30] "Confirmation in Historical Perspective," *The Lutheran Quarterly*, VII (May 1955), 111

tion. Procedures based on this approach, he writes, in no respect disparage

> the objective reality of the facts presented. They do, however, seek to arrange and present the essentials of Christianity in a manner most likely to result in Christian experience. They find very interesting precedent in Luther's own stated and implied differentiation between the Bible as a collection of books and the Word or the Gospel preached and taught in such a way as to be effective in the life of its hearers.[31]

In his two volumes, *Teaching the Way* and *Learning the Way*, Donald F. Irvin made even more use of modern teaching methods. In defense of his methods Irvin writes,

> Procedures in the catechetical class cannot continue without change generation after generation. Pupils respond best to the procedures that are practiced in the public schools they attend. For instance, not to use modern techniques such as audio-visual aids would be to miss opportunities for helpful teaching. The books prepared for this course are intended to help the pastor use procedures which will make the truths of the Catechism vital in the life of the catechumen.[32]

In addition to these catechetical books, many catechism workbooks and tests have been produced either as independent helps or as aids to be used with an existing text. Filmstrips and other teaching aids have been welcomed by pastors, though the use sometimes made of these tools may leave much to be desired.

Unfortunately the number of books providing better theological content for the instruction have been few, though the educational helps themselves have often provided some fresh doctrinal insights. John W. Doberstein's translations of Herbert Girgensohn's two books on *Teaching Luther's Catechism* provide some needed help.[33]

[31] (Philadelphia: The Board of Publication of The United Lutheran Church in America, 1939), p. 8.

[32] *Teaching the Way: A Pastor's Guide for Catechetical Instruction*, ed. Arthur H. Getz (Philadelphia: The United Lutheran Publication House, 1951), p. 11. *Learning the Way: A Catechetical Guidebook for Youth* was also edited by Arthur H. Getz (Philadelphia: The United Lutheran Publication House, 1951).

[33] Philadelphia: Muhlenberg Press, 1959—60.

A most encouraging sign has been the eagerness with which pastors have been organizing seminars, workshops, and one-day institutes for discussion of problems related to confirmation. This constant churning should gradually work toward general improvement of confirmation practices in this country. One of the most significant of such workshops was held in Racine, Wis., Aug. 24–27, 1954. It was sponsored by the Intersynodical Committee on Parish Education and drew together approximately forty persons from seven different synods. The four-day study was a means of making various synodical boards of parish education more conscious of their needs and assisted materially in giving some necessary direction to the Lutheran Church. As Americans unite with other Lutheran educators and theologians throughout the world in the studies of the Lutheran World Federation, still other important improvements in confirmation may soon be realized.

CHAPTER V

THE THEOLOGICAL IMPLICATIONS

OF CONFIRMATION

The history of confirmation in the Lutheran Church clearly shows that no one type of confirmation has won acceptance everywhere at any time. Therefore one cannot speak of a uniform confirmation practice among Lutherans. Rather the practice has varied greatly from period to period and from place to place. Since confirmation has no Biblical basis that might serve as a norm, the Lutheran Church did not hesitate to sanction new emphases and directions of development according to changing circumstances and needs. As confirmation is practiced today, especially in the United States, it is cluttered with incoherent remnants of its historical development, the origins of which are rarely recognized. Just as some in the Church of the Reformation thought they were restoring confirmation in accord with the tradition of the early church, so many today suppose that their particular practice of confirmation is a Reformation heritage. Such notions have given confirmation an aura which has largely prevented the consideration and acceptance of major changes where necessary.

A study of confirmation as practiced in any given Lutheran congregation will likely reveal that many things are said and done that do not harmonize with the teachings of the Lutheran Church. Such inconsistencies have caused considerable confusion. They have contributed to some of the larger problems of which many pastors are aware and which have made an even greater number of laymen uneasy. It is therefore the task of Lutheran churches in America, as it has been the task in Europe for some time, to restudy theologically their practice of confirming baptized persons. Such a study should help to eleminate

155

accretions which do not meet present needs or which imply a contradiction of sound Lutheran doctrine. This will not be a simple task, because our confirmation tradition, though transplanted from Europe, has already become deeply rooted in the life of the church. Traditions are not easily disturbed; as Von Schenck put it, "It is easier to change a doctrine than a tradition."[1]

Yet if we are to get at the roots of some of the current problems in connection with confirmation, we must carefully evaluate our tradition and determine whether it is in harmony with Scripture and the Lutheran Confessions. If we are willing to do this, we have taken a long step toward a sound solution. If, on the other hand, we prefer first to tackle problems connected with the curriculum or methods or more effective administration, we will continue to consume our efforts in attempts to eliminate mere surface symptoms. The more prudent approach to solving our confirmation problems lies in formulating a sound theological basis for our practice. Such a basis will then govern the objectives, curriculum, teaching methods, and all the related practices of confirmation instruction and the closing rite.

With few exceptions, confirmation in the Lutheran Church has been built on the means of grace. It is suspended between the sacramental poles of Holy Baptism and the Lord's Supper. Confirmation is part of the nurturing of that faith which the Holy Spirit has created in Holy Baptism. Through instruction the church discloses to the catechumen the meaning and continued significance of the sacrament. Furthermore, confirmation prepares the child for joyful and reverent participation in the Lord's Supper and richer sharing of all that life in the body of Christ implies. Such nurture and preparation is performed through instruction by the Word, the power of life to life.

Holy Baptism
The Baptismal Covenant

When the Christian church, in obedience to the Lord's command, baptizes a child, it is privileged to perform a stupendous

[1] Berthold von Schenck, "Confirmation and First Communion," *Una Sancta,* XIV (Pentecost 1957), 3.

miracle in His name. In Holy Baptism, God seizes the sinner and makes him His own. In this act the sin, together with the old man, dies an instant death. God creates in the infant the miracle of faith, which clothes him with the righteousness of Christ and gives him the new life. In Baptism the child is born anew through faith in Christ Jesus. God says in effect, "You are My child, My own, through the merits of My Son."

In Holy Baptism, God makes a covenant with the infant. It is a unique covenant in every respect. It is unique not merely because the righteous and holy God makes an agreement with a sinner but also because the agreement established is a covenant of *grace*. Covenants are usually bilateral, that is, one party agrees to something to which a second party makes a corresponding promise. Two partners, as it were, reach an agreement, and each pledges himself to keep the agreement. Should one break his promises, the covenant is null and void. If there are any damages to the innocent party, he may even have recourse to law. On the other hand, the covenant may be renewed if both parties agree. Not so with the baptismal covenant. It is unilateral. It is not conditioned by any act or promise of man. Natural man is impotent and not in a position to drive any kind of bargain with God or to establish a covenant with Him. But in His mercy and love, God comes to man in his sin and with Baptism enters into a personal relationship. Therein He makes a promise of forgiveness, life, and salvation. Man merely accepts the promises and gifts of Baptism and thereby enters into the covenant relationship. Even this acceptance is the result of the regenerative work of the Holy Spirit.

The uniqueness of the baptismal covenant is heightened still more by its continuousness. God never breaks it. The covenant never ceases and needs no renewal. His promises are never withdrawn. "Therefore Baptism remains forever. Even though we fall from it and sin, nevertheless we always have access to it so that we may again subdue the old man." [2]

True, a baptized person can reject his baptism and can re-

[2] LC IV 77, in *BS*, p. 706; *BC*, p. 446; *CT*, pp. 750, 751.

fuse to believe, but this does not invalidate the covenant. Should he, by the grace of God, return to the covenant, he would not be renewing it. It was never made by him, nor can he break it, though he may lose his covenant relationship. When man returns, he places himself under God's covenant and again receives its precious benefits.

Although Baptism has made man righteous in Christ, it is equally true that man is still sinful according to his own flesh. This creates the tension of the two natures of the Christian as summed up in Luther's well-known phrase, *simul iustus et peccator*. The continuous combat of these two natures in the Christian is signified by Holy Baptism in the drowning of the old man and in the coming forth of the new man (Rom. 6:3-14). This significance of Baptism continues throughout life. Thus, while the sacrament is never repeated and the covenant cannot be renewed, its significance, or meaning, for the Christian is continuous. In that sense Baptism is not accomplished until death. The Small Catechism says that baptizing with water "signifies that the old Adam in us, together with all sins and evil lusts, should be drowned by daily sorrow and repentance and be put to death, and that the new man should come forth daily and rise up, cleansed and righteous, to live forever in God's presence." [3]

Here the covenant idea is particularly helpful. In Baptism God renews us. Through it His Spirit mortifies our sinful nature and prepares us "for death and the resurrection at the Last Day." In addition, God gives us the desire for more and more of the new life, the will to remain in the covenant and to mortify sin more and more till the day we die. "This too God accepts. He trains and tests you all your life long with many good works and with all kinds of sufferings. Thereby he accomplishes what you in baptism have desired . . ." [4]

In commenting on this, Regin Prenter says:

[3] SC IV 12, in *BS*, p. 516; *BC*, p. 349; *CT*, pp. 550, 551.
[4] Martin Luther, *Eyn Sermon von dem heyligen Hochwirdigen Sacrament der Tauffe* ("A Sermon on the Holy and Blessed Sacrament of Baptism"), 1519, in *WA* 2, 730; *SL* X, 2218; *LW* 35, 33.

These sentences must be carefully considered. They tell us a great deal about Luther's conception of Baptism. The covenant concluded between God and you in Baptism is a personal relationship. Therefore you are not receiving something magical, with which you can purify yourself according to your own wishes and ideals and thus obtain a righteousness of your own. On the contrary! You are being put under an obligation toward another person, in this instance the obligation of taking the right attitude toward your God. You must ask and pray for that which God intends to work in you: to mortify your flesh and to make you a new creature in the resurrection with Christ. . . .

In concluding His covenant with us, God on His part has also accepted the consequences of such an unequal partnership. What are they? Luther answers: "Because this is your covenant with God, God on His part looks with grace upon you and promises that He will not impute the sins which remain in your nature after baptism. He will neither regard them, nor condemn you because of them; rather, He is satisfied and pleased with the fact that you are constantly trying and desiring to mortify them and to be rid of them in your death." [5]

In the light of this, how can we justify speaking of a renewal of the baptismal covenant in confirmation? If the covenant does not refer to the covenant of grace, is it perhaps being confused with the vow of the sponsors to renounce the devil and all his ways? If so, different terminology is needed. The thought of a renewal of the baptismal covenant, it will be remembered, was introduced into confirmation by the Pietists and their forerunners. They were interested in a pure congregation within the church *(ecclesiola in ecclesia)*, and the renewal of the baptismal covenant was part of their conversion theology. Others, like Theophil Grossgebauer (1627—61), believed that Holy Baptism was incomplete and needed confirmation as a complement. A renewal of the baptismal covenant tied the two together. Such ideas are scripturally untenable and unwarranted in Lutheran confirmation.

[5] "Luther on Word and Sacrament," *More about Luther*, in *Martin Luther Lectures*, II (Decorah, Iowa: Luther College Press, 1958), 93—95. Prenter quotes Luther's sermon on Holy Baptism cited above, n. 4, in *WA* 2, 731; *SL* X, 2118; *LW* 35, 34.

Confirmation

At confirmation the young Christian gives merely his personal affirmation of the covenant which God made with him at the time of his baptism and so reaffirms that he will live in that covenant. This affirmation is part of his continuous concern. Until he dies the Christian undertakes through Word and sacraments to remain true to the baptismal covenant and in faith to mortify his flesh. Such a confirmation affirmation is similar to the remembering of the covenant called for in several early Lutheran church orders before Pietism had effected a change in the confirmation practice.

Membership in the Church

Since in Holy Baptism we have put on Christ (Gal. 3:27) and share in His death and resurrection (Rom. 6:3, 4), the baptized person is a member of the body of Christ, His church (Eph. 4:3-6). Membership in this church is the only kind spoken of in Scripture. Membership in a local congregation has meaning and validity in the sight of God only because it is derived from membership in the holy Christian church. Membership in the congregation is not a higher kind of membership, nor is it more real because we can see someone's signature on the books.

The different types of membership which an organization may devise for the sake of order or its own efficiency, such as baptized, communicant, and voting memberships, do not indicate third-, second-, and first-class members in the church of Christ but are convenient tags to indicate various levels of rights or responsibilities that the members have accepted. The term "full membership," used frequently at confirmation to indicate communicant membership, is a misnomer; it implies bestowal of some privilege or right that adds to or completes the membership given in Baptism. It would be equally invalid to apply "full membership" to voting membership, for by the same token the designation would then imply that nonvoters have not as full a membership. If degree of responsibility is the criterion for "full membership," not all the voters are full members either, and the church would have to calibrate its membership scale even more precisely. God knows of no graduated membership.

Baptism makes us members of the only church He knows, the body of Christ. (Rom. 12:4, 5)

When a child is baptized, it is baptized into a definite faith, usually as expressed in the Apostles' Creed, the ancient baptismal confession. Baptism is normally administered by a minister of Christ who has been called by a particular group of Christians assembled about the means of grace, by the church in a given place. Even when a layman performs an emergency baptism, he does so by virtue of his membership in the holy Christian church. In such cases the child's newly created membership is normally inscribed in the records of an assembly of Christians who recognize him as a fellow member. But such assembled Christians do not exist in a vacuum. They profess membership in Christ through some confession of faith, more or less definitely defined, as they are assembled about the sustaining Word. They may call it Pilgrim Congregational, Christ Episcopal, St. Peter's Roman Catholic, the Lutheran Church of the Atonement, or some other confessional name. Hence the baptized child's membership in the holy Christian church is expressed and made more evident through the confession of the congregation which authorized or accepted his baptism. By virtue of his baptism a child becomes a member of the local congregation. The pastor who baptizes such a child therefore immediately assumes a pastoral relationship with it. The congregation that authorizes a baptism through its called and ordained servant of the Word or accepts a lay baptism also assumes a relationship of fellowship with such a baptized person, prays for him, and otherwise expresses its concern that he be strengthened, confirmed, in the grace of the almighty God unto life everlasting. The misconception that one is a member of the Christian church by Baptism and becomes a member of the Lutheran Church or of a local congregation by confirmation seems to be direct influence of Rationalism and reflects a faulty concept of the doctrine of the church.

When a baptized child is led to believe that his membership in the Lutheran Church begins with confirmation, a serious confusion is created. Even when in theory it is stated that while his membership began with Baptism, he now makes public acknowledgment of that fact, we confuse the issue for him and the congregation in attendance. Why ask him, "Do you desire to be a member of the Evangelical Lutheran Church and of this congregation?" at confirmation when he has already been a member since his baptism? To speak of membership in connection with a child's confirmation is not only confusing; it exalts a man-made rite and detracts from the initiatory sacrament which God has established.

Confession of Faith

At the time of Holy Baptism the sponsors confess in the child's stead the faith which the Holy Spirit creates by water and the Word. The confession expresses the faith in which the church embraces the child through his baptism. Since the sponsors' confession of faith is made in the name and stead of the child, it is as valid as if the child made it himself. The acts of parents or appointed guardians in behalf of minors are regarded as valid and binding. The child brought up in a Christian home soon learns to make confession of faith with his own lips. At first it may be a simple "Abba, Father." As his understanding grows, his confession becomes a little more precise, consisting perhaps of the words of the Apostles' Creed. In fact, he makes many confessions of faith during his childhood. Every time he seeks forgiveness of sin he makes such confession. Every attendance at Sunday school or church is, in a manner of speaking, a confession of faith. After he has been instructed, at confirmation he is asked to make a public confession through the examination and in the specific questions of the rite. Further confession is made at his first Communion, and by the grace of God he continues to confess through his life. The child is not confirming, as it were, the confession which his sponsors made for him at his baptism. This could easily be misunderstood as though it were something the child needs to make good, to validate, the confession made for him or even the Baptism itself and as though by confirmation he becomes eligible for certain rights and privileges. The point is that the confession of faith at confirmation is only an episode in the child's life. It represents a stage in the development of his personal faith. It is in effect a progress report in the presence of the congregation and an occasion for joy, thanksgiving, and prayer. Normally it is not a matter of "standing up and being counted," as some may wish to dramatize it. If in rare cases it happens to be that, then in an even more precise sense will this be true at first Communion, when the confirmand identifies himself with the body of Christ and shows forth the Lord's death.

Is the confession of faith at confirmation a confession of what is to be believed, or is it a confession of what the catechumen himself actually believes? This distinction between objective and subjective faith has been discussed throughout the history of confirmation. It seems that the majority of Lutherans in the 16th century had a confession of the objective faith in mind, although this cannot be proved with certainty in every instance. In more recent times, as mentioned earlier, Johann Michael Reu (1869 to 1943) was one of the strongest proponents of the objective view. He feared that every effort to elicit a subjective confession was, or might become, an interference in the work of the Holy Spirit. It is regrettable that his fears may often be well founded. Nevertheless, because we know that a living, saving faith was created by Baptism and normally nurtured by the home and the church through the Word, we should assume that this faith is still alive and further strengthened through confirmation instruction. Such a faith is ready always to express itself when witness is called for. We know that in some this faith may have died and the instruction may have been a formality under parental or social pressure. For this reason it is the responsibility of the pastor to show the confirmands the harm of making insincere confession. Beyond such admonition he cannot go. The final responsibility lies with the catechumen. Any effort to probe the catechumen's expressed faith to determine whether he is sincere is wholly unwarranted and highly dangerous. Even the Lord did not probe the confession of the Twelve (John 6:67-71), and Paul certainly did not suggest it to the Corinthian Christians (2 Cor. 2:5-11). In the final analysis, only the manifestly impenitent sinner may be turned away from confirmation.

Surrender to Christ and Obedience to Him

Baptism is not a passive sacrament. We do not merely become new creatures, put on Christ, and become members of His body. We are new creatures that we may walk in newness of life; we have been cleansed that we may serve Christ with "fruit unto holiness" (Rom. 6:22); we are members of Christ's body to give ourselves to Him and to His people. Baptism is an active sacrament implanting in us the dynamic of the Gospel. Through our sponsors we have been called to renounce the devil and all his works and to surrender ourselves, to use Bucer's term, to the obedience of Christ. Such surrender we promise daily as the continued significance of our baptism requires. This we do in a more formal way at confirmation or whenever the occasion demands it.

When we surrender to Christ and promise Him obedience, do we not by the same token then promise obedience to the church of which He is the Head? Yes, to *that* church and *in those things* with which He has charged His church. It is not carte blanche. When the catechumen is asked in the confirmation rite to surrender himself to the "discipline of the church," the church leaves itself open to serious question and becomes suspect. Such a requirement may be understood correctly. It may imply that the catechumen surrenders himself in obedience to the church only when it acts within its proper sphere and limits itself to the responsibilities specifically given it by Christ. However, in the light of history we know that such obligatory self-surrender can be seriously abused. When Christians get together in an organized way, they are easily tempted to make their predilections binding on others. When Bucer introduced the vow of obedience to the church, his purpose was to use confirmation to impose stricter discipline. As well-intentioned as Bucer may have been, he thereby sowed seed for new crops of popes where his formula was used. The same tendency is still prevalent when congregations attempt to legislate their members into higher sanctification by binding consciences in matters wherein Christ has set them free.

The Vow

The renunciation of the devil and all his works and the confession of faith by the sponsors are often referred to as the baptismal vow. Sometimes this vow is confused with the baptismal covenant. Such a confusion immediately poses the question: Is the vow of the sponsors regarded as the promise of the "second party" in the baptismal covenant? Then the baptismal covenant is no longer a covenant of grace. Then God's gifts are conditioned by man's action. Or is this a new covenant to be distinguished from God's covenant of grace but made in response to His covenant in Baptism? If so, who is the second party in this new covenant? God? What new promise is He making which He has not already made unilaterally and unconditionally in Baptism? It seems that we actually mean not a covenant but a vow when referring to the sponsors. Apparently the church sometimes falls into the inaccuracy of using the terms almost interchangeably. The vow of the sponsors in the child's stead is not a covenant. It is a promise made in response to God's gracious work in the child.

How should the confirmation vow be interpreted? Is it to be considered binding for life? There are many who regard it as such and give it the status of a solemn oath. But is the confirmation vow, strictly speaking, a lifetime promise of loyalty? Assuming that confirmation is not terminal and that Christian growth will continue through further instruction, is it not possible that the communicant will see implications in what he confessed — in what he thought he was confessing — which he did not and could not have seen at age 12 or even 16? If we can assume that it is possible for a conscientious Christian to accept, in error but without destroying his saving faith, a view of the Christian doctrine that is scripturally untenable but which he nevertheless sincerely believes, can we — dare we — bind his conscience and say that because of the vow he made at 14 he must now remain loyal to the Evangelical Lutheran Church? The problem becomes even more acute when the vow is interpreted as one of lifetime loyalty to a particular synodical body within the Lutheran Church, especially since the theological differences between synods, as important as they may be, are often difficult for the uninitiated to understand. Under such circumstances would a Christian whom we wish to bind with a lifetime vow be held to the Lutheran Church by the Law or by the drawing power of the Gospel? If he remains with the Lutheran Church merely because of a vow made in his youth, can he serve it in good conscience, fervently, and loyally?

Is it necessary that we attempt to hold any person on the basis of a man-made vow, a vow which may have been made under some pressure, parental or otherwise? Would it not be more prudent and more realistic to interpret the vow as an expression of the catechumen's sincere intent, devoutly and freely offered on the basis of his understanding at his level of maturity? By construing the confirmation vow as a declaration of intent, directly or by implication, to remain under the means of grace that alone can keep him in the faith, both the church and the catechumen would place their trust in the power of the Word and the work of the Spirit rather than in the promises of a person not yet mature.

Instruction in the Word

A child is brought to Baptism in response to Christ's command to make disciples by baptizing. At the same time the church and the parents are aware that in this injunction of the Lord they are bidden to teach their children "to observe all things whatsoever I have commanded" (Matt. 28:20). With Holy Baptism, then, both the home and the church assume the duty to teach the baptized child. For this reason sponsors make the promise that they will hold themselves responsible that the parents meet this obligation, and if not, that they themselves will assume it. In effect the parents say at the baptism of their child: "We will try to bring up this child as a Christian in the faith here expressed and pledge ourselves to this purpose by our instruction and through our Christian example." The church promises in turn to assist the parents because it recognizes that it shares in this responsibility. Such teaching the Scriptures call nurture in the Lord. However, it is not terminal. It does not end at a given point in the life of the Christian or with a single rite. Nurture is growth; it is evidence of life. Christian education is therefore a lifelong process for the child, the youth, and the adult. (1 John 2:13)

Regrettably the church has not always been faithful to such a continuous responsibility. It has traditionally reserved its major emphasis on instruction for the period prior to the child's confirmation. Such a concentration of effort has placed the church in a dilemma. Since it has permitted confirmation to become a fixed terminus of formal instruction for the majority of its members, it has attempted to gain additional time for its task by postponing confirmation as long as possible, often regretting that it cannot postpone it even longer. But with such postponement the church also defers the child's first Communion and deprives him for several years of the spiritual power and assurance that the Lord intends for His own.

Instead of postponing confirmation as long as possible, congregations need to recover the Reformation principle that Christian instruction is to continue after the Christian's first Communion. Confirmation should not be regarded as a sort of temple curtain beyond which the church need not guide and direct the young Christian through further religious instruction. In fact, as with the force and meaning of Baptism, Christian nurture ends only when the sinner-saint is transformed into a saint of the Church Triumphant. In such a continuing instruction the church assists the Christian in making his life a *coming into* his baptism, helping him constantly to appropriate the gifts received in the sacrament.

The Lord's Supper

Since the Christian's whole life is a continuous spiritual baptism, what is the relation of the Word and the Lord's Supper to Baptism? Are they subordinate to it? Not at all. As Prenter points out, it is just because the baptismal covenant implies the necessity of a lifelong exercise of man's faith under that covenant that there is need "for a continuous sanctifying activity of the living Word, not in competition with, but in consequence of, the regenerating activity of the living Word in Baptism. In this sanctifying activity preaching, absolution, and above all the Lord's Supper assume necessary functions." [6] The Lord's Supper is an indispensable help in the lifelong struggle of the sinner-saint.

With the exception of the traditional type of confirmation, preparation for the Lord's Supper has been historically one of the major goals of confirmation, and as such this sacrament is the second sacramental pole. Confirmation is to help meet the responsibility of both the parents and the church for the instruction implied in Baptism and for the Communion preparation required in 1 Cor. 11:23-30. However, confirmation does not give the catechumen the right to partake of the Lord's Supper. This right flows out of Baptism. It is a right given him because he is a child of God. Through confirmation the church acknowledges that the catechumen is ready to exercise his right because he is now able to prepare himself for the Lord's Supper. Conceivably a child may partake of the Lord's Supper without being confirmed. In fact, newly baptized adults should normally exercise their right to partake as soon as possible and without the rite of confirmation. It is a misunderstanding to regard confirmation as a rite which extends the privilege of participation in the Lord's Supper. It is even more incorrect to affirm this "extension" with a handshake, as though it were a lifetime guarantee. Confirmation merely indicates that the confirmed person has shown that he is able to discern the Lord's body and, as far as the congregation can determine, is spiritually fit to receive the gift of the Lord's Supper. With each subsequent participation the catechumen, with all other communicants, goes through essentially the same preparatory steps.

To say that the Lord's Supper has been associated with confirmation through most of its historical development is not to overlook the array of extraneous acts which have at one time or another been connected with confirmation and which have on occasion relegated preparation for the second sacrament to a somewhat subordinate position.

Members of the Erlangen school and others since then have tried to dissociate confirmation and the Lord's Supper altogether.

[6] Op. cit., p. 100.

However, if the church is to be faithful to its more historical tradition, then the Lord's Supper must retain a prominent position along with Holy Baptism. If the church finds it necessary to add a second purpose to confirmation instruction, such as making it serve as a terminal educational agency, the secondary purpose should not come to govern and determine the objectives for confirmation.

What are the Scriptural requirements for worthy participation in the Lord's Supper? If we can dissociate ourselves from the traditions of our own practices, whatever they may be, and allow ourselves to be guided solely by the Scriptures, we see that the requirements for a worthy eating and drinking are quite modest. The first requirement is that the communicant be able to distinguish between the bread and wine in the Lord's Supper and the bread and wine of an ordinary meal, that is, that he recognize the real presence of the body and blood of our Lord in the Sacrament. Second, the communicant must know and accept in faith the purpose for which the sacrament has been instituted. This implies more than a mere understanding of Christian doctrine, especially the doctrine of the Lord's Supper. The very purpose of the Sacrament requires that the communicant recognize his sinfulness, for this was the "first cause" behind God's gracious act, and that he repent of his sin and cling to the promises and merits of Christ for his forgiveness. Such faith will enable him to disown any other hope for forgiveness and salvation and to trust in Christ alone. Such faith will create both the earnest resolve to amend his sinful life and "the fervent love toward one another."

Hear Luther as he summarizes what worthy participation requires. In the Small Catechism he says,

> Who, then, receives this sacrament worthily?
> Answer: Fasting and bodily preparation are a good external discipline, but he is truly worthy and well prepared who believes these words: "for you" and "for the forgiveness of sins." On the other hand, he who does not believe these words, or doubts them, is unworthy and unprepared, for the words "for you" require truly believing hearts.[7]

---

[7] SC VI 9, 10, in *BS*, p. 521; *BC*, p. 352; *CT*, pp. 556, 557.

Elsewhere Luther said, "But if they believe and trust that at the sacrament they will receive grace, *then this faith alone makes them pure and worthy.*" [8] This is all that a faithful, i. e., worthy, participation in Holy Communion requires. Cannot this requirement readily be met by a 10- or 12-year-old Christian if church and home live up to their baptismal obligations?

But how, in actual practice, has the church interpreted worthy participation? In speaking of the faith necessary for the Lord's Supper the church has frequently interpreted it to mean a particular state of faith or amount of faith as evidenced by knowledge and understanding, something which can be measured and determined in a catechetical examination. In other words, understanding of the doctrine has been substituted for participation in faith.

To be sure, even when the church is prepared to settle for faith rather than a degree of knowledge, it still faces a dilemma, because faith rests on a knowledge of God's saving act. We must still answer the question of how much knowledge is necessary. While the Reformation practice set the standards at a minimum — namely, a knowledge of the Ten Commandments, the Apostles' Creed, the Lord's Prayer, the baptismal command, and the words of institution, all of which a 12-year-old can grasp — over the centuries since then the Lutheran Church has, without any Scriptural authority attempted gradually to raise the standards as high as possible, with an eye to advancing confirmation to a still later age and to requiring even more of the catechumen. This it has done not because it believed that our Lord actually laid down such rigid requirements for worthy participation but because it associated with the goal of confirmation such extraneous aims as conversion, church membership, or Christian education and allowed one or more of these to determine the standards for admission to first Communion.

Partaking of the Lord's Supper earlier than is now customary

[8] *Divi Pauli apostoli ad Hebreos epistola* ("Lectures on Hebrews"), 1517—18, in *WA* 57 III, 171; *Luther: Early Theological Works,* trans. and ed. James Atkinson (Philadelphia: Westminster Press, 1962), p. 107.

seems to be warranted by the social climate in which we live. Recognizing that the Lord's Supper is a means of grace established by God for the sole purpose of building up His church and for helping the individual to remain within His baptismal covenant, the church should be very loathe to oblige a baptized child to wait till he is 14 or 15 before he gets this additional help and protection offered by Christ. In the days of the Reformation the church faced many problems that are current today. A little reading in the writings of Luther, in the reports of the church visitations, and in the introductions attached to the church orders will dispel all romanticism about the world at that time. The Church of the Reformation did not develop in a Christian society. In such a milieu 16th-century Lutherans pressed the cup of forgiveness to the lips of the children at a very tender age.

Yet in one respect the social climate today is different from that of the 16th century. It is an important difference. In that day the enemy did not deny that the Scriptures were the Word of God, that man was accountable to God, that all things were under the rule of God. All this was self-evident even to the coarsest worldling, except that he did not follow through with it in life. This is not the case today. True, the climate in the United States cannot be said to be antireligious, but this is only because man is not concerned enough with religion even to oppose it. Man is so wrapped up in himself and in his activities that God has been ruled out of his conscious thought. Even when he is not engrossed in making a living, his growing amount of leisure time is appropriated by the entertainment and amusement industry. Meanwhile the youth of the land are guided by schools that are largely committed to a scientific secularism that substitutes scientific laws for God, scientific precision for holiness, scientific objectivity for faith, and scientific amorality for the will of God. It would seem that the church that has to compete with such naked materialism would use every means of grace at its disposal to safeguard its youth and would offer the Lord's Supper as early as possible as another means by which God confirms the individual's spiritual life.

The Lord's Supper a Church Sacrament

The Lord's Supper is a highly personal sacrament; in it God's gifts are given to the individual in a very direct way, and the words "for you" require him to believe. Yet the Lord's Supper is also a corporate sacrament in a sense not true of the Word and Baptism. The church preaches the Word to all; the church administers Baptism to all for whom it has some assurance that Christian instruction will follow. Among adults the Word precedes Baptism, and Baptism confirms the faith created by the Word. The Lord's Supper is unique in that the church administers it only to the church.

In giving the individual Christian Holy Communion the church, as Christ's agent, offers the gift of fellowship, not only with the Lord Himself but also with all the saints. The bond of union, among the saints which has existed since Baptism, is strengthened by Holy Communion. Hence Luther says of the sacrament of fellowship:

> See to it also that you give yourself to everyone in fellowship and by no means exclude anyone in hatred or anger. For this sacrament of fellowship, love, and unity cannot tolerate discord and disunity. You must take to heart the infirmities and needs of others, as if they were your own. Then offer to others your strength, as if it were their own, just as Christ does for you in the sacrament. This is what it means to be changed into one another through love, out of many particles to become one bread and drink, to lose one's own form and take on that which is common to all.[9]

Because the Lord's Supper is a corporate sacrament, the congregation is concerned about the spiritual maturity of every participant, especially at his first Communion. This is in harmony with the Augsburg Confession, which says, "it is not customary to administer the body of Christ except to those who have previously been examined and absolved."[10] Sharing in the fellowship of the Lord's Supper is not simply an individual matter to

---

[9] *Eyn Sermon von dem Hochwirdigen Sacrament des Heyligen Waren Leychnams Christi Und von den Bruderschafften* ("A Sermon on the Blessed Sacrament of the Holy and True Body of Christ, and the Brotherhoods"), 1519, in *WA* 2, 750; *SL* XIX, 439; *LW* 35, 61, 62.

[10] AC XXV 1 (Latin), in *BS*, p. 97; *BC*, p. 61; *CT*, pp. 68, 69.

be decided by the Christian alone or by the pastor or parent with the catechumen; it is to be decided under God by the congregation. For this reason, even where confirmation had not yet been instituted in the Reformation church and where the catechumens were examined privately or together with communicants who had come to confession, the pastor later announced to the congregation that such catechumens had come to confession and asked the congregation to intercede in their behalf. When confirmation was later established, as either a private or a public ceremony, public prayers were always offered for the confirmands by the congregation.

If participation in Holy Communion had been considered merely a private matter, the catechumen or his parents could have determined when he was ready for first Communion without any reference to the congregation or its appointed representatives. This was never the practice in the Lutheran Church. Instead the church set up regulations which it deemed necessary for deciding when and under what circumstances persons might participate in the Lord's Supper. That the church has not been scrupulously careful in requiring neither more nor less than is scripturally warranted has not meant its forfeiture of this responsibility.

In trying to meet its responsibility the church immediately faces some practical problems. In a large congregation it is obviously impossible to consider each catechumen separately to determine exactly when he is prepared. When the backgrounds and homes of the children vary greatly, especially where an intensive mission program has been under way for some time, it will be extremely difficult to decide individual preparedness without a broad governing policy. Such a policy must be kept broad if its administration is not to become legalistic. If, for instance, the minimum age is set at 11 or 12, some flexibility must still be retained if the policy is to be administered according to Scriptural principles. Granted that in isolated instances so general a policy may still prove arbitrary because it postpones unnecessarily some child's first Communion, it can generally be administered in an evangelical manner.

All this is not to say that the preparations for admission to first Communion are essentially different from those for any subsequent participation. What happens at confirmation is nothing else than what is expected of every communicant.[11] To be sure, at confirmation the preparation for first Communion takes on a structure that is different, but this is due only to the rite. In addition there is a special pastoral concern which will not be present later. But the rite and the special concern are accidental to the preparation. Every successive preparation for the Lord's Supper will be a repetition of confirmation in miniature.[12]

It is an error to look upon the observance of the confirmation rite as the occasion when the catechumen receives the right to partake of the Lord's Supper; the error is all the greater if this extension is regarded as a lifetime guarantee, affirmed often with a handclasp. Confirmation merely indicates that the confirmand has shown that he is able to discern the Lord's body and, as far as the congregation can determine, is spiritually fit to receive the gift of the Lord's Supper.[13] At every subsequent participation the Christian must go through the same steps — though of course not structured as in confirmation — as he prepares himself for worthy participation in Holy Communion. Hence the term "communicant membership" does not imply a special kind of membership, as though the Christian were a card-carrying member — in this case a certificate-carrying member — of the church, but it means simply that he has at one time shown that he can properly prepare himself for worthy participation in the sacrament.

Time for First Communion

It is interesting to note how with the development of confirmation the occasion when the catechumen receives his first

---

[11] Der Liturgische Ausschuss der Vereinigten Evangelisch-Lutherischen Kirche Deutschlands, *Begleitwort Zur Ordnung Der Konfirmation für evangelischlutherische Kirchen und Gemeinden,* ed. Chr[isthard] Mahrenholz (Berlin: Lutherisches Verlagshaus, 1952), p. 6.

[12] Ibid., p. 6.

[13] Some of the agendas took note that this was not an unconditional invitation. Thus Pennsylvania A, 1855 and 1860, read "so long as you remain faithful to your present profession and promises." So also United Synod in the South A, 1888.

Communion has come to be secondary. Originally, when the catechetical practice was almost universal in the Lutheran Church, participation in the Lord's Supper was of primary importance. With the development of a confirmation rite in liturgical form, there arose the option of separating the Lord's Supper from the rite. As the rite became more elaborate, exercise of the option became normal practice, though confirmation itself was usually observed at a secondary service. As time went on, the examination gained such prominence that two services were no longer sufficient and a third was added. Under such circumstances the Lord's Supper became even more detached from confirmation, and in the popular mind it became somewhat anticlimactic as the rite of confirmation appropriated major importance. Small wonder that because of this exaggeration of a human ceremony some have suggested that confirmation be abolished altogether and no further contempt be shown the Sacrament or that a form of the traditional type be revived in which there is a complete separation of first Communion and confirmation, but with first Communion preceding confirmation.

Instead of the three services usually observed, the church should attempt to combine the Lord's Supper and confirmation in one service.[14] If tradition is so strong that an extensive examination is required not merely to make a confession of faith but to show the congregation how far the catechumens have advanced in Christian understanding, then two services may be necessary, one for the examination at some secondary service and one for confirmation and the Lord's Supper. Then the service will not only remind the members of the congregation of their baptism but also serve better to remind all that confirmation belongs with the Lord's Supper and forfeits much of its meaning by itself. Celebration of both in a single service might also help to deemphasize confirmation and refocus attention on the sacraments as precious gifts of the Lord for His church.

[14] After some additional study of confirmation, Löhe recommended that the Lord's Supper be celebrated in behalf of the confirmands with the parents and sponsors immediately after the rite. See his rev. eds. of 1859 and 1884 (with J. Deinzer). A few other agendas made provisions suggesting that the Lord's Supper be celebrated in the confirmation service. E. g., see United Synod in the South A, 1888.

Confirmation

Is Confirmation Essential?

The question whether confirmation is essential is not an academic question. It is asked to help point up what is essential and what is not. The German agenda of the Missouri Synod stated that before the catechumen may be permitted to attend the Lord's Supper, he *must* give assent to his baptismal covenant and solemnly renew it before God. The implication was that this must be done publicly, as at Confirmation. What was meant by the "must"? The Wisconsin A, 1909, which followed the Missouri A quite closely, was more discreet and stated that the Catechumen "ought" to do this. Granted that only a baptized Christian can partake of the Lord's Supper and that the church will, as far as is possible, permit only the worthy participants to receive the Sacrament, the question still remains: Need there be a public confession of faith? What is more, need there be a public ceremony such as confirmation before one can be admitted to the Lord's Supper? Obviously not. The Lutheran Church has always regarded confirmation as a human institution and during its early history permitted the majority of its members to receive first Communion without confirmation. Now that confirmation is deeply rooted in the practice of the Lutheran Church, such instances are rare, but the principle is still maintained in cases of emergency and when persons are baptized as adults. In fact, such persons ought not first be confirmed but should normally be admitted immediately to the second sacrament.[15]

Among the current reform proposals are some suggestions that the children normally be admitted to the Lord's Supper without confirmation. This would require a new rite for first Communion and use of the term confirmation for a later rite associated only with the baptismal catechumenate. In principle this is a return to the traditional type, though confirmation usually

[15] The Synodical Conference A, 1949, allows the option of baptizing and confirming adults contrary to a strong Lutheran tradition. Thus, e. g., C[arl] M[anthey] Zorn, *Allerlei aus Gottes Garten* (Zwickau, Saxony: Johannes Hermann, n. d.), pp. 166, 167, says that those baptized as adults "are, of course, not to be confirmed" and relates how he baptized a young woman in a public ceremony and in the same service gave her Holy Communion.

preceded first Communion. Proposals of this kind are similar to the suggestions of Johann F. W. Höfling and Carl A. G. von Zezschwitz in the 19th century.[16] It is doubtful whether present circumstances warrant the return to some unusual form of the traditional type of confirmation. It would appear more suitable to retain confirmation for what it usually has been, a practice associated with both sacraments. The present wholesome trend in the Lutheran churches of America toward a more thorough instruction for all age levels must not be jeopardized. If a new rite needs to be introduced, it might be for a later period, such as age 18, to serve as an initiatory rite for voting membership and other formal participation in the work of the congregation. The introduction of such a rite would still not relieve the church of its obligation for some type of lifelong instruction, for which there can be no terminal rite except the Christian burial service.

What, Then, Is Confirmation?

Obviously confirmation is not a divine ordinance; it is not a sacrament. This has to be said, not because anyone in the Lutheran Church has taught it to be such but because the aura about confirmation and the esteem in which it is held make it practically as untouchable as some divine ordinance. Nor does the importance of confirmation lie in the rite. During the major portion of the Lutheran Church's history, confirmation was not universally observed with a ceremony. The heart of confirmation lies in the instruction in the Word that precedes the rite. The real confirmation takes place in the confirmation of faith by the Word, for through the Word God continues to confirm the faith begun in Baptism and nurtured by the home and the church. When pastors use confirmation instruction for children who have not been baptized or who have not previously been instructed, they utilize it in a way not originally intended. They must therefore make the necessary modifications to meet this special need. But basically the period of instruction is the confirming period. Therefore the word confirm should be used not for anything the catechumens do but for what God does. When

[16] See above, pp. 89, 91.

the term is used in referring to the pastor or congregation as the one who confirms, it is used only in a derived sense; pastor and congregation act under God's command.

As previously pointed out, the association of confirmation instruction with both sacraments creates a tension. By association with Baptism there is a tendency to postpone confirmation instruction as long as possible. Conversely the association with first Communion tends to fix the time for instruction as early as possible. Similarly the tension is felt when other matters related to confirmation come under consideration; for example, the objectives, the curriculum, the length of the instruction period, and the needs of postconfirmation youth. Yet the tension has value. It can serve as a wholesome check on extremists in either direction.

The Lutheran practice of confirmation helps the home and church to focalize for the child what an important gift God has given him in the Lord's Supper. The child is made more keenly aware of the concern which his parents and fellow Christians have for his spiritual welfare. Furthermore, the ceremony gives the catechumen the opportunity to make a personal, formal confession of faith, not as though this is either the first or the last time that he will acknowledge the baptismal covenant but rather as one of a new series of such witnesses that he will make every time he partakes of the Lord's Supper.

For members of the congregation, confirmation is a public witnessing of such confession and a solemn reminder of personal responsibility for these young Christians and all other members of the body of Christ. It further reminds them of the gifts God shares with them in His means of grace. It gives the members an opportunity to examine themselves whether the meaning of their baptism is daily manifest in their lives, whether they are still using the Word for its sustaining power, and whether theirs is the earnest desire to partake worthily of the Lord's Supper.

Because the congregation has a personal interest in the spiritual welfare of the confirmands, the members intercede for them in prayer and petition God to impart the gifts of His Holy Spirit. The pastor personalizes the prayers of the congregation with the laying on of hands, reminding the members that all sustaining help must come from God and giving them assurance that the prayers of a righteous people availeth much. Some have contended that the laying on of hands should be eliminated because the act can easily be misunderstood. Theodor Kliefoth is convinced that even though theologians generally avoid a sacramental view, the average person still feels that in a rite so solemnly observed by the pastor "something" must have taken place.[17] Perhaps more frequent use of the laying on of hands would dispel the notion where it exists. Since this ancient practice, rooted in the history of God's people since the days of the Old Testament, retains intrinsic values for both catechumen and congregation, it should not be lightly given up as long as there is no serious misunderstanding in connection with its use.

What are the essential elements of confirmation? From all that has been said, it seems that there are but three such elements: the instruction in the Word, the confession of faith, and the intercession of the congregation, accompanied by the laying on of hands. If confirmation is to be observed properly, the disturbing elements still attached to it, those that lead to serious misunderstandings, must be eliminated. Such extraneous elements are chiefly the renewal of the baptismal covenant, the reception into church membership, and the vows when they are meant as lifelong promises. To them may be added the handclasp when it is used either to exalt and dramatize the vow or to bestow new rights and privileges of church membership.[18]

[17] *Die Confirmation,* in *Liturgische Abhandlungen,* III, 1 (Schwerin: Stiller'schen Hof-Buchhandlung, 1856), 152, 153.

[18] In the Buffalo A, 1888, the handclasp was used with a vow in which the confirmand renounced the devil and promised to remain faithful in his baptismal covenant. Similarly the German Missouri A, 1856 and thereafter, associated the handclasp with the vow. Until the 1922 rev. the vow was referred to as an oath. The English Missouri A, beginning with the Abbetmeyer ed., 1904, spoke of the handclasp "as a pledge of your promise." The English Missouri A, 1881, a trans. of the German agenda, still referred to the vow as an oath and associated it with the handclasp.

The Ohio A, 1864, associated the handclasp with the vow, fellowship, and the bestowal of privileges: "Upon this your voluntary profession and promise, I hereby declare you to be confirmed members of this Christian congregation, and give you the right hand of Christian fellowship and love, and extend to you the privilege to join us in the celebration of the Lord's Supper, and to

Confirmation

Since confirmation has been subject to so much buildup through dramatic effects, the tendency to exaggerate its importance has become all the greater. The Christian's baptism and his first attendance at Holy Communion are rarely regarded as highpoints in his life, but confirmation nearly always is. Every overemphasis of confirmation is at the expense of God's means of grace. Instruction in the Word becomes terminal, Baptism is thought to need some completing act or further confirmation, and preparation for worthy participation in the Lord's Supper becomes an intellectual exercise. However, when confirmation receives its proper and more humble place, it becomes an edifying practice leading the young Christian closer to his Savior and to his church through reverent and joyful use of the means of grace.

participate in all our spiritual blessings, so long as you remain faithful to your present profession and promises." Similarly the Ohio Selection of Forms, 1870.

The United Lutheran Church A, 1918, 1930, and 1943, associated the handclasp with becoming a member of the local congregation and the authorization "to receive the Lord's Supper and to participate in all the spiritiual privileges of the Church."

The Tennessee A, 1843, stated that in view of the voluntary promises made "we give you the right hand of brotherly fellowship and love; and invite you to join us in the celebration of the Lord's Supper."

CHAPTER VI

THE STRUCTURE

OF CONFIRMATION

Despite an overemphasis on confirmation in the Lutheran Church and despite some erroneous and contradictory views associated with the practice, few Lutherans will be inclined to do away with confirmation. Lutheranism, by nature conservative, will seek rather to reconstruct this time-honored practice in such a manner that it will become more effective under present-day circumstances. But as attempts are made to reconstruct confirmation, no effort should be made to structure a uniform practice for all of Lutheranism. Confirmation must be accepted as an unsolved problem in the Lutheran Church, and as such, diversity will be recognized as not only permissible but desirable so long as the different practices are in harmony with Lutheran theology and fulfill sound purposes. Conditions in Europe, the United States and Canada, and among the "younger churches" are often so different that any attempt at uniformity will be unnatural and will in time prove unsatisfactory. Even among various church groups in the same country, diversity should be accepted as wholesome as long as it does not become an end in itself. The structure of confirmation suggested in this chapter is intended for the United States and Canada. If the general theses are accepted that sound Lutheran principles are to serve as norms and that the best educational theories for the prevailing circumstances are to serve as guides to congregations and pastors, differences in detail will be unimportant. The mobility of population will of itself be an important deterrent to still greater diversity of practice.

Confirmation

The Age of the Catechumen

At what age should the congregation, under normal circumstances, confirm its children? As stated previously, in the history of confirmation we search in vain for a uniform age among the catechumens. The customary ages varied, depending on the theological traditions of the time and on the social, cultural, and educational environment of the confirmands. During the 16th and the early part of the 17th century it was customary to confirm children at an age which today seems unusually early.[1] Less emphasis was placed on the catechumens' age and more on their understanding and the desire of their parents or sponsors to have them partake of the Lord's Supper. The catechumens were expected to know from memory Luther's Small Catechism without explanation. It was assumed that confirmands had participated in the parish catechizations and a brief preparation immediately before confirmation. The chief purpose of the preparation was to review the catechism and learn the answers to the confirmation questions to be asked in the presence of the elders or congregation. When church schools came to be established, it was usually assumed that the children had also attended them for a time. At the time of Reformation, and for some time after that, the church did not expect the confirmand to know the arguments against false teaching. If the children really knew the catechism, the implication was that they rejected false teachings, an implication that did not necessarily follow.

The early age at which children were permitted to be confirmed and to partake of the Lord's Supper during the first one and a half centuries of Lutheranism is particularly significant when one remembers how low the level of Christian education then was, particularly in the homes. For this reason the church orders emphasized the need for catechization whenever communicants attended confession before partaking of Holy Communion.

When confirmation began to be regarded as terminal rather than as merely an important part of the normal teaching respon-

[1] See above, p. 56.

sibility assumed with Holy Baptism and when first Communion ceased to be the primary goal to which confirmation instruction was to lead the catechumen, there was a tendency to postpone the age for confirmation. Pietism's emphasis on the subjective, including the confirmand's personal vow of commitment and his renewal of the baptismal covenant, made it logical for the confirmand to be at least 14 years of age. With Rationalism an even later age seemed to be desirable, especially when civic, economic, and social privileges were associated with confirmation.[2] With the rise of state schools in Germany during the 18th century, a minimum age for confirmation was laid down more definitely and generally, allowing little leeway for congregations to vary from that which was normative.[3]

During this shift, confirmation gradually came to mark the end of formal Christian education. Hence any efforts during the last century and during the first part of this century to reduce the age for confirmation was regarded by most Lutherans as attacks on the church's responsibility to indoctrinate its youth. It became almost axiomatic that confirmation is terminal and that any effort to conduct a serious program of Christian education after confirmation is simply impossible. Proposals for confirmation at an earlier age were therefore usually equated with indifference to sound doctrine.

The Lutheran Church now faces a serious predicament as a result of these accretions. There is, on the one hand, a desire to postpone confirmation to an even later date. Postponement is argued in the interest of giving the church more time for an extended program of education. Furthermore, it is asserted that if the vow is to be taken seriously as a lifelong obligation, the confirmand should be more mature before he is expected to commit himself to it. At a more advanced age the confirmand, it is also said, would find his instruction more meaningful than he can at the beginning of his adolescence. On the other hand, some are beginning to feel uneasy about postponing the child's

[2] See above, pp. 81, 82.
[3] Martin Doerne, *Neubau der Konfirmation* (Gütersloh: C. Bertelsmann, 1936), p. 150.

first Communion till 14 or a later age. They sincerely believe that any unwarrantable delay in sharing the Lord's Supper with the young people is not in harmony with a sound view of the sacrament of the Lord's Supper. The dilemma is especially acute in Europe, where the church for generations has relied on the state schools to teach children the Christian doctrine and has done little on its own. The situation becomes even more problematic when with confirmation the children are said to assume majority rights as church members. Quite obviously any instruction that terminates in early confirmation cannot prepare the child adequately for assuming full congregational responsibilities. Fortunately this particular complication arises infrequently in the United States, where majority rights are usually not assumed till about 21. Nonetheless, the misconception that confirmation is or can be terminal for the religious education of the children is probably just as widespread and just as deeply rooted in the United States as it is in Europe. Regrettably most American congregations have a much weaker program of education after confirmation than they have prior to it. One can well appreciate the suggestions made in both Europe and the United States that perhaps one of the best solutions of the dilemma is to separate first Communion and confirmation. The proposal in the United States is most often for either a very early or a very later confirmation.

A 1954 report on an intersynodical questionnaire on catechetical instruction in 1,162 congregations revealed that a little over half of the children are confirmed at age 14 and a little over one third at 15.[4] Another survey, reported in 1959, showed that in some 1,136 congregations of four Lutheran synods slightly more than half of the children confirmed were in the eighth grade and

[4] "Report on the Results of the Intersynodical Questionnaire on Catechetical Instruction," in "Report to the Seminar on Confirmation and Confirmation Instruction, August 24—27, 1954," Racine, Wis., p. 2.

	Ages 12	13	14	15	16
American Lutheran Church		23	97		
Evangelical Lutheran Church			230	335	
United Evangelical Lutheran Church			52	29	
United Lutheran Church of America	39	122	194	35	6
	39	145	573	399	6

about a fourth were in the ninth grade.[5] Similarly a survey in the Missouri Synod (1947) indicated that a little over 50 percent of the congregations required the catechumen to be at least 13 at the time of confirmation. Slightly less than a third set the minimum age requirement at 14. It is significant that approximately 8 percent of those reporting stated that their congregations specified no minimum age requirement for confirmation.[6]

It is interesting to note that when pastors who received the 1954 intersynodical survey questionnaire reported on the question what they considered the best age for confirmation, there was a recognizable tendency to set a later date than was commonly practiced. Only 38 percent favored 14; approximately one third preferred 15. Significantly almost 16 percent thought 16 a more ideal age for confirming children.[7] The chief reason given for not requiring a higher age in actual practice was the pastors' conviction that confirmation must take place before the child enters high school. But those who favored 15 felt that the young people were then more mature and needed the guidance of their pastor during the first year of high school.

Age Levels Proposed for Confirmation

Confirmation at 14

The overwhelming preference in the Lutheran Church for confirming children at approximately 14 is due to the tradition which has been built around this age. Those in the United States who favor a late date recognize that 14 is perhaps as late as they can get children to attend confirmation instruction before

[5] The Boards of Parish Education of the American Evangelical Lutheran Church, Augustana Lutheran Church, Suomi Synod, United Lutheran Church of America, "The Functional Objectives for Christian Education," ed. W. Kent Gilbert, II (1959), Table D-1.

[6] A[rnold] C. Mueller, "Report on Confirmation Instruction, May 13, 1941," p. 1. Of the 885 congregations that reported, the following age requirements were indicated: age 11 — 1 congregation, 12 — 33, 12½ — 17, 13 — 456, 14 — 289, 15 — 12, 16 — 4, 17 — 1, and no rule — 72.

[7] "Report on the Results of the Intersynodical Questionnaire . . ." (see n. 4), p. 2. The following was the age range for "the best age for confirmation": age 12 — 48 respondents, 13 — 101, 14 — 434, 15 — 388, 16 — 145, 17 — 3, and 18 — 10.

they become involved in the social and academic demands of high school. Where children must travel some distance to attend a consolidated high school, additional demands prevail. In spite of a strong tradition favoring 14 as the most practical age level for confirmation, there is ample experience to indicate that the church ought to reevaluate whether this is actually the most suitable time for so important a stage of Christian education.

One of the most valid reasons against confirming at 14 is that the preparatory instruction then falls into the period of puberty. Far from being a peculiarly receptive period, puberty is one during which the instructor may anticipate difficulties. During this stage of physiological development that marks the beginning of adolescence, the child experiences rebellion against the adult world, and the ethical and moral patterns which confirmation seeks to establish easily become a challenge to him. His natural inclination, more so during adolescence than at any other time, is to throw off every possible restriction.

The influence of the home is definitely on the wane during puberty. By 13, certainly by 14, most children withdraw from family activities. They tend to display this withdrawal whenever possible in family worship, attendance at public services, and in partaking of the Lord's Supper. Young adolescents often feel embarrassed by their families for no other reason than that they are adolescents and their families represent adulthood. Patterns which the home has been unable to establish are almost impossible to set up in this period of striving for personal independence.

Pastors who teach the children during the two crucial years before confirmation at 14 find that in addition to the normal range of individual differences there are varying degrees of maturation among boys as well as a growing gulf between boys and girls, as girls rapidly mature toward young womanhood.[8]

[8] On the basis of data supplied by F. K. Shuttleworth, "The Physical and Mental Growth of Girls and Boys Age Six to Nineteen in Relation to Age at Maximum Growth," *Monographs of the Society for Research in Child Development*, IV, 13 (1939), p. 5, Henry P. Smith cites the following cumulative percentages of boys and girls becoming pubescent between 12 and 14:

Chronological Ages	12	12½	13	13½	14
Girls	36.8	56.8	76.1	89.0	95.4
Boys	1.1	3.1	7.7	15.9	31.9

Psychology in Teaching (New York: Prentice-Hall, Inc., 1954), p. 32

It is an error to suppose that at age 14 the children can have the proper understanding of Christian doctrine to make a commitment for life. This is no more true at 14 than it is at 18 or at any other period. Commitment for the Christian life is a daily need and a lifelong task and requires continuous growth in faith and understanding.

When confirmation coincides with graduation from the eighth grade or from junior high school, the idea that confirmation terminates formal religious instruction is accentuated. If there ever was a need to tie confirmation to the elementary school, the need disappeared long ago; today most children intend to go beyond elementary school. Any approach which suggests that confirmation is terminal is self-defeating.

The same high school activities and adolescent interests that make a still later age impractical for confirmation also tend to interfere with church activities and make it very difficult to set up Christian behavior patterns not yet established.

Perhaps the most serious argument against confirmation at 14 is that the church must then withhold the Sacrament of Holy Communion from younger children even though some of them apparently have both the ability and spiritual maturity to partake of the Sacrament, often without formal confirmation instruction. Strong Lutheran emphasis on the efficacy of the Lord's Supper and the blessings which the Lord offers to His church in the Sacrament should make pastors hesitate to postpone the time when the young Christian is permitted to share in this fellowship. Any unnecessary postponement of first Communion only encourages a wrong interpretation of 1 Cor. 11:23-30 or encourages many to become lackadaisical in their use of this blessed sacrament.

Confirmation Later than 14

The suggestion that confirmation be postponed beyond 14 seems to be prompted by a belief that 14-year-olds are not sufficiently mature to partake of the Lord's Supper or, what is more frequently held, that since so many assume that confirmation is to be terminal, the period of Christian instruction should be prolonged as much as possible. The strong emphasis on a lifelong vow has made many, especially among the laity, consider a later confirmation age more desirable. The misconception of some that the confirmand is making a major life decision and is in effect making an adult decision when he is not yet an adult has been added inducement to consider an age considerably later than 14 as more desirable.

In spite of some practical considerations which may from time to time tempt pastors to prefer a later age for confirmation, Lutherans must recognize that as long as first Communion is associated with confirmation, there is no Scriptural warrant whatever that normally permits withholding the Lord's Supper from a Christian till he has reached the age of 16 or 18. This procedure is followed only when some intellectual requirement becomes the deciding criterion for determining what makes one worthy to receive the Sacrament. Such postponement deprives youth of a means of grace that was intended to help them too in the personal struggles they face from day to day in passing from childhood to adulthood.

Postponing confirmation instruction beyond age 14 must imply a strong program of indoctrination throughout the adolescent years; otherwise the inroads which the adolescent period makes on Christian living eventually bring about a great loss in membership before the children are confirmed. It is folly to assume that without a continuous program of education the children will remain faithful to the church and their Lord while merely waiting for confirmation till they are more mature. Furthermore, waiting till a later age assumes that a commitment made at that time in life is based on better understanding and therefore will be more lasting. This seems to be a subtle identification of knowledge and understanding with living, saving faith.

Psychologically considered, patterns of conduct, including Christian conduct, are usually fixed at adolescence. This observation does not mean that after adolescence the Spirit no longer has the power to break through conduct patterns inimical to the Christian faith, but it does mean that by then the existing bad habits create a formidable barrier. In fact, humanly speaking, it may be easier to make a positive impact on the lives of young adults and adults than on the average high school youngster.

The personal influence of the adolescent without confirmation instruction or its equivalent is deficient; such an adolescent Christian often lacks the insights and attitudes needed for effective witness to his peer group in and out of school or at work.

The increasing mobility of population in the United States compounds the difficulties of postponing the age for confirmation.[9]

Confirmation at 8

Postponement of the use of the Lord's Supper to 14 or later has prompted a small number of pastors to suggest that children be permitted to partake of first Communion when they are approximately 8 years old. However, a few of these hesitate to combine this with an early confirmation for fear that the deeply ingrained idea that confirmation is terminal will make it virtually impossible for the church to conduct an effective program of Christian instruction after the child's first Communion. Proponents of early first Communion and confirmation argue that a child of 8, and certainly one of 10, can be taught the elements of Christian faith so that he is able to partake of the Lord's Supper in a worthy manner. In Holy Scripture there is certainly nothing contrary to this point of view, and in the Lutheran Church we find a long tradition that substantiates such an early Communion. If the practice is associated with a strong emphasis on education as Christian nurture and is applied within the framework of a strong educational program in which both church and home participate for many years after first Communion, then such an early date for confirmation would seem to be unassailable.[10]

[9] For a thought-provoking brief in behalf of confirmation at about 17 see Llyod E. Sheneman, "Instruction and Admission to Communion in Our Time," *The Lutheran Quarterly*, XV (Nov. 1963), 304—307.

[10] A good case against the separation of first Communion and confirmation is made by Sheneman, 300—304. A plea for first Communion as a sort of family ritual for infants or very small children is set forth by Paul G. Bretscher, "Communion Ought to Precede Confirmation?" *Confirmation in the Vocation of the Church: [Proceedings of the] Third Annual Conference of Lutheran Workers with Youth, Valparaiso University, Valparaiso, Indiana, February 19—21, 1963*

In actual practice, however, it may be difficult to follow through with such an extremely early period for confirmation. The aggressive mission program so characteristic today of the Lutheran Church in the United States makes one hesitate to encourage confirmation at age 8. Where the mission outreach has been successful, the congregations can no longer count on the support of as large a proportion of strong Christian homes with a long Lutheran tradition behind them. While the homes of novices may be Christian, the doctrinal level is usually quite elementary. We must realize, too, that the average Sunday school is incapable of following through with a strong Christian program of indoctrination without the help of the home. Parishes that support Lutheran day schools and even a high school may be able to maintain a strong program for follow-through even though the home backing is weak. Obviously a radical shift downward in the age of the confirmand would place a still heavier responsibility on the home. It is questionable whether in general the church is, at this time, able to provide the necessary help.

Age as a Criterion for Confirmation

Perhaps the church should face the fact that age is always a questionable criterion for determining when to confirm. Its use is based on the assumption that the normal readiness of all children takes place at practically the same age or stage in life. This assumption Doerne calls a *heidnisch-natur-religiöse Vorstellung.*[11] It reflects a failure to reckon with the normal individual differences among children of similar age and background, and it overlooks the even more important differences that exist among children of widely varying religious backgrounds. This is an especially important point to remember when the present mission emphasis brings into our confirmation classes children with virtually no previous instruction in Christian doctrine and life.

As stated above, the Lutheran Church has not always used

[St. Louis: Concordia Publishing House, 1963], pp. 18—29. For a more Lutheran view see Martin J. Heinecken, "Confirmation in Relation to the Lord's Supper," *The Lutheran Quarterly,* XV (Feb. 1963), 23—28; Sheneman, 297—299.

[11] Doerne, p. 146.

age as a primary factor for determining when to confirm; rather it left the age fluid and based its decision on the child's actual readiness and on the judgment of Christian parents. Wilhelm Loehe's views are particularly appropriate at this point. He emphasized that when a child is able to examine himself according to the command of 1 Cor. 11:28, he should no longer be restrained from partaking of the Holy Supper.[12] Loehe felt that admission to confirmation instruction should not be determined according to age and proposed that the required ability as outlined in 1 Cor. 11:28 should be decisive in every case.[13]

12 as a Proposed Age Level

Loehe was nonetheless willing to accept a stipulated age level as a "comfortable church ordinance," a rule of thumb that may serve to avoid unnecessary embarrassment. With this, and with only this in mind, it is proposed that 12 is the more desirable age at which to confirm children. Such a proposal must not be considered an absolute rule; it is merely a suggestion of a time when the average child, under present circumstances, may be adequately prepared. Such a norm should allow for confirmation at an earlier age when feasible. Occasionally, when the child's background is deficient in religious instruction, as when the initial contact is made at 12, deferral of confirmation should also be permitted. In determining the right time a pastoral concern for the individual catechumen will be as important a factor as any proposed age level.

Twelve is a more desirable age for confirmation because it seems to be most suitable psychologically. By 12 most children have emerged from the childhood period but have not yet become distractingly entangled in the problems of puberty. A two-year period of preconfirmation instruction would utilize

12 See above, pp. 125, 126.

13 So also E[ugen] A[dolf] W[ilhel]m Krauss (1851—1924) of Concordia Seminary, St. Louis. In a letter of Nov. 6, 1909, he further relates how he, while pastor in Baden, Germany, "gave the Lord's Supper to a hopelessly ill, 11-year-old, unconfirmed schoolgirl; when she later recovered, she further received thorough instruction for confirmation! Under similar circumstances I would do the same today." *Grüsse* (Milwaukee: Northwestern Publishing House, 1928), p. 33.

the full benefits of the childhood plateau normally found at this age level.

Furthermore, confirming at age 12 would allow children to partake of first Communion at least two years earlier than is the custom at present. It would indicate that the church is serious when it says that the Lord's Supper is a means of grace, a power so valuable that it should not be postponed unnecessarily in the life of any Christian. It would be an added source of comfort and strength to the young Christian as he enters his adolescent struggle.

Since confirmation instruction does not attempt merely to reach the understanding of children but hopes to affect their total Christian life, it is easier for both church and home to establish desirable attitudes and conduct patterns at the age of 12. The home has relatively greater influence at 12 than at 14, though perhaps less than at 10 and 11. The Christian home pattern generally is smoother at age 12 than it is either immediately before or after. Under the guidance of the home, Christian patterns, especially those of partaking of the Lord's Supper, church attendance, and the daily use of the meaning of Holy Baptism, can be practiced for two years before the adolescent break begins. During this time the home can serve better as a "nest" for Christian life.

Granted that children are more mature and need their pastor's guidance after age 12 and especially at 14, it is equally true that any Christian counseling and any decision made by an individual must be based on the insights that he has received from the Word through the Holy Spirit. The best time for a person to become indoctrinated is not when he is in the midst of a spiritual problem, unless we can assume that he will normally turn to his pastor, his parents, or a mature Christian for guidance. It is preferable that he fortify himself through previous indoctrination for the hour when he will face more serious problems.

Confirming a child two years before he graduates from elementary school or three years before graduation from junior high school will certainly help to diminish the "confirmation complex," the faulty assumption that confirmation is terminal. If confirmation coincides with no terminal point in educational life, neither the parents nor the child will be inclined to suppose that confirmation ends formal religious instruction. At this early date it should be more evident both to the home and to the child that he has not yet reached the end of Christian instruction, if there is no indication during the period of instruction that confirmation terminates his contact with the church and if the home is properly prepared to guard against any such misunderstanding. Under such circumstances there should be a reasonable assurance that the child will continue his study under the guidance of the church and home. He must be made to realize that there is nothing magical and certainly nothing final about confirmation. Through postconfirmation study he will learn that his previous instruction only began to prepare him for the new problems that he faces and that there are additional insights awaiting him for the issues that he continues to face day after day.

The Educational Frame for Confirmation

Confirmation occurs within an educational frame in which instruction properly precedes and follows it and in which both home and church participate. Broadly speaking, the age from birth to 6 may be regarded as the *first* stage. During this time mainly the Christian home assumes full responsibility for Christian nurture, though the church stands by ever to assist through its prayers, guidance, personal interest, and later through such agencies as the nursery department and kindergarten. For this and every other level the church must make every effort to strengthen the homes which form its congregations.

As the child grows in years and enters the *second* stage, from 7 to 12, the parish finds itself increasingly able to offer assistance for the cultivation of the Christian life in a more formal setting. The parents of children of elementary school age will look to the church for help through its Sunday school, vacation Bible school, the Christian day school, or whatever other agency the congregation is able to maintain. While parents will expect the church's aid, their reliance on it should not be interpreted as encouragement for the church to harbor the idea that it may

Confirmation

usurp parental responsibility or that it may serve as an adequate substitute for the Christian home.

Toward the end of this period, beginning at 10, the church will show its particular concern for the young Christian's growing maturity by intensifying and focalizing previous training through confirmation instruction so that the child may be better equipped to meet his growing responsibilities and opportunities.

With confirmation instruction completed, the child enters the *third* stage of his catechumenate, which continues till he is 18. Particularly during this period, it must be emphasized, the Christian home plays a vital and important part in the instruction of the adolescent. Church and home must work together vigorously and prayerfully to help the youth grow in Christian maturity. If the church has in the past been negligent in following through with a sound program of Christian education after the child's confirmation at 14, it would be nothing short of disastrous for the church to fail to the same degree, were it to accept 12 as the age at which to confirm children. Regardless of the age for confirmation the church must face the fact that much more serious efforts to nurture youth through a sound and intensive program of Christian education are absolutely necessary for its own survival. Similarly the home must be aware that it cannot follow the growing American pattern of surrendering to the adolescent, cannot weakly stand by as he is lost to His Savior and His church.

The choice of age 18 as the close of the third stage seems obvious. For most young persons this period marks a separation point, a time when many temporarily leave home for college or service in the military or, if they remain at home, attend a streetcar college, get married, or take employment. At any rate, Christian education will in most instances come to them in a less formal manner after 18.

How formal the third six-year period of instruction may be depends much on local circumstances and resources. For some it may mean one or more years of very intensive instruction one evening a week. For others it may be limited to a Sunday morning hour. Still others may enjoy the resources of a Lutheran high school. Christian nurture need not be limited to one agency but may come through many teaching channels. Where possible, persons of this age should become involved in congregational activities commensurate with their maturity.

It is further proposed that near the close of the third stage, perhaps some six months before it ends, a special course be given, summarizing previous instruction and preparing the youth for even more active participation in congregational life. To make this possible it is further proposed that the age for voting membership in the congregation be set at 18 rather than 21, so that the youth, especially the young men at home, may become more involved in the affairs of the congregation. In this we will not be wiser than the world, which at 18 permits young men and women to participate in its labor organizations and in social, civic, and other economic groups. Where young women are not granted voting membership, opportunities may be opened to permit them to serve more actively on congregational committees.

The *fourth* stage of the catechumenate remains open-ended and continues throughout life. Circumstances usually force a congregation to become less formal in its educational activities among those over 18, and the chief emphasis comes through public worship, adult Bible classes, and the activities of organizations centered in the continued cultivation of the life in Christ. When young men and women temporarily leave the home congregation for the military or for academic pursuits, the home pastor will make every effort to follow through so that they, too, are kept with the Word. On their return they may again take up life in the community and continue to make use of every opportunity to grow in the grace of their heavenly Father.

Objectives for Confirmation Instruction

Having discussed to what extent age is a criterion for determining when a child should be confirmed and having considered also what is the general educational structure in which confirmation plays an important role, we are prepared to discuss what the objectives should be, that is, what changes should take place in the catechumen as learner. Formulating the outcomes of confirmation instruction does not imply that the church thereby assumes for itself the work of the Holy Spirit. The church is not unmindful that all spiritual growth is solely the work of God through His Spirit. But Christians know that God works through the means of grace which He has given the church to carry out His purposes. He has commanded His church to "make disciples of all nations" (Matt. 28:19) even though Christians are merely the agents through whom He effects His will. Therefore it is in harmony with the New Testament for the church to formulate its objectives in a manner which assumes that spiritual outcomes can be arrived at effectively through Christian nurture.

Not only does the Holy Spirit "give the increase"; He alone can evaluate whether the church actually attains the outcomes for which it strains. No instrument has yet been devised whereby church and home can accurately measure how well they are achieving objectives for spiritual growth. Not even the overt actions of a catechumen can be evaluated with certainty. No one can determine whether desirable habits or behavior are prompted by the Law or by the Gospel, the difference between death and life.

Actually it is unnecessary for the Christian teacher to know with absolute certainty whether the goals of Christian nurture are being achieved. His task, according to the best of his ability and in harmony with sound educational principles, is rightly to divide the Word, making a clear distinction between the Law and the Gospel, and to leave the final outcome to God. The educational principle that no objective should be set up which cannot be evaluated does not apply to goals pertaining to the faith life.

Since the catechumen has normally had previous instruction in both the home and the church, the objectives will be stated developmentally to indicate this. The objectives are stated developmentally also because it is assumed that Christian education will continue after confirmation and that the learner will grow in his Christian faith life.

In formulating objectives the church must guard against the historic fallacy that at the popular level identified instruction with knowledge or understanding. Since the power of the Gospel permeates the whole person, Christian instruction must be directed at the total personality of the learner — his understanding, his emotions, his skills, and his behavior patterns, which includes his will. It is true that the Scriptures say, "This is life eternal that they might *know* Thee, the only true God, and Jesus Christ, whom Thou hast sent" (John 17:3), but this knowing is not to be understood in the Greek sense, where it is limited to the intellect, but is to be understood in the Hebrew sense, which involves the whole person, the fusion of all the facets of the human personality. The objectives for confirmation instruction will therefore be concerned not merely with understanding but also with the attitudes, skills, and behavior patterns of the learner.

Finally, the objectives are best stated in terms of the learner, that is, in terms of what the instructor, with the aid of the Holy Spirit, seeks to achieve in the learner. When objectives are stated in terms of the instruction or the teacher, the emphasis can easily be deflected from the learner in whom the changes are to take place. But by stating the objectives in terms of the learner the instructor will be forced to look away from his lesson plans, his methods, and even the curriculum and be constantly reminded that the changes to be effected in the learner are of primary concern and that everything else is a means to accomplish the objectives.

By stating the objectives in terms of the learner the implication will become clearer that the teacher must consider the catechumen's level of maturity and that in both formulation and interpretation the objectives must be limited to the learner's capacities, interests, and needs.[14]

With this in mind we are prepared to formulate the objectives for confirmation instruction. As stated repeatedly, we have defined confirmation instruction as revolving about both sacra-

[14] For a more complete discussion on the objectives of Christian education see the material issued by the Lutheran boards of parish education: "A Study Guide for the Objectives of Christian Education," "The Objectives of Christian Education," and "The Age Group Objectives of Christian Education," issued in 1958 as part of "A Long Range Program of Parish Education," ed. W. Kent Gilbert. The material is available at 2900 Queen Lane, Philadelphia, Pa. 19129.

ments, Holy Baptism and the Lord's Supper. We recognize further that confirmation instruction is only part of the total instruction which the home and the church give. Therefore, in the broad meaning of the term, "confirmation" precedes formal confirmation instruction — it begins with the baptismal catechumenate — and such confirmation continues long after the child has been confirmed. However, in the formal meaning of the term, confirmation instruction is the intensification and focalization of all previous instruction so that as a maturing Christian the confirmand may meet his growing responsibilities. Therefore the objectives for confirmation instruction are for every confirmand, as a baptized child of God and as a member of the body of Christ,

> *to possess a more developed personal faith life in response to the means of grace, so that as a maturing Christian he (1) more fully live the life in Christ and (2) be able to participate in the sacrament of Holy Communion in a worthy manner.*

To this end the confirmand, appropriate to his level of maturity, (A) possesses a growing desire and ability to live under Christ and serve Him in His kingdom, (B) manifests a more reverent and deepened devotional life of faith and adoration to God, and (C) has a maturing realization of his privileges and responsibilities as a member of the Evangelical Lutheran Church.

While the last two objectives may well be subsumed under the first, they are lifted out for special emphasis as major areas of concentration appropriate to confirmation instruction. At an earlier or a later age one may wish to have other emphases more appropriate to those levels.

What is implied in the three objectives set forth?

A. *The confirmand possesses a growing desire and ability to live under Christ and serve Him in His kingdom.*

  1. *He has a greater assurance of the gracious love of God in Christ as a forgiven sinner* (forgiveness).

  In spite of the catechumen's misgivings regarding his own unworthiness and his inability to measure up to the stan-

199

dards of God, his family, or even his friends, the confirmand should have the certainty that in Christ he is a *forgiven* sinner. This assurance should be his mainstay especially when the moodiness and loneliness of adolescence begin to haunt him.

2. *He exhibits an increasing awareness of God as the Lord of the universe* (creatureliness).

Although every newspaper headline and every television and radio program may make it appear that man is in control of space, power, and speed, the confirmand should become more aware that God has not surrendered to man, nor is He in any danger of being replaced. The catechumen needs to know that God is not asleep somewhere on a whirling planet but that He is in control as Lord of lords and King of kings.

3. *He recognizes God's all-embracing claim on him and all his gifts and talents* (stewardship).

Because God is his Lord, the confirmand must recognize more fully that every area of his life is God's concern; that his every gift, every power, every enjoyment, and every opportunity are to be used in grateful service and to the glory of his God.

4. *He seeks to reflect in concrete ways God's love for him in his personal relationship with those of the household of faith* (witness).

As a maturing Christian he will show in his life a richer and fuller understanding of the significance of being a member of the body of Christ. He will begin to recognize that although he was redeemed as an individual, as part of the Christian fellowship he leaves wholly separate existence behind him and becomes an interacting member of the body. He will therefore have a more personal concern for every other member of that body, especially for his peer group, and because of this concern he will witness among them by admonishing, strengthening, encouraging, and sharing with the brother.

5. *He develops an earnest, active concern to share the Gospel and its gracious gifts with all men* (evangelism).

Children at this age may soon tend to lose the missionary zeal so characteristic of brash 8–10-year-olds. They will soon reach the stage when they feel it embarrassing to "speak the Word." An effective measure against such feelings of embarrassment is to impress on them beforehand that evangelism is not an option and that it cannot be transferred either to the little ones or to adults. Unchurched friends are not merely to be enjoyed but to be given the message of the Gospel.

6. *He practices his various callings faithfully* (vocation).

At this point we are reminded of Luther's words in Confession and Absolution and apply them to his Table of Duties. "Reflect on your condition in the light of the Ten Commandments: whether you are a father or mother, a *son* or *daughter* . . .[15] These "conditions" indicate the callings of children, pupils, junior citizens, paper boys, baby-sitters, and so forth, each one requiring faithfulness and each one a preparatory step for other callings as the years pass. Above all, the catechumen will practice the call which he has received from God — the call to serve Him with the talents, time, and opportunities which his other callings give him.

B. *The confirmand manifests a more reverent and deepened devotional life of faith and adoration of God:*

1. *He responds to the Spirit's work in him with a holy and sacrificial life, a "worship offered by mind and heart."*

The essence of true worship is the total response of the Christian to the grace and mercy of God. This is the life Paul refers to when he implores the Christians of Rome to offer their "very selves to Him: a living sacrifice, dedicated and fit for His acceptance, the worship offered by mind and heart." (Rom. 12:1 NEB)

[15] SC V 20, in *BS*, p. 517; *BC*, p. 350; *CT*, pp. 552, 553.

Confirmation

2. *He regularly and reverently sets aside moments and hours for private and corporate worship.*

Thus the catechumen will (a) hear God address him in His Word; (b) daily apprehend more fully the rich and comforting meaning of his baptism; (c) receive frequently the gracious assurance of divine forgiveness and the comfort and joy of Christ's presence in the Lord's Supper; (d) concentrate on God's goodness and mercy toward him; and (e) respond to God in prayer and praise and offer the sacrifice of heart and lips.

3. *He recognizes that worship, especially corporate worship, is an opportunity for strengthening the bond of fellowship, for giving witness to the brother, and for hearing his witness.*

With this recognition the confirmand will understand that in corporate worship he is not participating merely as an individual, hearing God address him and in turn addressing the Lord in song and prayer. Instead the confirmand will understand that in corporate worship he is participating as a member of a body, strengthening that bond and being strengthened by it, particularly in the prayers, the confession, the hymns, the music, and the sacraments.

4. *He possesses the skill to prepare himself inwardly for such worship.*

Worship is work, and for it we need the help of the Holy Spirit. Setting aside a few moments for meditation on the propers for the coming Sunday is one among many ways of preparing oneself inwardly for the public worship.

5. *He has had practice in the meaningful use of the more common aids to worship.*

The hymnal is more than a hymnbook. The first 170 pages of *The Lutheran Hymnal* and the first 284 pages of the *Service Book and Hymnal* contain many aids for private and corporate worship. These aids the catechumen should learn to use.

C. *The confirmand has a maturing realization of his privileges and responsibilities as a member of the Evangelical Lutheran Church.*

1. *He has a growing understanding and appreciation of the purpose, content, and uses of the Holy Scriptures.*

Since the Scriptures are the only norm of Christian doctrine and the one great source of power for the Christian faith, they will naturally be the center of Lutheran confirmation instruction.

2. *He has an increasing understanding and appreciation of Luther's Small Catechism as a major confession of the Lutheran Church.*

Since the confirmand is a member of the Lutheran Church, he should obviously know the enchiridion, Luther's Small Catechism, not merely as a systematic summary of Christian doctrine but as a confession of his faith.

3. *He possesses a growing consciousness of the precious heritage which has come down to him through the Christian church, particularly through the Lutheran Church.*

As time will allow, the confirmand should become acquainted with some of the great men and events of church history as a means of acquiring an appreciation of God's care and love for His church throughout the ages.

4. *He shows a growing confessional loyalty to the Lutheran Church.*

The confirmand should learn to distinguish the tenets of the Lutheran Church from those of Protestantism and from those of the Roman Catholic Church, not in polemical spirit and manner but through emphasis at his level of maturity particularly such distinctively Lutheran teachings as the means of grace, the proper distinction of Law from Gospel, the holy Christian church, and justification by faith.

5. *He participates adequately as a faithful steward in the activities of the Lutheran Church in parish and community, in church and world.*

203

Such participation may be limited at this age level, but the confirmand should become involved as much as possible in the accomplishment of the local and synodical goals of the parish where he lives and where his fellow Christians are at work.

6. *He becomes progressively acquainted with some of the problems, dangers, and opportunities facing the Christian church today.*

The world of the confirmand is much broader today than it was a few generations ago. Through television, radio, and other means of mass communication he is aware of some of the problems of his culture and world: integration, the "new nations," the exodus from the inner city, the conformity of suburbia, changes in rural life, and others. All these problems have created a new field for the church, for good or for ill, and the implications of some of them for the church must also begin to dawn in the life of the confirmand.

Although the objectives stated above may not be suitable in every instance — congregations do vary — they can serve as guides. It should be emphasized again that the objectives aim at a maturity possible for 12-year-olds and must be implemented with this age group in mind. We must not interpret the objectives in terms of young adults, for this would be a fatal mistake. Trusting in the Spirit's operation through the means of grace, we may prayerfully work toward the achievement of these objectives at the maturity level of 12-year-old children.

Cooperating with the Home and Enlisting Its Support

Any church program of Christian education must realistically take into account that without the cooperation of the Christian home the church can normally accomplish very little of its assigned task. This is true whether we confirm at age 10, 12, 14, or 16. After all is said and done, the Christian pastor or teacher must remember that the home has the primary and divinely given responsibility for teaching the child, a responsibility which it cannot transfer. Christian parents assume this responsibility with the baptism of their children. Unfortunately, many parents feel unable to meet their responsibility and are frustrated by the obstacles set forth within our society. Therefore they readily succumb to the temptation to surrender their obligation to anyone who assures them that he can do a better job. One of the more eager aspirants to substitution for the parents in educating children is the state. It is very anxious to give ethical training to its citizens. In its attempt to reach the total man the state, knowingly or unknowingly, begins to take over the child's total life. But the state has competitors. Social workers with their teen towns and youth centers, camps with their appeal through crafts and camping, neighborhood clubs, and the church all stand in line ready to take over any part of the task that the home is willing to relinquish.

For Christian parents the church seems a most likely agency to take over the task of training their children. And the church, instead of helping the home do a better job, has been tempted to by-pass it or even to write it off as a failure. In doing this the church fails to remember that the strength of its work with children and youth lies not so much in what it can do through confirmation instruction or any of its educational agencies but in the cooperation it can give to and get from the home. The church must therefore be adamant in its refusal to assume the home's responsibility as teacher and should do everything in its power to help the home do its part. Only when the home fails to fulfill its God-given responsibility may the church attempt to take over the parents' task so that young Christians may receive the needed spiritual help.

Home cooperation is essential for achieving the best results during confirmation instruction and the years that lie ahead. While most pastors know of instances in which children continue in the Christian faith without the support of the home or know of children who first learned their Savior in confirmation instructions, these instances are exceptions. Normally the home is by far the greatest single influence in a child's life. Those who doubt that a child should be confirmed at age 11 or 12 should not forget that confirmation at any age is precarious without the help of the Christian home.

Home support must be enlisted before the child begins confirmation instruction. Christian parents need to be reminded that Christian education is a continuous process throughout life, during every hour of each day of life. The pastor should explain to the parents that he plans to help them fulfill the responsibilities they assumed in Baptism. He may find it necessary to show specifically how the parents can cooperate and how he proposes to help them. Such contacts should be made not merely at the beginning of confirmation instruction but throughout the sessions. As confirmation instruction draws to a close, the pastor may wish to impress on the parents the importance of the child's regular use of the means of grace after he has been confirmed. It may be necessary to inform parents specifically how they should follow through after confirmation, for example, through private devotions, continued church attendance and regular partaking of the Lord's Supper, continued instruction of the child in Sunday school or Bible class, and through keeping in mind the importance of youth work within the framework of the congregation. The pastor may further point out how parents can assist the child in choosing his lifework as a Christian and how they can help him in the choice of wholesome friends.

The Congregation's Part in Working with Its Youth

Perhaps the most important task that lies before us in getting the congregation to assume its responsibility for the continued spiritual growth of its youth is to instruct it in the proper meaning of confirmation and to help it in gaining a more Scriptural understanding of Holy Baptism and the Lord's Supper. Since God alone can give spiritual life and strength, the congregation should be invited to pray for its youth and to show continuous concern for keeping its young people in close contact with the Gospel.

For postconfirmation youth a strong program of Christian education should be established as the third stage so that by the time the young people reach age 18 they have solid ground for their faith and have acquired the habit of nurturing their Christian faith life through the means of grace.

The congregation's program for the third stage of the cate-chumenate should be concentrated on meeting the basic needs of adolescent Christians. At the risk of oversimplifying this difficult area of Christian nurture, we suggest seven basic youth needs as a guide for the congregation in formulating its objectives for this age level.[16]

The principal and most pressing need of the youth is to rec-ognize his *immanent relationship with God*. As a Christian he knows about the God who has revealed Himself in Christ Jesus. But he needs a maturing understanding and faith in the Christ, who has redeemed him and whose child he has become through the work of the Holy Spirit. A youth, like the adults who shape his patterns of thinking, easily slips into the climate of thought in which God is supposed to be merely one who serves and is to be used. The youth needs to have his newfound doubts answered, especially in his beginning brush with intellectuals for whom God is irrelevant. He needs to know that God is relevant even though in many places there seems to be a conspiracy of silence and it isn't the thing to talk about God in a familiar way. In sum, the youth needs to see the relevance of God in his own life. He needs to possess a growing faith commensurate with his total development. He needs to grow with his religion.

If the youth's first need is to recognize the immanent rela-tionship of God to Himself and to mankind in general, his second is to *understand himself*. If man's greatest problem is man, then surely the youth needs to recognize himself for what he is. He needs to know his limitations and complete dependence on God. He needs to understand himself, why he is restless and anxious, why his handicaps let him down, why he does what he does, and how he tries to rationalize his actions. In his attempt to understand himself the youth may become particularly con-

[16] For a more detailed study by the author see *Proceedings of the Thirty-Sixth Convention of the Texas District of The Lutheran Church — Missouri Synod, April 7—11, 1958*, pp. 26—60; or a somewhat shorter form in the *Proceedings of the Thirty-Sixth Convention of the Atlantic District of The Lutheran Church — Missouri Synod, June 27—July 1, 1960*, pp. 30—48.

fused about what is right and wrong and need help to formulate the proper ethics of Christian behavior.

The third need of the youth is to *understand his place in the church*. Before he can understand his place in it, he must understand what we mean when we talk about the Christian church. Too often adults give the youth the idea that the church is a sort of club that he joins. Perhaps Christians need to be reminded again that the primary meaning of church is the body of believers, a fellowship that is joined together, a living organism in Christ. The youth needs to recognize the implications of such a fellowship. He needs to know what it means when he is thus united to Christ on the one hand, with his fellow believer on the other, and that as a redeemed and regenerated person he cannot live unto himself as a rugged individualist.

Fourth, youth needs to *understand and be understood by his family*. Since the youth, to a degree, represents conflict against authority, it is only natural that his greatest conflict is often with those who represent the closest authority, his family. He needs to know that as much as he needs independence, he needs shelter; as much as he needs freedom, he still needs discipline. As a maturing Christian he must recognize that both he and his parents need to continue to adjust to one another. He must know that the shortcomings of his parents that he comes to recognize more clearly through his growing insights are the same kind of sin to which he is heir. Both parents and youth need daily forgiveness before the throne of God. As a growing individual in the home the youth must learn to accept his responsibilities as well as the privileges which he demands.

Fifth, the youth needs to *find his place within his peer group*. From his own point of view, status among his peers is perhaps his greatest need. He wants to be accepted. He wants to find his place in the crowd in which he moves. Much of the conflict that the youth has with parents and church and even in relationship with God stems from his desire to fit in with his friends. He needs to recognize that while status in his community is important and acceptance by his group desirable, the group must never dominate him, never be his final authority. He needs to know what friends are for. He must recognize that they are not given him merely to enjoy or to give him status. He needs to know that every friend and acquaintance whom God has given him is to be used to His glory, either to strengthen his friends in the body of Christ or to witness to them that they might be one with Him.

As the youth passes through one phase of adolescence after another, he becomes more conscious of *the need to find a vocation.* The choice of a vocation is most difficult in our age of specialization. In spite of the emphasis on vocational guidance, it is still one of the major needs the youth want to have met. The youth needs to know the purpose of his vocation. He needs to know what a Christian vocation is. He must recognize that the purpose of his vocation is more than making money, more than happiness, more than animal satisfaction. He needs to make a vocational selection commensurate with his abilities and interests.

Finally, a basic need for youth is to *find a life mate.* With all our emphasis on sex in American life, as a nation we are in many ways immature in our preparation for marriage. While sex has been taken out of its "plain wrapper," we have gone from one extreme to the other. Youth needs to know that sex is a gift of God to be used but not abused and that while men may glorify sex, God has sanctified it.

Above all, the youth needs help in preparing for Christian marriage. He needs to know the obligations, responsibilities, joys, and sorrows that are part of Christian marriage. To those for whom it becomes impossible to marry there must come the recognition that while marriage does offer special potential for living a full life, the unmarried state can also be one of happiness and fulfillment.

To keep adolescents close to the church, emphasis should be placed on actually accepting and treating them as members. Corporate worship may be encouraged by helping them have their own choir. They may be urged to serve as ushers in the minor services, as instrumentalists on festive occasions, and as special participants in Easter, Christmas, and Pentecost services.

Normally they should not be encouraged to teach in Sunday school but rather to continue as learners. To place them in full-time teaching positions is not fair to them or to the children of the Sunday school.

Congregations may wish to give thought to finding a place for the adolescent in an advisory capacity on some of the congregation's committees. Adolescents can make contacts with their peers and can be used to visit youth their own age in behalf of the congregation's various committee projects. In this way youth, like other Christians, will learn that the Word is both a gift and a trust; it is for them, and it is for giving away.

CHAPTER VII

THE CONFIRMATION SERVICE

While the confirmation service is admittedly an important occasion, it must be kept within its proper sphere. Nothing happens in the rite which has not previously taken place. No extraordinary change occurs in the catechumen through the prayers of the congregation or in the rite. The prayers are in behalf of the catechumen, but they do nothing to him in an unusual way. Conversely God comes to men with His grace in Holy Baptism and in the Lord's Supper, but not so in confirmation. In marriage, ordination, and installation, persons enter into an estate or office which God has created, but not in confirmation. As Kliefoth points out, in all these ceremonies God acts through men. In confirmation it is not God but the church that acts. To be sure, God acts through the Word before and after confirmation, but not in the rite.[1] Hence the Lutheran Church must qualify the importance which the confirmation service has assumed over the years, for as the rite is now observed, in the minds of the laity it very frequently overshadows the acts and means ordained by God Himself.

The Examination

As stated earlier, the Lutheran Church has in effect so glorified confirmation that it has normally not only separated it from the Lord's Supper, the sacrament for which it prepared the catechumen; it has even separated the examination from the ceremony proper and so given the rite an additional pretension with which it overshadows both holy sacraments.

[1] Theo[dor] Kliefoth, *Die Confirmation*, in *Liturgische Abhandlungen*, III, 1 (Schwerin: Stiller'schen Hof-Buchhandlung, 1856), 35.

The concept that the examination is to be a testing or a probing of what the catechumen knows and believes is a product of Pietism. Originally the examination was a brief confession of faith drawn from the catechumen through catechization. Through Pietism a large segment of the Lutheran Church was influenced to make the catechization an examination for determining whether the child was a sincere Christian, whether he had been properly instructed, and perhaps whether the pastor had performed his duty. The better to fulfill these purposes, the Pietists separated the examination from the rite and reserved it for a special service. If the questioning is to serve today primarily as an examination, it may well be kept as a special service and observed during the week prior to confirmation or at a vesper service. It is not necessary for the entire congregation to be present. The examination may be conducted in the presence of the parents, sponsors, elders, and friends of the families.

Even this type of questioning is not a real examination as the word is ordinarily understood. All the children who participate are expected to pass, that is, to be confirmed and then permitted to partake of the Lord's Supper. If any screening has to be done, the pastor will have already taken the necessary step with the knowledge of his elders and the parents of the catechumen.

The pietistic element of probing and testing has no place in a truly Lutheran confirmation. An examination held separately may have a twofold purpose: (1) to show that the demands of both Holy Baptism and the Lord's Supper have thus far been complied with, that is, that the parents have been faithful in following through with the Christian instruction which both sacraments imply; and (2) to give the children an opportunity by their answers to confess their faith personally in the presence of their sponsors and the representatives of the congregation.

An examination of this type must not degenerate into an exhibition of individual achievement. The questions should not be limited to the factual or to the material memorized. The purpose is not to offer evidence that the children "know the whole catechism." Rather the questions, put in an informal conversational way, should indicate that the confirmands understand what they are confessing. When, as it will happen frequently, the one or the other child cannot answer a question, the incident will be accepted in a natural way with as little embarrassment and self-consciousness as possible.

In the event that none of the confirmands can answer a question the pastor will take opportunity then and there to explain the matter as unostentatiously as possible. Special care must be taken that the individual differences do not become a source of frustration, shame, or bitterness for those who are unable to do as well as others.

More in keeping with the earlier Lutheran tradition before it was affected by the Pietists is to conduct the examination together with the rite and the first Communion. Under such circumstances the examination will be brief and primarily a confession of the children's faith. It is not to be regarded as an evaluation of the class.

The Hymns

While most Lutheran hymnals now in use in America include a section for confirmation hymns, this has not always been the case.[2] Many of the hymns so listed were not originally intended for confirmation, while others written for the occasion reflect the influence of Pietism or some other aberration. Great care must therefore be taken that a proper selection is made. In general, hymns of praise and thanks and those pertaining to the church, justification, sanctification, the confession of faith, and the Holy Spirit will be found suitable. The use of Luther's "Come, Holy Ghost, God and Lord!" has a long tradition behind it. It is most suitable if there is nothing in the rite to suggest that the Spirit is coming in an extraordinary way. Another of Luther's hymns, "We All Believe in One True God," gives emphasis to the Creed and is reminiscent of the confession of faith at Holy Baptism.

The use of Matthew Bridges' hymn,

[2] The German hymnal of the Missouri Synod did not include a section for confirmation hymns until the 1917 ed. The hymnal of The English Ev. Lutheran Synod of Missouri and Other States (1909) did not include such a section either. Concordia Publishing House met some of the demand for a special confirmation hymn by reproducing Rambach's "Baptized into Thy Name Most Holy" on the back of printed confirmation vows supplied to the confirmands.

Confirmation

> My God, accept my heart this day
> And make it always Thine [3]

which was written in connection with Bridges' entrance into the Roman Catholic Church, seems to be indiscreet even though the average worshiper may not recognize what the hymn writer had in mind. Such lines as

> Let me feel Thy confirmation
> In Thy truth and fear today [4]

which John Mason Neale penned, are not in the true spirit of Lutheran theology. Johann Jakob Rambach's hymn, "Baptized into Thy Name Most Holy," [5] which originally bore the heading "For Daily Renewal of the Baptismal Covenant," has in the past been a favorite for confirmation. This was unfortunate, for when the lines

> My loving Father, Thou dost take me
> To be henceforth Thy child and heir

so appropriate for Holy Baptism, were applied by the worshiping congregation to confirmation, a wrong concept was implanted.

The Lection

The lection appointed for the day shall be used for the confirmation service. If an additional reading is desired, it may be read before the Epistle for the Day. One of the following may be found appropriate: Ps. 73:23-26; John 15:1-10; 17:1-21; 2 Thess. 2:13-17; 2 Tim. 3:14-17.

The selected reading should not emphasize the imparting of the Spirit (as Acts 8:14-17) or refer to reception of the children. Such a reception takes place in Holy Baptism but not in confirmation.

The Sermon

If the examination, the rite, and the first Communion take place in one service, the sermon may be dropped. If a sermon is included, it should stress that we obtain our membership

[3] *TLH* 336; *SBH* 289.
[4] "Blessed Savior, Who Hast Taught Me," *TLH* 333; *SBH* 290.
[5] *TLH* 298.

214

in the church through Holy Baptism and that we continue in it through the means of grace. The pastor will wish to keep in mind not only the catechumens but also the parents, the sponsors, and the entire congregation. All should be made aware of their life in the church and of the importance of continuing in the means of grace.

The Rite of Confirmation

Nothing in the rite should give the impression that the catechumens are renewing their baptismal covenant, that covenant which God has made with them by His grace. Nor should they be led to believe that not till then do they become members of the church.

The renunciation of "the devil and all his works and all his ways" can best be omitted. As Kliefoth points out, it applies to Holy Baptism but not to confirmation. If the child is ready for confirmation, he continually renounces Satan. If continual renunciation is meant in the rite, the wording is ambiguous and says too little.[6]

The confession of faith which each one answers personally should be twofold — a confession of the Apostles' Creed, the ancient baptismal creed, and a confession of the doctrine of the Evangelical Lutheran Church as they have learned to know it from Luther's Small Catechism. Any reference to specific elements of Christian doctrine seem to be superfluous in the confession of faith, for such elements are properly part of the examination.

If a vow is desired, the emphasis should be on a renewal of the vow made by the sponsors at the time of the confirmand's baptism, a renewal which should occur daily throughout the life of the confirmand. The vow should not be interpreted as a lifelong promise but as an expression of the sincere intent of the confirmand at the time of his confirmation. It may include his intent as a member of the Evangelical Lutheran Church to remain steadfast in the confession of that church and his intent

---

[6] Kliefoth, p. 186. Some German agendas used in America were more correct when they asked: "Dost thou renounce *anew* the devil and all his works and all his ways?" (Italics ours)

to conform faithfully all his life to the rule of the divine Word, to be diligent in the use of the means of grace, to walk as it becomes the Gospel of Christ, and in faith, word, and deed to remain true to the Triune God.

The laying on of hands, though often misunderstood, ought to be retained because of its Biblical tradition. Care must be taken that nothing in the rite suggests that the Holy Spirit is imparted by this act. The laying on of hands neither confirms Holy Baptism nor bestows absolution or any other special gift nor consecrates the individual for Holy Communion. The laying on of hands is an expression and a confession of the Holy Spirit's work and a sign, individually given, that God's blessing has been bestowed on the confirmand. As such it symbolizes what the congregation in its prayers and hymns is asking God to do for the confirmands through His means of grace.

The handclasp has such a close association with taking an oath or lifelong vow or with an extension of new privileges that it is best left out. The ease with which the handclasp may be dramatized suggests that not much is lost if it is eliminated. So far the church has not found it necessary to include the handclasp when administering the sacraments. Confirmation may well omit it also.

In line with the principles set forth in this book the following rite of confirmation was drawn up by the author at the request of the Commission on Worship, Liturgics, and Hymnology of the Synodical Conference.[7]

PROPOSED RITE OF CONFIRMATION FOR CHILDREN

It is preferable for the Examination to be held in connection with the Rite of Confirmation. If not, it may be incorporated

[7] The proposed rite first appeared for critical review and tentative use in substantially this form in a special clergy bulletin inserted in *Advance*, IX (April 1962). Most of the changes reflect suggestions that came in response to a request for constructive criticism.

For a review of rites currently used in the Lutheran Church in various parts of the world see Helge Fehn, "Konfirmations-Ordnungen in den Lutherischen Kirchen der Gegenwart," *Zur Geschichte und Ordnung der Konfirmation in den Lutherischen Kirchen,* ed. Kurt Frör (Munich: Claudius Verlag, 1962), pp. 108 to 121.

in the Order of Morning Service Without Communion or the Order of the Holy Communion and placed after the hymn following the Creed; in the orders of Matins or Vespers, after the Responsory or a hymn following the Lection.

THE EXAMINATION

The following introductory paragraph may be read.

DEARLY BELOVED: When children have come to know the truths of the Christian religion as they are contained in the Catechism so that, as directed by St. Paul (1 Cor. 11:28), they might examine themselves, they should be admitted to the Lord's Supper. However, before they receive the Holy Sacrament, they should give evidence of their knowledge and profess their faith in the presence of the assembled congregation.

The Minister may introduce the Examination by the following or another suitable Address.

[HOLY BAPTISM is the washing of rebirth and renewing of the Holy Spirit, whom God shed on us plentifully through Jesus Christ, our Savior, that being justified by His grace, we might in hope become heirs to eternal life. Through this sacrament God receives little children into His covenant and Kingdom of Grace, working faith in them and making them members of Christ's church and temples of His Holy Spirit. And as God will not let His faithfulness fail but will keep His covenant and mercy, even so He says to each of His own: Be faithful unto death, and I will give you the crown of life. To the end that this purpose of God may be accomplished and children may grow in grace and Christian knowledge as they advance in years, the Lord commands parents: Bring up your children in the discipline and instruction of the Lord, and bids the church: Feed My lambs.

In accordance, then, with Christ's command, children should be instructed in the Christian faith and should daily give their hearts to God and observe His ways.

To encourage Christian knowledge, faith, and action the Rite of Confirmation is maintained in the Lutheran Church. The catechumens publicly make profession of the true faith, recalling the covenant God made with them in Holy Baptism. The church, the dispenser of God's mysteries, having assured itself that the catechumens possess such knowledge of Christian doctrine as will enable them to examine themselves and thus partake worthily of the body and blood of Christ, invites them to receive the Holy Supper. With the laying on of hands the church prays over them for the Holy Spirit of God that they may grow in grace, stand firm in their profession, become fruitful in every good work, and in the end receive the crown of life.]

THESE CATECHUMENS are now presenting themselves for Confirmation. We shall therefore give them the opportunity to give evidence of their true understanding of the Christian doctrine.

Then shall the Catechumens be examined briefly.

A Hymn may then be sung, followed by the Sermon.

If the Confirmation is held in a later service, the service will be concluded in the usual manner.

THE CONFIRMATION

The Order of Confirmation shall follow the General Prayer and Intercessions in the Order of Holy Communion and the Morning Service, the Hymn after the Sermon in the Order of Vespers.

Then may the Minister address the Catechumens thus:

DEARLY BELOVED: When you were little children, you were received into God's covenant of grace in Holy Baptism. By means of this blessed sacrament you were freed from the power of darkness and called to be disciples of Jesus Christ, your Lord. You have been instructed in the Word of God and in the true meaning of the Holy Sacraments according to the Confessions of the Evangelical Lutheran Church. As evidenced by your examination [in the presence of this Christian congregation], you now know what God has given you by His grace and what He requires of you as His child. You now can exercise the privilege of partaking of the Blessed Sacrament of the Lord's Supper, granted you by your Baptism. Lift up your hearts with me, therefore, to the God of all grace, and cheerfully confess the Christian faith which your sponsors and parents confessed at your Holy Baptism and be thereby reminded again of the covenant of grace which God made with you at that time.

The Minister, facing the altar, and Catechumens: I believe in God the Father Almighty, Maker of heaven and earth, and . . .

The Minister turns, facing the Catechumens: Now I ask you in the presence of God and this congregation, do you intend to continue in this Christian faith which you have again confessed?

Catechumens: Yes, with the help of God.

The Minister: Do you intend, as members of the Evangelical Lutheran Church, to continue steadfast in the confession of this church as you have learned to know it in Luther's Small Catechism?

Catechumens: Yes, with the help of God.

The Minister: Do you intend with the help of God to conform your life to the rule of the divine Word: to be diligent in the use of the means of grace, to conduct yourselves worthy of the Gospel of Christ, and in faith, word, and deed to remain true to the Triune God?

Catechumens: Yes, by the grace of God.

Then shall the Minister invite the Congregation to make Intercession as follows:

SINCE it is God alone who enables us both to will and do His good pleasure, it is fitting for us, dear friends in Christ, to call on Him for these young members of this Christian congregation, that He would graciously complete the good work which He has begun in them by the water and word of Holy Baptism and continued in them by instruction in His holy Word. Let us therefore [kneel and] pray.

ALMIGHTY AND EVERLASTING GOD, who makest us both willing and able to do those things which are good and acceptable to Thy divine majesty, we humbly come to Thee for these

Thy servants. We implore Thee that Thou let Thy fatherly hand ever be over them; may Thy Holy Spirit ever be with them; and so lead them in the knowledge and obedience of Thy Word that in the end they may obtain everlasting life; through our Lord Jesus Christ, who, with Thee and the Holy Spirit, ever one God, livest and reignest eternally.

The Congregation shall say:

Amen.

Or

LORD GOD, heavenly Father, we thank and praise Thee for bringing these Thy servants to the knowledge of Thy Son Jesus Christ through the precious Gospel revealed in the Scriptures. We ask Thee to continue to enlighten and strengthen them by Thy Holy Spirit, that they may daily increase in faith, in godly fear, in patience under trials, in true knowledge of Thee, and in all other things profitable to their eternal salvation. Grant that they continue to bring forth fruits of faith and remain firm to the victorious day when all who have fought the good fight of faith shall receive the crown of righteousness; through Jesus Christ, Thy Son, our Lord, who, with Thee and the Holy Spirit, ever one God, livest and reignest eternally.

Or

ALMIGHTY AND EVERLIVING GOD, we thank Thee that Thou hast brought these Thy servants to Thy Son Jesus Christ in Holy Baptism, cleansed them by His blood, buried them with Him by Baptism into His death, and raised them with Him to newness of life, dead unto sin and alive unto Thee. And we implore Thee of Thy great goodness to renew in them the gift of the Holy Spirit that their hearts may be filled with the light of Thy Gospel. Increase in them pure knowledge and true faith that they may firmly believe in Thee, the only true God, and in Jesus Christ, whom Thou hast sent, and ever hold fast to Thee with firm confidence. Fill their hearts and minds with the peace of Christ, the joy of the Holy Spirit, and love to Thee and all mankind. Supply them richly with the gifts of Thy heavenly grace that they may be led into all truth, put to death evil deeds of the body and soul, overcome the attacks and temptations of the wicked one, and serve Thee in Thy church with uprightness of heart all their days. Grant that together with all true believers they may with joyful hearts and watchful prayer and in modest and godly living hope and wait for the coming of the Savior, to the honor of Thy holy Name; who, with the Son and the Holy Spirit, ever one God, livest and reignest eternally.

Or

ALMIGHTY AND EVERLASTING GOD, who of Thine infinite mercy hast added to Thy church these Thy servants by causing them to be born again of water and the Holy Spirit and hast given them knowledge of their redemption in Christ and power to own and confess Thee in the presence of Thy people, we thank Thee for the steadfast love Thou hast been pleased to show them. We implore Thee, continue to strengthen them by Thy Holy Spirit, and daily increase in them the various gifts of Thy grace, the spirit of wisdom and understanding, the spirit of counsel and might, the spirit of knowledge and of the fear of the Lord, that they may be kept in the kingdom and covenant of Christ through faith. Strengthen them against the attacks of sin. Let not Satan overpower them. Keep them from the evil that is in the world. Help them to walk by the Spirit that they may not gratify the evil desires of body and soul but serve Thee with uprightness of heart all their days. Defend them against all false doctrine and error, from desertion and unbelief. Keep them faithful unto death that no one may take from them their crown. And grant that, remaining firm in faith and hope, they may at the end share the inheritance of the saints in light; through Jesus Christ, Thy Son, our Lord, who, with Thee and the Holy Spirit, ever one God, livest and reignest eternally.

Then shall the Minister address the Catechumens:

DEARLY BELOVED: What we as a Christian congregation have here asked our heavenly Father to confer on you all, we will now pray Him to grant to each of you.

Then shall the Catechumens come forward one by one or in groups and kneel before the altar.

Then shall the Minister, laying his hands upon each separately, pronounce the name of the Catechumen and the Benediction — he may add a Scripture passage as a memorial of Confirmation — saying:

N., GOD, the Father of our Lord Jesus Christ, give you His Holy Spirit, the Spirit of Wisdom and knowledge, of grace and prayer, of power and strength, of sanctification and the fear of God.

Or

N., THE FATHER in heaven for Jesus' sake renew and increase in you the gift of the Holy Spirit and make you strong in faith and grant you growth in grace, patience in suffering, and the blessed hope of everlasting life.

Or

N., THE GOD of all grace, who has called us to His eternal glory by Christ Jesus, make you perfect, establish, strengthen, settle you, and keep you through faith for life eternal.

Or

N., THE GOD of peace sanctify you wholly and keep you sound in spirit, soul, and body, without fault when our Lord Jesus comes.

Or

N., MAY GOD, who has begun a good work in you, bring it to completion at the day of our Lord Jesus Christ.

The Minister shall say to the Catechumens:

YOUR CHURCH now invites you to partake of the Blessed Sacrament of the Lord's Supper. Accept this invitation with deep reverence and holy joy and regard your communing at the Lord's Table as a precious privilege given you by God through His church; receive this Sacrament thankfully and often. The peace of the Lord be with you all.

222

Catechumens:

Amen.

When persons not yet baptized are in the group of Cate-chumens, they obviously shall not be confirmed. Instead they shall receive the Sacrament of Holy Baptism either immediately before or after the Confirmation of the others.

Then may be sung a hymn.

Normally the Catechumens should partake of their first Communion at the Confirmation service. The service therefore continues in the usual manner with the Order of the Holy Communion. If the Lord's Supper is not celebrated, the service is to close as usual with a Collect and the Benediction.

Confirmation Certificates

Sometime during the 18th century the practice of issuing confirmation certificates arose in the Lutheran Church. As might be expected, the pietistic and rationalistic influences were clearly reflected in the certificates printed. Thus they frequently certified that the confirmand became a member of the Lutheran Church or the local congregation by the rite of confirmation or that he then entered into "full communion" with the congregation or the Lutheran Church. The rationalistic influence was more clearly seen in the statement that in confirmation the child became "a member of said organization," that is, of the Lutheran Church. The expression "full communicant membership," found on a number of certificates, seems to have been a fusion of "full communion" and "communicant membership." The pietistic influence was expressed in such statements as "restate and confirm your part of the solemn covenant that God made with you in Baptism" or "having been found worthy of membership in the Church of God, was admitted into full communion with the Evangelical Lutheran Church, by the solemn rite of confirmation" or "having vowed faithfulness thereto [the Lutheran Church] until death, was confirmed."

In other instances the certificates testified also that the confirmand had finished his schooling and with his confirmation was "solemnly dismissed." Some certificates stated that the candidate was confirmed "to the Evangelical Lutheran Church, by the imposition of hands and prayer."

A more wholesome influence was seen in those certificates which were issued simply as a token of the person's confirmation or as a witness that he "had been confirmed in the confession of faith."

Because some of the unhealthy influences of the past are still in evidence in the certificates currently on the market, the pastor will take great care in his selection, lest the unwholesome effects of the past be perpetuated.

Memory Verses

The custom of assigning memory verses to the confirmands has evoked much sentiment, certainly much more than the practice warrants. Very often little is made of the memory verse until the day of confirmation, when the children are wholly unprepared for the importance which is then assigned to the memory verse. If the memory verse is to have any real value at all, the catechumen should have a voice in its selection. Instead of having the verse chosen for him, often not from Scripture but from a prescribed number of verses listed in a catalog, it would be much more profitable and meaningful if early in his instruction the catechumen were alerted to choose, with the help of the pastor, some passage which has particular meaning for him. If in addition he is asked to write briefly on why he has selected the particular passage, he will be led to meditate on it. In an interview the pastor may use it as a basis for discussion. The memory verse may then be handwritten on the confirmation certificate and spoken either by the confirmand or by the pastor during the laying on of hands or during the consecration.

Song by the Catechumens

While a song by the confirmation class is a fairly common custom, it must be kept within bounds, lest it add to the general overemphasis of the occasion. Where the catechumens have previously sung at a service their appearance on the day of their confirmation will not be unusual. If there is a junior or a children's choir available, its participation may be more appropriate and will be less likely to give the occasion a climactic effect.

The selected song should obviously be a church hymn rather than some spiritual folk song. It should avoid the extremely subjective and sentimental, for example, Julia Hausmann's "Take Thou My Hand and Lead Me."

Since a hymn sung in two or more voices usually needs a director and since a confirmation class frequently has some members whose gifts do not include musical prowess, it may be most desirable that the hymn be sung in only one voice. A hymn like "God the Father, Be Our Stay," [8] based on a medieval litany and revised by Luther, seems to be more appropriate than one about "These Thy frail and trembling sheep." [9]

The Confirmation Day

That Palm Sunday is still the most common day for the observance of confirmation is unfortunate. From the history of confirmation we know that the selection of this date has no liturgical tradition. Even a superficial study of the propers for the day bears this out. The choice of Palm Sunday was due chiefly to the fact that during the 18th and 19th centuries confirmation was coupled with the closing of the school term. The association of confirmation with Palm Sunday is incongruous because it ushers in Holy Week. The spirit of the preparation for confirmation and of the observance of the day itself is one of joy and quite inappropriate for the Lenten season. From the administrative point of view the selection of Palm Sunday has some other handicaps. The time is unsuitable for the pastor, whose final preparation of the class may hinder his own preparation for the special services of Holy Week. Since the date for Palm Sunday is so flexible, in some years the period of instruction may be unduly shortened.

A much more appropriate time for confirmation would seem

[8] *TLH* 247.

[9] *TLH* 338; *SBH* places it under "Consecration" (Hymn 511) and omits the stanza containing this line.

to be during the Easter cycle, especially on Jubilate or Exaudi, provided that latter does not encourage postponement of first Communion till Pentecost. In many ways the Feast of Pentecost seems to be ideal, provided that the annual observance of confirmation on this high feast day does not prove a distraction. When confirmation was first introduced in the Lutheran Church, it was frequently observed on Easter, Pentecost, or even Christmas, but at that time confirmation was fortunately not given the importance it has today. It was therefore less likely to become a distraction in the observance of a high festival.

First Communion

Since confirmation and the Lord's Supper are so closely related, every effort should be made to have the catechumens receive first Communion on the day of their confirmation. This will help them recognize that the Lord's Supper, not confirmation, is the real climax of the day. Attendance at the Lord's Supper will be part of remembering Christ's work for us, which is the basis for Holy Baptism. Where congregations observe the Lord's Supper every Sunday, the association of first Communion with confirmation will be a natural one.

External Preparations

If confirmation had not become such a festive occasion in the Lutheran Church, one might suggest that the confirmands be expected to wear no special attire for confirmation. However, we recognize that this is wholly unrealistic. Even if no special confirmation garments were expected or taken for granted, Christian parents, being what they are, would soon have their children appearing in special dress, adorned with jewelry, flowers, and what not. If pomp and circumstance have invaded even kindergarten "graduations," can less be expected for confirmation? For this reason it is strongly recommended that the custom of having the catechumens wear white robes be encouraged. This gives all children, rich and poor alike, a more uniform appearance. It is strongly urged, however, that flowers and jewelry be discouraged. The occasional custom of having children wear "confirmation stoles" should be discouraged. It has no place in a Lutheran confirmation. Confirmation is not a lay ordination of any kind, nor does it symbolize taking on the yoke of discipleship. All such accretions unnecessarily dramatize the day and detract from the holy sacraments.

Because Lutheran confirmation is and will remain an unsolved question, church bodies and larger districts within a synod should be encouraged to experiment in order to find better solutions to meet the varying needs of the Lutheran Church today. Once the clergy and the laity, particularly in the United States and Canada, become more aware that confirmation is truly an adiaphoron with an involved history influenced by many trends and tendencies, a more relaxed attitude toward wholesome experimenting will be taken. If this book may contribute to such an awareness and cultivate such an attitude even in a modest way, sections of the Lutheran Church will become more ready for responsible reconstruction of confirmation for our day.

Let us pray for our *catechumens,* that our Lord God would open their hearts and the door of His mercy, that they too receive the remission of all their sins by the washing of regeneration and evermore be found in Christ Jesus, our Lord:

O ALMIGHTY and everlasting God, who dost always provide new children for Thy church, increase the faith and understanding of our catechumens, that being born again in the waters of Baptism, they may be numbered among Thine adopted children, through Jesus Christ, our Lord. *Amen.*

A Bidding Prayer from the
Schwäbisch-Hall CO, 1543

AGENDAS, SERVICE BOOKS

AND CONFIRMATION RITES

American Lutheran Church. *The Altar Service Book of the American Lutheran Church.* Authorized 1936. Columbus, Ohio: The Wartburg Press, 1947.

Augustana Evangelical Lutheran Church. *Church Book of the Evangelical Lutheran Augustana Synod in North America.* Rock Island, Ill.: Lutheran Augustana Book Concern, 1898.

————. *Kyrko-Handbok för Augustana-Synoden.* Adopted 1895. Rock Island, Ill.: Lutheran Augustana Book Concern, 1899.

————. *The Hymnal and Order of Service.* Authorized by The Evangelical Lutheran Augustana Synod. Rock Island, Ill.: Augustana Book Concern, 1925.

————. *Church Service Book and Ministerial Acts of The Evangelical Lutheran Augustana Synod.* Rock Island, Ill.: Augustana Book Concern, 1928.

————. *Proposed Orders: Baptism of Infants, Adult Baptism and Confirmation, Confirmation of Children, Confirmation of Adults, Order for Marriage, Burial of the Dead.* Prepared by the Commission on Lutheran Liturgical Theory and Practice of The Evangelical Lutheran Augustana Synod. Rock Island, Ill.: Augustana Book Concern, 1944.

————. *Church Service Book and Ministerial Acts of the Augustana Evangelical Lutheran Church.* Rock Island, Ill.: Augustana Book Concern, 1951. Reprint of the 1928 ed. except for change in the church body's official name.

Australia, Evangelical Lutheran Synod in. *Agende für evangelisch-lutherische Gemeinden in Australien.* Zwickau [Saxony]: Johannes Hermann, 1912.

Buffalo, Lutheran Synod of. *Evangelisch Lutherische Agende, auf Grund der alten Pommerschen und Sächsischen Agenden bearbeitet und mit den nötigen Zusätzen für hiesige Bedürfnisse vermehrt.* Hrsg. von der Lutherischen Synode von Buffalo, N. Y. Buffalo: Reinecke & Zesch, 1888.

English Evangelical Lutheran Church in New York. *The Liturgy. Gospels and Epistles of the English Evangelical Lutheran Church in New York.* New York: C. Totten, 1806.

The English Evangelical Lutheran Synod of Missouri and Other States. *Lutheran Forms for Sacred Acts,* ed. C[arl A.] Abbetmeyer. Pittsburgh: American Lutheran Publication Board, 1904.

Evangelical Lutheran Church of America. *Altar Book with Scripture Lessons and Collects.* Minneapolis, Minn.: Augsburg Publishing House, 1952 printing.

General Council of The Evangelical Lutheran Church in North America. *Church Book for the Use of Evangelical Lutheran Congregations.* Philadelphia: Lutheran Book Store, 1868.

————. *Church Book. For the Use of Evangelical Lutheran Congregations.* Philadelphia: F. W. Weiskotten, Agent, 1891.

Confirmation

————. *Kirchenbuch für Evangelisch-Lutherische Gemeinden.* Philadelphia: General Council Publication Board, 1892.

————. *Church Book. For the Use of Evangelical Lutheran Congregations.* Philadelphia: General Council Publication Board, 1903.

General Synod of The Evangelical Lutheran Church. *A Liturgy for the Use of the Evangelical Lutheran Church.* Published by Order of the General Synod of the Evangelical Lutheran Church in the United States. Baltimore: Publication Rooms of the Evangelical Lutheran Church, 1847.

————. *The Liturgy of the Evangelical Lutheran Church.* Prepared and Published by Order of the General Synod. Philadelphia: Lutheran Publication Society, 1881.

Hessisches Kirchenbuch, enthaltend die Bekenntnisse der hessischen Kirche, Auszüge aus der Kirchenordnung und die Presbyterial-Ordnung. Cassel: Aubel'-schen Buchdruckerei, 1842.

Iowa and Other States, Evangelical Lutheran Synod of. *Agende für christliche Gemeinden des Lutherischen Bekenntnisses.* Auf Grund der Agende von Wilhelm Löhe. Chicago: Wartburg Publishing House, 1919.

Jacobei, Pavel. *Duchovní Poklad Modliteb Křestánských.* 1732. Revised by Kristian Eduard Popspíšil. Turnov [Bohemia]: F. Vonka, 1891.

Löhe, Wilhelm. *Agende für christliche Gemeinden des Lutherischen Bekenntnisses.* Nördlingen: C. H. Beck'schen Buchhandlung, 1844.

————. *Agende für christliche Gemeinden des lutherischen Bekenntnisses.* Part II. 2d, supplemented ed. Nördlingen: C. H. Beck'schen Buchhandlung, 1859.

————. *Agende für christliche Gemeinden des lutherischen Bekenntnisses.* Part II. 3d ed., executed by J. Deinzer. Nördlingen: C. H. Beck'schen Buchhandlung, 1884.

Lutheran Free Church. *Ministerial Acts.* Authorized by the Annual Conference of the Lutheran Free Church [1948]. Minneapolis: The Messenger Press, n. d.

Missouri Synod, The Lutheran Church —. *Kirchen-Agende für Evangelisch-Lutherische Gemeinden ungeänderter Augsburgischer Confession.* Zusammengestellt aus den alten rechtgläubigen Sächsischen Kirchenagenden und herausgegeben von der Allgemeinen deutschen Evangel.-Lutherischen Synode von Missouri, Ohio u. a. St. St. Louis: Druckerei der Deutschen Ev. Luth. Synode v. Missouri, O. u. a. St. 1856.

————. *Kirchen-Agende für Evang.-Luth. Gemeinden ungeänderter Augsburgischer Confession.* Zusammengestellt aus den alten rechtgläubigen Sächsischen Kirchenagenden und herausgegeben von der Allgemeinen deutschen Evangel.-Lutherischen Synode von Missouri, Ohio u. a. St. [2d ed.] St. Louis: M. C. Barthel, General Agent, 1866.

————. *Kirchen-Agende für Evang.-Luth. Gemeinden ungeänderter Augsburgischer Confession.* Zusammengestellt aus den alten rechtgläubigen Sächsischen Kirchenagenden und herausgegeben von der Allgemeinen deutschen Evang.-Lutherischen Synode von Missouri, Ohio u. a. St. 3d ed. St. Louis: M. C. Barthel, General Agent, 1876.

————. *Kirchen-Agende für Evang.-Luth. Gemeinden ungeänderter Augsburgischer Confession.* Zusammengestellt aus den alten rechtgläubigen Sächsischen Kirchenagenden und herausgegeben von der Allgemeinen deutschen Evang.-Lutherischen Synode von Missouri, Ohio u. a. St. 4th ed. St. Louis: M. C. Barthel, General Agent, 1880.

in the Lutheran Church

————. *Church Liturgy for Evangelical Lutheran Congregations of the Unaltered Augsburg Confession.* Published by the German Evangelical Lutheran Synod of Missouri, Ohio and other States. St. Louis: Concordia Publishing House, 1881.

————. *Kirchen-Agende für Evang.-Luth. Gemeinden ungeänderter Augsburgischer Confession.* Zusammengestellt aus den alten rechtgläubigen Sächsischen Kirchenagenden und herausgegeben von der Allgemeinen deutschen Evang.-Lutherischen Synode von Missouri, Ohio u. a. St. 5th ed. St. Louis: Lutherischer Concordia Verlag, 1890.

————. *Kirchen-Agende für Evang.-Luth. Gemeinden ungeänderter Augsburgischer Confession.* Zusammengestellt aus den alten rechtgläubigen Sächsischen Kirchenagenden und herausgegeben von der Allgemeinen deutschen Evang.-Lutherischen Synode von Missouri, Ohio u. a. St. St. Louis: Concordia Publishing House, 1896.

————. *Kirchen-Agende für Evang.-Luth. Gemeinden ungeänderter Augsburgischer Confession.* Zusammengestellt aus den alten rechtgläubigen Sächsischen Kirchenagenden und herausgegeben von der Allgemeinen deutschen Evangel.-Lutherischen Synode von Missouri, Ohio u. a. St. St. Louis: Concordia Publishing House, 1902.

————. *Liturgy and Agenda.* St. Louis: Concordia Publishing House, 1917.

————. *Liturgy and Agenda.* St. Louis: Concordia Publishing House, 1921.

————. *Kirchen-Agende für Ev.-Luth. Gemeinden ungeänderter Augsburgischer Confession.* Zusammengestellt aus den alten rechtgläubigen Kirchenagenden und in mehrfach veränderter Form herausgegeben von der Evangelisch-Lutherischen Synode von Missouri, Ohio u. a. St. St. Louis: Concordia Publishing House, 1922.

————. *Liturgy and Agenda.* St. Louis: Concordia Publishing House, 1936.

National Lutheran Council. *Service Book and Hymnal of the Lutheran Church in America.* Authorized by the Churches cooperating in The Commission on the Liturgy and The Commission on the Hymnal. Music ed. 1958. Minneapolis, Minn.: Augsburg Publishing House; et al.,

New York, Evangelical Lutheran Synod of. *A Liturgy, for the use of Evangelical Lutheran Churches.* Published by order of the Evangelical Lutheran Synod of the State of New York. Philadelphia: G. & D. Billmeyer, 1814.

————. *A Liturgy for the use of Evangelical Lutheran Churches.* Published by Order of the Evangelical Lutheran Synod of the State of New York. Philadelphia: G. & D. Billmeyer, 1817.

————. *A Liturgy for the Use of Evangelical Lutheran Churches.* Published by Order of the Evangelical Lutheran Synod of the State of New York. New, enlarged ed. Philadelphia: G. & D. Billmeyer, 1834.

Norwegian Evangelical Lutheran Synod of America. *Church Liturgy for Evangelical Lutheran Congregations,* trans. from the Norwegian. Published by the Norwegian Evangelical Lutheran Synod of America. Decorah, Iowa: Lutheran Publishing House, 1891.

————. *Alterbog til Brug ved den offentlige Gudstjeneste og de kirkelige Handlinger for Synoden for den nosk-ev-luth. Kirke i Amerika.* Decorah, Iowa: Den norske Synodes Forlag, 1901.

Ohio and Other States, Evangelical Lutheran Joint Synod of. *Liturgy or Formulary for the Use of Evangelical Lutheran Churches.* Compiled by the Synod of Ohio and Ordered to be printed. Lancaster, Ohio: John Herman, 1830.

Confirmation

————. *Agende für Gemeinden des Evangelisch-Lutherischen Bekenntnisses,* hrsg. von der Allgemeinen, Evangelisch-Lutherischen Synode von Ohio u. a. St., A. D. 1863. Columbus, Ohio: Reinhard and Fieser, 1864.

————. *Selection of Forms for the Use of Evangelical Lutheran Ministers.* Columbus, Ohio: Schulze & Gassmann, 1870.

————. *Agende für Evangelisch-Lutherische Gemeinden Ungeänderter Augsburgischer Konfession.* Hrsg. von der Allgemeinen Evangelisch-Lutherischen Synode von Ohio und anderen Staaten. Columbus, Ohio: Lutheran Book Concern, 1909.

Pennsylvania and Adjacent States, Ministerium of. *Kirchen-Agende der Evangelisch-Lutherischen Vereinigten Gemeinen in Nord-America.* Philadelphia: Melchior Steiner, 1786.

————. *Liturgie oder Kirchen-Agende, der Evangelisch-Lutherischen Gemeinen in Pennsylvanien, und den benachbarten Staaten.* Baltimore: Schäffer und Maund, 1818.

————. *Liturgie oder Kirchen-Agende, der Evangelisch-Lutherischen Gemeinen in Pennsylvanien und den benachbarten Staaten.* Zweyte, vermehrte Auflage. Libanon: Heinrich Diezel, 1838.

————. *Liturgie und Kirchenagende für die Evangelisch-Lutherischen Gemeinden in Pennsylvanien, Neu York, Ohio und den benachbarten Staaten* [1st ed.]. Philadelphia: Julius Bötticher, 1842.

————. *Liturgie und Agende: Ein Kirchenbuch für die Evangelisch-Lutherische Kirche in den Vereinigten Staaten.* Hrsg. mit kirchlicher Genehmigung [2d ed.]. New York: Heinrich Ludwig, 1855.

————. *A Liturgy for the Use of the Evangelical Lutheran Church.* By authority of the Ministerium of Pennsylvania and Adjacent States. Philadelphia: Lindsay & Blakiston, 1860.

Repp, Arthur C[hristian]. "Proposed Rite of Confirmation for Children," special 11-page clergy bulletin insert in *Advance,* IX (April, 1962).

Richter, Ae[milius] L[udwig]. *Die evangelischen Kirchenordnungen des 16. Jahrhunderts.* 2 vols. Weimar: Landes-Industriecomptoirs, 1846.

Runge, Kenneth. "The Lutheran Rite of Holy Confirmation in Zion Lutheran Church, Detroit, Michigan, on The Holy Feast of Pentecost, June 10, 1962."

Schleswig-Holsteinsche Kirchen-Agende. Schleswig: Joh. Gottl. Röhss, 1797.

Sehling, Emil. *Die Evangelischen Kirchenordnungen des XVI. Jahrhunderts.* 6 vols. Leipzig: O. R. Reisland, 1902—13. 3 vols. Tübingen: J. C. B. Mohr (Paul Siebeck), 1955— .

South, United Synod of the Evangelical Lutheran Church in the. *The Book of Worship for the Use of the United Synod of the Evangelical Lutheran Church in the South.* Columbus, S. C.: W. J. Duffie, 1888.

Sweden, Lutheran Church of. *Kyrko-Handbok, hwarnti stadgas, huru Gudstjensten i Swenska Fösamlingar skall sörrättas.* Stockholm: P. A. Norstedt & Söner, 1854.

Synodical Conference of North America, Evangelical Lutheran. *The Lutheran Agenda.* St. Louis: Concordia Publishing House [1949].

Tennessee Synod, Evangelical Lutheran. *Liturgy, or Book of Forms for the use of the Evangelical Lutheran Church.* Compiled and Published by order of the Evang. Lutheran Tennessee Synod. New Market, Va.: Solomon Henkel, 1843.

Twietmeyer, Arvin. "The Confirmation for Concordia Lutheran Church, Granite City, Illinois." [1962]

in the Lutheran Church

The United Lutheran Church. *The Occasional Services.* From the *Common Service Book* of the Lutheran Church. Philadelphia: The Board of Publication of The Lutheran Church in America, 1918.

United Norwegian Lutheran Church in America. *Altar Book with Scripture Lessons and Collects.* Minneapolis, Minn.: Augsburg Publishing House, 1915.

Vereinigte Evangelisch-Lutherische Kirche Deutschlands. "Ordnung der Konfirmation." Vorabdruck aus *Kirchliche Handlungen. Agende für evangelischlutherische Kirchen und Gemeinden,* Vol. III. Berlin: Lutherisches Verlagshaus, 1952.

Wisconsin and Other States, Evangelical Lutheran Joint Synod of. *Agende.* Hrsg. von der Evang.-Luth. Synode von Wisconsin u. a. Staaten. Milwaukee: Northwestern Publishing House, 1896.

BOOKS, ESSAYS, AND THESES

Achelis, E[rnst] Chr[istian]. *Lehrbuch der Praktischen Theologie.* Vol. II. 3rd ed. Leipzig: J. C. Hinrich'sche Buchhandlung, 1911.

Adam, Adolf. *Das Sakrament der Firmung nach Thomas von Aquin.* Freiburg [im Breisgau]: Verlag Herder, 1958.

[Aepinus, Johann (Johannes Höck)]. *Bekentniss unnd Erklerung auffs Interim.* Magdeburg: Christian Roedinger [1548].

"The Age Group Objectives of Christian Education," ed. W. Kent Gilbert. Prepared in connection with the Long-Range Program of Lutheran Boards of Parish Education. Mimeographed, 1958. Available from the ed., 2900 Queen Lane, Philadelphia, Pa. 19129.

Andrén, Carl-Gustaf. *Konfirmationen i Sverige under medeltid och reformationstid.* Bibliotheca Theologiae Practicae, Vol. I, ed, Ake Andrén and Sven Kjöllerström. Lund: Berlingska Boktryckeriet, 1957.

Anrich, Gustav [Adolf]. *Martin Bucer.* Strassburg: Karl J. Truebner, 1914.

Bachmann, Johann Fr. *Die Confirmation der Catechumenen in der evangelischen Kirche.* Berlin: Wilhelm Schultze, 1852.

Backus, Donald Wm. "An Analysis of the Extent of Growth in Doctrinal Knowledge of Saint Louis Children in the Nine Months After Confirmation." Unpub. B. D. thesis, Concordia Seminary, St. Louis, Mo., 1951.

Bäumler, Christof. "Zur Frage der Konfirmation." Vortrag bei der Tagung der hauptamtlichen Jugendleiter im Januar 1960. No place given.

Balthasar, Jac. Henr[icus]. *Erste Sammlung Einiger zur Pommerischen Kirchen-Historie gehörigen Schriften.* Part I. Greifswald: Andreas Bussen, 1723.

Barth, Karl. *The Teaching of the Church Regarding Baptism,* trans. Ernest A. Payne. London: S. C. M. Press, 1948.

Die Bekenntnisschriften der evangelisch-lutherischen Kirche, herausgegeben im Gedenkjahr der Augsburgischen Konfession 1930. 4th, rev. ed. Göttingen: Vandenhoeck & Ruprecht, 1959.

Belfour, E[dmund] "The History of the Liturgy in the Lutheran Church in Denmark." *Memoirs of the Lutheran Liturgical Association.* Vol. II. Pittsburgh: Lutheran Liturgical Association, 1906.

Benze, Cha[rle]s Theo. "The Liturgical History of Confirmation." *Memoirs of the Lutheran Liturgical Association.* Vol. III. Pittsburgh: Lutheran Liturgical Association, 1907.

Confirmation

Bertermann, E[rnst] H. "Instructing the Catechumens Preparatory to Confirmation." Essay delivered at the 1955 [convention of the] Minnesota District of The Lutheran Church — Missouri Synod. Mimeographed, 1955.

The Book of Concord: The Confession of the Evangelical Lutheran Church, trans. and ed. Theodore G. Tappert in collaboration with Jaroslav Pelikan, Robert H. Fischer, Arthur C. Piepkorn. Philadelphia: Muhlenberg Press, 1959.

Bretschneider, Karl Gottlieb. Handbuch der Dogmatik der evangelisch-lutherischen Kirche. Vol. II. 2d, rev. ed. Reutlingen: J. J. Mäcken'schen Buchhandlung, 1823.

Caspari, Walter. Die evangelische Konfirmation, vornämlich in der lutherischen Kirche. Erlangen and Leipzig: And. Deichert, 1890.

Chemnitz, Martin. Examen Concilii Tridentini, ed. Ed[uard] Preuss. Berlin: Gust. Schlawitz, 1861.

The Concordia Pulpit for 1947. Vol. XVIII. St. Louis: Concordia Publishing House, 1946.

Concordia Triglotta: Die symbolischen Bücher der evangelisch-lutherischen Kirche, deutsch-lateinisch-englisch, als Denkmal der vierhundertjährigen Jubelfeier der Reformation, anno Domini 1917, herausgegeben auf Beschluss der evangelisch-lutherischen Synode von Missouri, Ohio und andern Staaten. St. Louis: Concordia Publishing House, 1921.

Confirmatio: Forschungen zur Geschichte und Praxis der Konfirmation, ed. Kurt Frör. Munich: Evang[elischer] Presseverband für Bayern, 1959. Of it Gustav K. Wiencke has prepared a mimeographed "English Digest and Summary," 1961.

Confirmation: History, Doctrine, and Practice, ed. Kendig Brubaker Cully. Greenwich, Conn.: The Seabury Press, 1962.

Confirmation in the Vocation of the Church: [Proceedings of the] Third Annual Conference of Lutheran Workers with Youth, Valparaiso University, Valparaiso, Indiana, February 19—21, 1963. Sponsored by Youth Leadership Training Program in cooperation with Valparaiso University, Board for Young People's Work, Lutheran Laymen's League, Walther League. [St. Louis: Concordia Publishing House, 1963.]

Delekat, Friedrich. Die heiligen Sakramente und die Ordnungen der Kirche. Berlin: Furche Verlag, 1940.

Diehl, Wilhelm. Zur Geschichte der Konfirmation: Beiträge aus der hessischen Kirchengeschichte. Giessen: J. Ricker, 1897.

Dix, Gregory. The Shape of the Liturgy. 2d ed., reprinted. Westminster: Dacre Press, 1947.

————. The Theology of Confirmation in Relation to Baptism. Westminster: Dacre Press, 1946.

Documentary History of the Evangelical Lutheran Ministerium of Pennsylvania and Adjacent States. Philadelphia: Board of Publications of the General Council of the Evangelical Lutheran Church in North America, 1898.

Doerne, Martin. Neubau der Konfirmation. Gütersloh: C. Bertelsmann, 1936.

Duus, Olaus, Fredrik. Frontier Parsonage: The Letters of Olaus Fredrik Duus, Norwegian Pastor in Wisconsin, 1855—1858, trans. Verdandi Study Club of Minneapolis and ed. Theodore C. Blegen. Northfield, Minn.: The Norwegian-American Historical Association, 1947.

Eells, Hastings. Martin Bucer. New Haven: Yale University Press, 1931.

238

in the Lutheran Church

Ernsberger, C. S. *A History of the Wittenberg Synod of the General Synod of the Evangelical Lutheran Church, 1847—1916.* Columbus, Ohio: Lutheran Book Concern, 1917.

Ernst, August, and Johann Adam. *Katechetische Geschichte des Elsasses bis zur Revolution.* Strassburg: Friedrich Bull, 1897.

A Family of God, ed. Daniel Nystrom. Rock Island, Ill.: Augustana Press, 1962.

Fritz, John H[enry] C[harles]. *Pastoral Theology: A Handbook of Scriptural Principles Written Especially for Pastors of the Lutheran Church.* 2d, rev. ed. Saint Louis: Concordia Publishing House, 1945.

"The Functional Objectives for Christian Education," ed. W. Kent Gilbert. Prepared in connection with the Long-Range Program of the Boards of Parish Education. Vol. II. Mimeographed, 1959. Available from the ed., 2900 Queen Lane, Philadelphia, Pa. 19129.

Gerberding, G[eorge] H[enry]. *The Lutheran Catechist: A Companion Book to "The Lutheran Pastor."* 4th, rev. ed. Philadelphia: The Lutheran Publication Society, 1915.

Gill, Joseph. *The Council of Florence.* Cambridge: University Press, 1959.

Girgensohn, Herbert. *Teaching Luther's Catechism,* trans. John W. Doberstein. 2 vols. Philadelphia: Muhlenberg Press, 1959—60.

Graebner, Theodore. *Our Faith Victorious.* New York: Ernst Kaufmann, n. d.

Graff, Paul. *Geschichte der Auflösung der alten gottesdienstlichen Formen in der evangelischen Kirche Deutschlands.* 2d, rev. ed. 2 vols. Göttingen: Vandenhoeck & Ruprecht, 1937—39.

Grossgebauer, Theophilum. *Wächterstimme auss dem verwüsteten Zion.* Frankfort on the Main: Joachim Wildens, 1661.

Haendschke, Martin. "The Emerging Objectives of Instruction for Confirmation as Currently Practiced in The Lutheran Church — Missouri Synod." Unpub. S. T. M. thesis, Concordia Seminary, St. Louis, Mo., 1957.

Hamel, Johannes. *Christ in der DDR.* Berlin: A. Seydal, 1957.

Hammelsbeck, Oskar. *Der kirchliche Unterricht: Aufgabe — Umfang — Einheit.* Munich: Chr. Kaiser Verlag, 1947.

Hansen, Emil. *Geschichte der Konfirmation in Schleswig-Holstein.* Kiel: n., pub., 1911.

Harms, Claus. *Pastoral-Theologie in Reden an Theologiestudirenden.* 3 vols. Stuttgart: Christian Hausmann, 1834.

Harnack, Th[eodosius]. *Die freie lutherische Volkskirche.* Erlangen: A. Deichert, 1870.

Hauschildt, Karl. *Konfirmation ganz anders.* Kiel: Evangelischer Presseverband Schleswig-Holstein, 1958.

———, and Johannes Schröder. *Arbeitshilfen für die Unterweisung der Konfirmanden.* Neumünster: G. Ihloff & Co., 1955.

Herzer, J. H. *Evangelisch-Lutherische Katechetik.* St. Louis: Concordia Publishing House, 1911.

Heubach, Joachim. "Study Document on Confirmation," *Commission on Education.* Report 1957—1963. Document No. 16. Fourth Assembly of The Lutheran World Federation, July 30—August 11, 1963. Helsinki, Finland.

Höfling, Joh[ann] Wilh[elm] Friedrich. *Das Sakrament der Taufe.* Vol. II. Erlangen: Palm'schen Verlagsbuchhandlung, 1848.

Confirmation

Hoffmann, Gerhard. *Der Stoff des Konfirmandenunterrichts: Seine Abgrenzung, Anordnung, und Gliederung.* Munich: Evangelischer Presseverband für Bayern, 1950.

Irvin, Donald F. *Teaching the Way: A Pastor's Guide for Catechetical Instruction,* ed. Arthur H. Getz. Philadelphia: United Lutheran Publication House, 1951.

Kansanaho, Erkki. *Konfirmaatio: Liturgishistoriallinen tutkimus konfirmaatioaktista.* Helsinki: Suomalainen Teologinen Kirjallisuusseura, 1956.

Kehre Wieder! Worte der Liebe an einen früheren Konfirmanden von seinem lutherischen Pastor. St. Louis: Luth. Concordia Verlag, 1883.

A Kierkegaard Anthology, ed. Robert [Walter] Bretall. Princeton, N. J.: Princeton University Press, 1946.

Klett, Paul E. "A Reevaluation of Protestant Confirmation." Unpub. master's thesis, Andover Newton Theological School, Newton Centre, Mass., 1960.

Kliefoth, The[odor]. *Die Confirmation. Liturgische Abhandlungen,* Vol. III, 1. Schwerin: Stiller'schen Hof-Buchhandlung, 1856.

Kline, J. J. "The Lutheran Church in New Hanover, Montgomery County (Falckner Swamp)." *The Pennsylvania-German Society.* Vol. XX. 1911.

Koehler, Robert T. "A Survey of the Confirmation Instruction of the Children Within a Pastoral Conference," Unpub. B. D. thesis, Concordia Seminary, St. Louis, Mo., 1948.

Koepchen, Paul K. "A Survey of Confirmation Instruction for Children," Unpub. B. D. thesis, Concordia Seminary, St. Louis, Mo., 1952.

Konfirmation: Ein Studienbuch zur Frage ihrer rechten Gestaltung, ed. Wilhelm Rott. Berlin: Burckhardthaus-Verlag, 1941.

Krause, L[eberecht] F[riedrich] E[hregott]. "*Chronica* der evangelisch lutherischen Kirche in Town Nine Washington County, Territory of Wisconsin, Nord Amerika, deutscher Zunge zur Freystatt." 1848. The original is in the archives of Trinity Lutheran Church, Freistadt, Wis. (Mequon, 3W).

Kraushaar, Chr. Otto. *Verfassungsformen der Lutherischen Kirche Amerikas.* Gütersloh: C. Bertelsmann, 1911.

Krauss, E[ugen] A[dolf] W[ilhel]m. *Grüsse.* Milwaukee: Northwestern Publishing House, 1928.

Kreider, Harry. *History of the United Lutheran Synod of New York and New England.* Philadelphia: Muhlenberg Press, 1954.

Kressel, Hans. *Die Liturgik der Erlanger Theologie: Ihre Geschichte und ihre Grundsätze.* 2d ed. Göttingen: Vandenhoeck & Ruprecht, 1948.

Kunze, John C[hristoph]. *A Hymn and Prayer-Book. For the Use of such Lutheran Churches as use the English Language.* New York: Hurtin and Commardinger, 1795.

Kurtz, Benjamin. *Why Are You a Lutheran? or A Series of Dissertations.* Baltimore: Evangelical Lutheran Church, 1843.

Lampe, G[eoffrey] W[illiam] H[ugo]. *The Seal of the Spirit.* London: Longmans, Green and Co., 1951.

Langemack, Gregorio. *Histor. Catecheticae, oder Gesammleter Nachrichten zu einer Catechetischen Historie.* Vols. I and II. Greifswald and Stralsund: Samuel Gottlieb Lochmann und Jacob Löffler, 1729—33.

"Lectures for the International Seminar on Confirmation." Commission on Education in Cooperation with the Commission on Theology. The Lutheran World Federation, April 18—21, 1961. Loccum, Germany.

in the *Lutheran Church*

Lilja, Einar. *Den Svenska Katekestraditionen Mellan Svebilius och Lindblom.* Vol. 16 in *Acta Historico-Ecclesiastica Suecana*, ed. Hilding Pleijel. Stockholm: Svenska Kyrkans Diakonistyrelses Bokförlag, 1947.

Lindemann, F[rederick]. Letter to H[einrich] G. Sauer, Jan. 5, 1896. Photocopy in the possession of the author.

Lindhol, Stig. *Konfirmandundervisning: Metodiska elementa.* Stockholm: Svenska Kyrkans Diakonistyrelses Bokförlag, 1954.

Littel, Franklin H. *The Anabaptist View of the Church.* 2d rev. ed. Boston: Stan King Press, Beacon Hill, 1958.

Der Liturgische Ausschuss der Vereinigten Evangelisch-Lutherischen Kirche Deutschlands. *Begleitwort zur Ordnung der Konfirmation für evangelisch-lutherische Kirchen und Gemeinden*, ed. Chr[isthard] Mahrenholz. Berlin: Lutherisches Verlagshaus, 1952.

Löhe, Wilhelm. "Neuendettelsauer Briefe, 1858," 3 in *Gesammelte Werke*, III, 1. Neuendettelsau: Freimund Verlag, 1951. Pp. 221—228.

Luther, Martin. *D. Martin Luthers Werke: Kritische Gesammtausgabe.* Weimar: Herman Böhlau and Hermann Böhlaus Nachfolger, 1883— .

———. *Dr. Martin Luthers Briefe, Sendschreiben und Bedenken*, ed. Wilh[elm] Martin [Leberecht] de Wette. 5 vols. Berlin: G. Reimer, 1825—28.

———. *Dr. Martin Luthers Sämmtliche Schriften*, ed. Joh[ann] Georg Walch. New, rev. ed. 25 vols. St. Louis: Lutherischer Concordia-Verlag, 1880—1910.

———. *Luther: Early Theological Works*, trans. and ed. James Atkinson. Philadelphia: Westminster Press, 1962.

———. *Luther's Works.* American ed. Jaroslav [Jan] Pelikan and Helmut T. Lehmann, general eds. St. Louis: Concordia Publishing House; Philadelphia: Muhlenberg [later Fortress] Press, 1955— .

The Lutheran Church — Missouri Synod. *Reports and Memorials (Eingaben) for the Twenty-third Delegate Synod (Thirty-eighth Regular Convention) Assembled at Fort Wayne, Indiana, June 18—28, 1941.* St. Louis: Concordia Publishing House, 1941.

———. *Vierter Synodal-Bericht: Verhandlungen der deutschen evangelisch-lutherischen Synode von Missouri, Ohio und anderen Staaten*, 1850. St. Louis: M. Niedner, 1851.

The Lutheran Hymnal. Authorized by the Synods Constituting The Evangelical Lutheran Synodical Conference of North America. St. Louis: Concordia Publishing House, 1941.

Lynch, Kilian F. *Texts.* Vol. I in *The Sacrament of Confirmation in the Early-Middle Scholastic Period.* Franciscan Institute Publications, Theology Series, No. 5, ed. Eligius M. Buytaert, O. F. M. St. Bonaventure, N. Y.: The Franciscan Institute, 1957.

Maassel, Richard G. "A History of the Early Catechisms of the Missouri Synod." Unpub. S. T. M. thesis, Concordia Seminary, St. Louis, Mo., 1957.

Maurer, Wilhelm. *Gemeindezucht, Gemeindeamt, Konfirmation.* Kassel: Johannes Stauda Verlag, 1940.

Mayer, E[mmanuel] A. *Geschichte der evangelisch-lutherischen St. Lorenz-Gemeinde U. A. C. zu Frankenmuth, Mich.* St. Louis: Concordia Publishing House, 1895.

Mehl, Oskar Joh. *Das liturgische Verhalten: Beiträge zu einem evangelischen Zeremoniale und Rituale.* Göttingen: Vandenhoeck & Ruprecht, 1927.

Confirmation

Mertz, Georg. *Das Schulwesen der deutschen Reformation im 16. Jahrhundert*. Heidelberg: Carl Winter's Universitätsbuchhandlung, 1902.

Metzger, Wolfgang. *Die Konfirmation Zwischen Gesetz und Freiheit*. Stuttgart: Calwer Verlag, 1962.

Mueller, A[rnold] C. "Report on Confirmation Instruction, May 13, 1941." Mimeographed, 1941.

Muhlenberg, Henry Melchior. *The Journals of Henry Melchoir Muhlenberg*, trans. Theodore G. Tappert and John W. Doberstein. 3 vols. Philadelphia: Muhlenberg Press, 1942—58.

Nagel, William. *Probleme der Konfirmation*. Berlin: Evangelische Verlagsanstalt, 1959.

Neunheuser, Burkhard, O. S. B, *Taufe und Firmung*, in *Handbuch der Dogmengeschichte*, ed. Michael Schmauss, Josef Geiselmann, and P. Aloys Grillmeyer, Vol. IV, 2. Freiburg im Breisgau: Verlag Herder, 1956.

Nicum, J[ohann]. *Geschichte des Evangelisch-Lutherischen Ministeriums vom Staate New York und angrenzenden Staaten und Ländern*. New York: Verlag des New York Ministeriums, 1888.

"The Objectives of Christian Education," ed. W. Kent Gilbert. Prepared in connection with the Long-Range Program of the Boards of Parish Education. Mimeographed, 1957. Available from the ed., 2900 Queen Lane, Philadelphia, Pa. 19129.

Olson, Oscar N[ils]. *Pioneer Period, 1846—1860. The Augustana Lutheran Church in America*, Vol. 1. Rock Island, Ill.: Augustana Book Concern, 1950.

Pohle, Joseph. *The Sacraments: A Dogmatic Treatise*, adapted and ed. Arthur Preus. Vol. I. St. Louis: B. Herder Book Co., 1915.

Prenter, Regin. "Luther on Word and Sacrament." *More about Luther. Martin Luther Lectures*, Vol. II. Decorah, Iowa: Luther College Press, 1958. Pp. 63 to 122.

Quistorp, J[ohann Nicholaus]. *"Pia Desideria IX" in Variorum Auctorum Miscellanea Theologica*, ed. Johann Gottlob Pfeiffer. Leipzig: Impensis Lankisianorum Haeredum, 1736.

Reformation der Konfirmation: Grundsätzliche Besinnung und praktischer Vorschlag eines Arbeitskreises, ed. Georg Gründler and Ernst Klessmann. Göttingen: Vandenhoeck & Ruprecht, 1960.

Rendtorff, F[ranz]. *Das Problem der Konfirmation und der Religionsunterricht in der Volkschule*. Leipzig: Dörffling und Francke, 1910.

Rendtorff, Heinrich. *Konfirmation und Kirche*. Dresden: C. Ludwig Ungelenk, 1928.

"The Report to the Seminar on Confirmation and Confirmation Instruction, August 24—27, 1954." Racine, Wis. Mimeographed, 1954.

Repp, Arthur C[hristian]. "The Pastor and Parish Education." Ch. xv in *The Pastor at Work*. St. Louis: Concordia Publishing House, 1960. Pp. 231—258.

———. "Reconstructing Confirmation for Our Day." Essay delivered to the Iowa District East of The Lutheran Church — Missouri Synod in 1960 and in revised form to the Synod's Western District in 1961.

Reu, [Johann] M[ichael]. *Catechetics or Theory and Practice of Religious Instruction*. 2d, rev. ed. Chicago: Wartburg Publishing House, 1927.

———. *D. Martin Luthers Kleiner Katechismus: Die Geschichte seiner Entstehung, seiner Verbreitung und seines Gebrauchs*. Munich: Chr. Kaiser Verlag, 1929.

———. *Quellen zur Geschichte des kirchlichen Unterrichts in der evangelischen Kirche Deutschlands zwischen 1530 und 1600.* Gütersloh: C. Bertelsmann, 1904—35.

Richter, Ae[milius] L[udwig]. *Die evangelischen Kirchenordnungen des sechszehnten Jahrhunderts.* 2 vols. Weimar: Landes-Industriecomptoirs, 1846.

Rietschel, Georg. *Lehrbuch der Liturgik.* 2d ed., rev. Paul Graff. Göttingen: Vandenhoeck & Ruprecht, 1952.

Ritter, Karl Bernhard. *Die Konfirmandenstunde.* Kassel: Johannes Stauda Verlag, 1961.

Rohne, J[ohn] Magnus. *Norwegian American Lutheranism up to 1872.* New York: Macmillan Company, 1926.

Rohnert, Wilhelm. *Die Dogmatik der evangelisch-lutherischen Kirche.* Braunschweig: Hellmuth Wollermann, 1902.

Rosenbloom, Enns. *Gemeindeaufbau durch Konfirmandenunterricht.* Gütersloh: Gütersloher Verlagshaus Gerd Mohn, 1962.

Roth, Donald. "Confirmation Instruction in the Light of Adolescent Psychology." Unpub. S. T. M. thesis, Concordia Seminary, St. Louis, Mo., 1951.

Schempp, Paul. *Gesammelte Aufsätze.* Munich: Chr. Kaiser Verlag, 1962.

Schleiermacher, Friedrich [Ernst Daniel]. *Der christliche Glaube nach den Grundsätzen der evangelischen Kirche.* Vol. II. 4th ed. Berlin: G. Reimer, 1843.

Schmauk, Theodore E[manuel]. *Old Salem in Lebanon.* Lebanon: Press of Report Publishing Co., 1898.

Schuppius, Joh[annus] Balthasaris. *Lehrreiche Schrifften.* Title page missing. [1663?]

Schweizer, J[ulius]. *Zur Neuordnung der Konfirmation in den reformierten Kirchen der Schweiz.* Basel: Helbing und Lichtenhahn, 1938.

Sehling, Emil. *Die Evangelischen Kirchenordnungen des XVI. Jahrhunderts.* 6 vols. Leipzig: O. R. Reisland, 1902—13. 3 vols. Tübingen: J. C. B. Mohr (Paul Siebeck), 1955—.

Service Book and Hymnal of the Lutheran Church in America. Authorized by the Churches cooperating in The Commission on the Liturgy and The Commission on the Hymnal. Music ed. Minneapolis, Minn.: Augsburg Publishing House; et al., 1958.

Sheatsley, C[larence] V[alentine]. *History of the Evangelical Lutheran Joint Synod of Ohio and Other States.* Columbus, Ohio: Lutheran Book Concern, 1919.

Shepherd, Massey H[amilton]. *The Worship of the Church.* Greenwich, Conn.: The Seabury Press, 1952.

Smith, Henry P[eter]. *Psychology in Teaching.* Prentice-Hall Psychology Series. New York: Prentice-Hall, Inc., 1954.

Spener, Philipp Jacob. *Theologisches Bedenken Und andere Briefliche Antworten.* Vols. III, IV. Halle: Verlegung des Wäysenhauses, 1715.

"A Study Guide for the Objectives of Christian Education," ed. W. Kent Gilbert. Prepared in connection with the Long-Range Program of Lutheran Boards of Parish Education. Mimeographed, 1957. Available from the ed., 2900 Queen Lane, Philadelphia, Pa. 19129.

Thieme, Karl. *Der wahre lutherische Konfirmationsbegriff.* Giessen: Alfred Töpelmann Verlag, 1931.

Confirmation

Thornton, L[ionel] S[pencer]. *Confirmation: Its Place in the Baptismal Mystery.* Westminster: Dacre Press, 1954.

Thurian, Max. *Die Konfirmation: Einsegnung der Laien,* trans. from the French by Richard Bochinger. Gütersloh: Gütersloher Verlagshaus, 1961.

"The Trappe Records." *The Pennsylvania-Germany Society.* Vol. III. 1896.

20 Confirmation Sermons by Pastors of the Evangelical Lutheran Church. Minneapolis, Minn.: Augsburg Publishing House, 1951.

Velthusen, Johann C. *Nordcarolinische Kirchennachrichten.* Vol. I. Leipzig: Siegfried Lebrecht Crusius, 1790.

Vischer, Lukas. *Die Geschichte der Konfirmation.* St. Gallen: Evangelischer Verlag AG., Zollikon, 1958.

Von Hofmann, Johann Chr[istian] K[onrad]. *Encyclopädie der Theologie,* ed. and produced by H. J. Bestmann. Nördlingen: C. H. Beck, 1879.

V[on] Zezschwitz, Carl Adolph Gerhard. *Der Katechumenat oder die Lehre von der kirchlichen Erziehung. System der christlich-kirchlichen Katechetik,* Vol. I. Leipzig: Dörffling und Francke, 1863.

"Wachet, stehet im Glauben!" Eine Sammlung von Konfirmationsreden, ed. Emil Ohly. Leipzig: G. Strübig, 1894.

Wackernagel, Philipp. *Das deutsche Kirchenlied.* 5 vols. Leipzig: B. G. Teubner, 1864—77.

Walther, C[arl] F[erdinand] W[ilhelm]. *Americanisch-Lutherische Pastoraltheologie.* St. Louis: Druckerei der Synode von Missouri, Ohio, u. a. Staaten, 1872.

——. *Briefe von C. F. W. Walther an seine Freunde, Synodalgenossen und Familienglieder,* ed. L[udwig Ernst] Fürbringer. Vol. I. St. Louis: Concordia Publishing House, 1915.

——. *Festklänge: Predigten über Festtexte des Kirchenjahrs,* comp. C. L. Janzow. St. Louis: Concordia Publishing House, 1892.

Williams, George Huntston. *The Radical Reformation.* Philadelphia: The Westminster Press, 1962.

Williston, Ralph. *A Choice Selection of Evangelical Hymns from Various Authors for the Use of the English Evangelical Lutheran Church in New York.* New York: J. C. Totten, 1806.

Witt, Karl. *Konfirmanden-Unterricht: Neue Wege der Katechetik in Kirche und Schule.* Göttingen: Vandenhoeck & Ruprecht, 1959.

Yelverton, Eric E[sskildsen]. *An Archbishop of the Reformation: Laurentius Petri Nericius, Archbishop of Uppsala, 1531—73: A Study of His Liturgical Projects.* London: The Epworth Press; Minneapolis, Minn.: Augsburg Publishing House, 1959.

Zorn, C[arl] M[anthey]. *Allerlei aus Gottes Garten.* Zwickau, Saxony: Johannes Hermann, n. d.

Zur Geschichte und Ordnung der Konfirmation in den lutherischen Kirchen, ed. Kurt Frör. Munich: Claudius Verlag, 1962.

PERIODICALS

A., N. "To Our Newly Confirmed Readers," *Lutheran Standard,* LXXXVIII (March 28, 1931), 2.

——. "The Proper Age for Confirmation," ibid., XC (May 13, 1933), 3, 4.

Achelis, E[rnst] Chr[istian]. "Bemerkungen zu dem Waldeckschen Konfirmations-

in the Lutheran Church

bekenntnis aus dem Jahre 1529," *Neue Kirchliche Zeitschrift*, XI (1900), 423—427.

"After Confirmation," *Lutheran Standard*, LXII (April 9, 1904), 232, 233.

Anderson, O. B. "Three Approaches to the Post-Confirmation Problem," *American Lutheran*, XXV (January 1942), 18, 19.

Arndt, W[illiam Frederick]. Review of Harold L. Yochum, *Confirmation Sermons* (Columbus, Ohio: The Lutheran Book Concern [1933]), *Concordia Theological Monthly*, V (Aug. 1934), 653.

B. "The Examination of Catechumens," *Lutheran Standard*, LXII (Nov. 5, 1904), 708.

B., S. "Catechization," *Lutheran Standard*, XXXI (July 12, 1873), 187.

Banting, H. M. J. "Imposition of Hands in Confirmation: A Medieval Problem," *The Journal of Ecclesiastical History*, II (Oct. 1956), 147—159.

"Baptism and Confirmation," *The Lutheran and Missionary*, XIV (April 8, 1875), 102.

Belfour, Edmund. "The Rite of Confirmation in the Jewish and in the Christian Church," *Lutheran Church Review*, XVIII (1899), 231—237.

B[ente], Fri[edrich]. "Eine katechetische Besprechung des Konfirmationsgelübdes mit der Konfirmandenklasse," *Magazin für Ev.-luth. Homiletik*, XXXVII (Feb. 1913), 86—95.

Bergstresser, P. "Catechisation and Confirmation in the Lutheran Church," *Lutheran Quarterly*, XXI (Oct. 1891), 515—524.

"Bericht über den Gegenwärtigen Bestand unserer in den letzten fünf Jahren Konfirmierten," *Der Lutheraner*, LXXXVII (June 2, 1931), 182.

"Bf." "Zur Konfirmation," *Der Lutheraner*, LXXVII (March 8, 1921), 69, 70.

Braaten, Carl E. "Communion before Confirmation?" *Dialog*, I (Summer 1962), 61, 62.

Brenner, Leo. "Geschichte und Bedeutung der Confirmation," *Lehre und Wehre*, LI (Feb.—March 1905), 64—76, 124—135.

Brokering, Herbert. "Rethinking Confirmation," *The Lutheran Standard*, I (Sept. 12, 1961), 11, 12.

Brown, Edgar S. "Children at Communion," *The Lutheran*, XLIV (Feb. 14, 1962), 24—26.

Brueggemann, M. "Instruction for Confirmation," *The Lutheran Witness*, XXXIV (Oct. 5, 1915), 307.

Brunner, Hans Heinrich. "Mit der Konfirmation kam der Bruch," *Evangelischer Pressedienst*, Feb. 18, 1961, pp. 11, 12. "The Catechetical Class," *The Lutheran and Missionary*, V (Jan. 18, 1866), 50. "Catechization," *Lutheran Standard*, I (Oct. 26, 1842), 2.

Christensen, J. P. "Holding Our Youth," *Lutheran Standard*, C (May 23, 1942), 3.

"Church Membership and Confirmation," *Lutheran Standard*, LXXV (March 31, 1917), 193, 194.

"Confirmation," *American Lutheran*, XXVIII (Feb. 1945), 45.

"Confirmation," *Lutheran Standard*, II (April 6, 1844), 2.

"Confirmation," *Lutheran Standard*, XXXI (April 12, 1873), 84, 85.

"Confirmation," *Lutheran Standard*, XXXII (April 4, 1874), 108, 109.

"Confirmation," *Lutheran Standard*, XXXIII (March 20, 1875), 92.

"Confirmation," *The Lutheran Witness*, XVIII (Feb. 7, 1900), 130, 131.

Confirmation

"Confirmation," *The Lutheran Witness*, XXXIV (March 23, 1915), 94.

"Confirmation a Fixed Day," *Lutheran Standard*, LXVII (April 10, 1909), 226.

"The Confirmation Vow," *Lutheran Standard*, LXXVIII (March 27, 1920), 193.

"Communion Before Confirmation," *The Lutheran*, XLIV (July 11, 1962), 14—19.

Conrad, F. W. "The Lutheran Doctrine of Baptism," *The Quarterly Review of the Evangelical Lutheran Church*, IV (Oct. 1874), 477—556.

Craemer, Friedrich Aug. "Über die sacramentale Auffassung der Confirmation," *Lehre und Wehre*, VIII (April 1862), 110—116.

Cressman, Mark S. "The Relation of Baptized Children to the Church," *Lutheran Quarterly*, XX (Jan. 1890), 45—54.

Dorn, Harold. "The Confirmation Instruction of Children, a Survey," *Concordia Theological Monthly*, XXIV (March 1953), 177—193.

"The Earnestness of Confirmation," *Lutheran Standard*, LXXII (April 4, 1914), 213, 214.

E[ckstein, Richard]. "Zur Konfirmationsnot ein Konfirmations-Chaos?" *Evangelisch-Lutherische Kirchenzeitung*, XV (Jan. 1, 1961), 5.

————. "Die Neuordnung der Konfirmation," ibid., XIV (March 15, 1960), 89—91.

————. "Schafft diese 'Konfirmation' ab!" ibid., XV (June 1, 1961), 173.

Eckstein, Richard. "Internationales Gespräch über die Konfirmation," *Evangelisch-Lutherische Kirchenzeitung*, XV (June 15, 1961), 190—193.

————. "Um die Neuordnung der Konfirmation," ibid., XIII (Feb. 15, 1959), 49—52.

"Die Einheit der Konfirmation soll bleiben: Beschlüsse der Synode der EKD," *Evangelischer Pressedienst*, Feb. 18, 1961, p. 8.

Erskine, Dr. "Catechising," *Lutheran Standard*, I (Dec. 7, 1842), 2.

F., A. "Ihr habt einen andern Geist!" Part II, *Der Lutheraner*, LXVIII (Feb. 6, 1912), 34—36.

Frenk, Erdman W. "Problems of Confirmation Instruction," *Lutheran Education*, LXXXIV (Sept. 1948), 17—25.

————. "Improving Confirmation Instruction," ibid., LXXXV (Nov. 1949), 119—129.

Frerichs, Supt. "Baptism and Confirmation in the Lutheran View," trans. N. N. April 15, 1958. Reprint; source not given.

Frör, Kurt. "Confirmation: A Lutheran World Federation Seminar," *Lutheran World*, VIII (Sept. 1961), 174—181.

————. "Konfirmation und Admission," *Evangelisch-Lutherische Kirchenzeitung*, XIII (May 1, 1959), 133—137.

————. "Neue Wege in den Konfirmationsordnungen," *Lutherische Monatshefte*, II (Dec. 1963), 594—601.

F[ürbringer], L[udwig Ernst]. "Zur kirchlichen Chronik: Die Confirmation," *Der Lutheraner*, LX (April 12, 1904), 118, 119.

————. "Zur kirchlichen Chronik: Die Konfirmation," ibid., LXIII (March 12, 1907), 86, 87.

————. "Ein Schlusswort an die Eltern unserer Confirmanden," ibid., LIV (April 19, 1898), 68.

G., E. "Catechisation," *The Lutheran and Missionary*, II (June 11, 1863), 129.

in the Lutheran Church

G[raebner], A[ugust Lawrence]. "Confirmation," *Theological Quarterly*, V (Jan. 1901), 53—58.

Graebner, A[ugust] L[awrence]. "Taufe und Confirmation," *Der Lutheraner*, LI (July 30, 1895), 127—129.

Graebner, Theodore. "Confirmation," *The Lutheran Witness*, XXXVII (March 5, 1918), 67—69.

———. "Touching a Sore Spot," ibid., XLII (Oct. 23, 1923), 339, 340.

Grewenow, Geo[rge] J. "Accent on Catechumen's Parents," *Lutheran Standard*, IC (Oct. 4, 1941), 5.

Hamsker, M. R. "Benefits and Solemnity of Confirmation," *Lutheran Quarterly*, XLI (April 1911), 208—213.

H[anser], A[dolf] T. "Der Tag der Konfirmation," *Der Lutheraner*, LXIX (March 4, 1913), 70, 71.

Harbaugh, H. "At What Age Should the Young be Confirmed?" *Evangelical Review*, XVII (July 1866), 402—417.

Hauschildt, Karl. "Abbau der Konfirmation? Darstellung und Kritik der Konfirmationsthesen von Johannes Hamel," *Evangelisch-Lutherische Kirchenzeitung*, XIII (July 15, 1959), 213—216.

———. "Die Reform der Konfirmation," *Informationsblatt*, IX (Aug. 4, 1960), 229—235.

Heinecken, Martin J. "Confirmation in Relation to The Lord's Supper," *The Lutheran Quarterly*, XV (Feb. 1963), 22—28.

Hoerr, "Confirmation," trans. J. Humberger from the German minutes of the Eastern District [Ohio Synod], June 8—14, 1887, *Lutheran Standard*, (Sept. 10, 1887, through Nov. 5, 1887), 289, 298, 305, 306, 313, 314, 338, 345, 346, 353.

Hope, Rich[ard]. "Spirituality in Teaching the Catechism," *American Lutheran*, IV (Oct. 1921), 8, 9.

Hübener, P. "Soll die Konfirmation auf ein späteres Alter verschoben werden?" *Der Lutheraner*, CXIV (April 1, 1958), 107, 108.

Ilse, Herman. "Confirmation Hymn," *The Lutheran Witness*, LXIV (March 13, 1945), 81.

"Instruction of Children and Confirmation," *The Evangelical Lutheran Intelligencer*, IV (July 1829), 145—147.

"Instruction of Children, and Confirmation," *The Lutheran Magazine*, III (July 1829), 131—133.

Jacobi, Gerhard. "Veränderung der Konfirmation?", *Informationsblatt*, IX (Aug. 4, 1960), 236, 237.

Jensson, J. C. "The Problem of Holding the Young, and How the United Norwegian Lutheran Church Is Solving It," *The Lutheran Church Review*, 17 (July 1897), 412.

Kaye, Bishop. "History of the Rite of Confirmation," *Lutheran Standard*, V (Aug. 4, 1847), 2.

"Keep Your Confirmation Vow," *Lutheran Standard*, LX (Jan. 18 and 25, 1902), 36, 37, 50—52.

Kenny, J. P., S. J. "The Age for Confirmation," *Worship*, XXXV (Dec. 1960), 4—15.

Knappe, J. H. "Training and Holding the Newly Confirmed," *The Lutheran Outlook*, XV (March 1950), 70—75.

Confirmation

Koehneke, M[artin] L. "We Aim to Please the Lord," *The Lutheran Witness,* LXXI (Sept. 2, 1952), 4.

"Konfirmation und Jugendweihe," *Evangelisch-Lutherische Kirchenzeitung,* XIII (Sept. 1, 1959), 284, 285.

"Zur Konfirmationsfrage: Eine Stellungnahme des Theologischen Ausschusses der Vereinigten Kirche zur gegenwärtigen Diskussion," *Nachrichten der Evangelisch-Lutherischen Kirche in Bayern,* XIII (Nov. 1958), 345.

Krenz, Otton. "Warnung vor unbedachter Frühkommunion," *Evangelisch-Lutherische Kirchenzeitung,* XIII (April 15, 1959), 126, 127.

Kuegele, F[riedrich]. "Confirmation-Address," *The Lutheran Witness,* IX (Jan. 7, 1891), 113, 114.

――――. "Your Confirmation Vow: An Open Letter," ibid., XIV (July 7, 1895, through March 21, 1896), 19, 26, 82, 89, 98, 105, 114, 122, 138, 154, 155.

――――. "Confirmation Sermon," ibid., XVI (June 7 and 21, 1897), 3, 10, 11.

Laubscher, Friedrich. "Aus der Sprechstunde des Pfarrers: 'Mein Sohn kommt aus der Schule . . .' Ein Gespräch mit einem Konfirmandenvater," *Evangelischer Pressedienst,* Feb. 18, 1961, pp. 13, 14.

Leyburn, John. "The Development and Direction of Lay Work," *Lutheran Quarterly,* XI (Oct. 1881), 463—465.

Lippold, Martin. "Die Konfirmationsfrage in den östlichen Gliedkirchen der EKD: Diskussion und Ergebnisse," *Evangelisch-Lutherische Kirchenzeitung,* XIV (Sept. 15, 1960), 273—275.

Lochner, Friedrich. "Kurze Form und Weise des Gebets für den Konfirmanden-Unterricht," *Liturgische Monatschrift,* 2d ser. (Dec. 1885), 137—139.

――――. "[Gebete] Für die Konfirmanden," ibid. (Feb. 1886), 153, 154.

[Löscher, Valentin Ernst]. "Allerhand neue Bücher," *Unschuldige Nachrichten von Alten und Neuen Theologischen Sachen,* IV (1713), 694, 695.

"A Lutheran Boy Takes His Vows," *Parade,* Dec. 4, 1955, pp. 8—10, 12, 13.

Luykx, Boniface. "Theology of Confirmation," *Theology Digest,* XI (Summer 1963), 79—84. Digest of original in *Paroisse et Liturgie,* XXXIV (1957), 180 to 201, 263—278.

Manschreck, Clyde L. "The Role of Melanchthon in the Adiaphora Controversy," *Archiv für Reformationsgeschichte,* XLVIII (1957), 165—181.

Mauder, Albert. "Zur Frage der Konfirmation in der Evang.-Lutherischen Kirche," *Evangelisch-Lutherische Kirchenzeitung,* XII (Nov. 15, 1958), 359—363.

Maurer, Wilhelm. "Das Ringen um evangelische Kirchenzucht und Einzelbeichte," *Evangelisch-Lutherische Kirchenzeitung,* VII (Feb. 15, 1953), 49—53.

M[ayer], E[mmanuel] A. "Zum Confirmationstag," *Der Lutheraner,* LX (March 15, 1904), 81, 82.

Mehnert, Gottfried. "Drei Aspekte der Konfirmationskrise," *Informationsblatt,* IX (Aug. 4, 1960), 241—244.

Menter, Norman. "The Enlistment of After-Confirmation Youth," *Lutheran Standard,* XC (May 27, 1933), 12, 13.

Mervyn, Bishop of Worchester. "Concerning Confirmation," *Theology,* LXI (Aug. 1958), 311, 312.

Morris, [John Gottlieb]. "Catechization and Luther's Catechism," *Lutheran Standard,* XXVI (Jan. 1, 1866), 8.

Morrison, Chester. "A Boy Confirms His Faith," *Look,* XXI (March 19, 1957), 91—96, 98.

in the Lutheran Church

Mosley, J. Brooke, William Fisher Lewis, and Edward Randolph Welles. "A Symposium," *The Living Church,* CXLII (May 21, 1961), 12, 13, 20.

Mueller, Arnold C. "Confirmation of the Mentally Retarded," adopted by the Board of Parish Education, May 7, 1963, *The Lutheran Witness,* LXXXII (June 25, 1963), 302.

Nagel, William. "Die pommersche Confirmatio und ihre Beseitigung im 19. Jahrhundert," *Theologische Literaturzeitung,* LXXXV (Dec. 1960), 905—910.

"Neue Drucksachen: 'Das feierliche Gelübde gottseliger Confirmation am Tage ihrer Confirmation,'" *Der Lutheraner,* XLV (Feb. 26, 1889), 40.

"Zur Neuordnung der Konfirmation: Stellungnahme des Theologischen Ausschusses der VELKD zu Einzelfragen der gegenwärtigen Diskussion über die Neuordnung der Konfirmation," *Evangelisch-Lutherische Kirchenzeitung,* XV (April 15, 1961), 127.

"Die 'neuralgischen Punkte' der Konfirmationspraxis," *Evangelische Welt,* XIII (Nov. 1, 1959), 642, 643.

Niebergall, Alfred. "Das Unbehagen an der Konfirmation," *Evangelische Welt,* XII (Nov. 16, 1958), 657—661.

Nordsieck, W[illiam H.]. "Confirmation Instruction," *Lutheran School Journal,* LXXV (Sept. 1939), 8—12.

Nyman, Helge. "Zur Konfirmationsfrage," *Theologische Literaturzeitung,* LXXXIII (March 1958), 175—178.

"The Object of Catechizing," *Lutheran Standard,* XXVII (April 1, 1867), 60, 61.

P., C. W. "The Public Examination of Catechumens," *Lutheran Standard,* LXIV (May 19, 1906), 306, 307.

Petersen, H. W. "The Pastor's Personal Relationship with His Confirmed Youth," *American Lutheran,* XIX (June 1936), 6—8.

Pf[otenhauer], A. "Ein freundliches Wort an die lieben Eltern unserer diesjährigen Confirmanden," *Der Lutheraner,* LVIII (Dec. 9, 1902), 388, 389.

Pf[otenhauer], F[riedrich]. "Unsere diesjährigen Konfirmanden," *Der Lutheraner,* LXXVII (March 8, 1921), 70.

"Proceedings of the Second District Conference of the Synod of Pennsylvania, assembled in Centreville, Northampton Co., Pa., in Christ's Church . . ." *The Lutheran and Missionary,* I (Nov. 21, 1861), 15.

"Questions and Answers," *The Lutheran Companion,* CVII (May 17, 1961), 15.

"Readers Comments: Letters to *Layman* Offer Clarification," *The Lutheran Layman,* June 1, 1955, p. 5.

Reisser, Horst. "Mein Gedenkspruch," *Evangelischer Pressedienst,* Feb. 18, 1961, pp. 10, 11.

"Report from Detroit," *The Lutheran,* XLIV (July 11, 1962), 5—8.

Repp, Arthur C[hristian]. "Manual for the Confirmation Instruction of Children," *Concordia Theological Monthly,* XXII (Aug. 1951), 600—607.

———. "Proposed Rite of Confirmation for Children," special 11-page clergy insert in *Advance,* IX (April 1962).

———. "The Theological Implications of Confirmation," *Concordia Theological Monthly,* XXXI (March-April 1960), 165—173, 227—235.

Ringstrom, Martin T. "The Significance of the Confirmation Vows," *Augustana Quarterly,* XVII (Jan. 1938), 59—66.

Rohr, A. F. "Confirmation," *Lutheran Standard,* XLVII (Dec. 28, 1889), 409, 410.

Confirmation

Runte, Heinrich. "Vom rechten Konfirmandenalter," *Informationsblatt*, IX (Aug. 4, 1960), 237—240.

Rupprecht, Walter. "Neuordnung der Konfirmation," *Evangelisch-Lutherische Kirchenzeitung*, XIV (July 15, 1960), 209—212.

S., C. F. "Confirmation," *The Lutheran Observer*, I (May 1 and 15, 1852), 289, 290, 307, 308.

S., G. H. "Care of the Confirmed," *Lutheran Standard*, XLIII (April 4, 1885), 108.

S., W. W. "You're in Christ's Army Now," *Lutheran Standard*, XCIX (May 17, 1941), 12, 13.

Schaefer, C. A. "Keep Your Confirmation Vow," *Lutheran Standard*, LX (Jan. 18 and 25, 1902), 36, 37, 50—52.

Schanze, Wolfgang. "Der dritte Band der Lutherischen Agende," *Evangelisch-Lutherische Kirchenzeitung*, XV (June 1, 1961), 174—177.

Schlerf, J. "Das Kirchenlied in der Konfirmationsfeier," *Lehre und Wehre*, LV (March 1909), 116—119.

Schmidt, Martin. "Konfirmation im Lichte von Schrift, Bekenntnis und Geschichte der Kirche," *Evangelisch-Lutherische Kirchenzeitung*, XIII (April 15, 1959), 124—126.

Schmucker, B. M. "The Rite of Confirmation in the Lutheran Church," *The Lutheran Church Review*, II (April and July 1883), 89—103; 230—253.

Schneider, Ino. "Auszug aus Kollege [B. F.] Zismers Katechese über die Konfirmation," *Evangelisch-Lutherisches Schulblatt*, XXVI (July 1891), 201—204.

Schultze, Victor. "Ein unbekanntes lutherisches Konfirmationsbekenntnis aus dem Jahre 1529," *Neue Kirchliche Zeitschrift*, XI (1900), 232—242.

————. "Ein Nachwort zur waldeckischen Konfirmationsordnung vom Jahre 1529," *Neue Kirchliche Zeitschrift*, XI (1900), 586—589.

Seidel, W. C. "Faithful Catechisation and Its Results," *Lutheran Quarterly*, XLI (July 1911), 424—436.

Seilhamer, Frank H. "The New Measure Movement Among Lutherans," *The Lutheran Quarterly*, XII (May 1960), 121—143.

Senter, J. M. "Catechisation," *Lutheran Standard*, LV (July 17, 24, and 31, 1897), 226, 233, 241.

Sheneman, Lloyd E. "Instruction and Admission to Communion in Our Time," *The Lutheran Quarterly*, XV (Nov. 1963), 291—307.

S[ieck], H[enry]. "Early Confirmations," *The Lutheran Witness*, XIV (Jan. 21, 1896), 121, 122.

Simon, W[ilhelm]. " 'Mein Schöpfer, steh mir bei!' " *Evangelisch-Lutherisches Schulblatt*, XL (May 1905), 129—136.

"The Small Catechism by Martin Luther: A New Translation: A Handbook of Basic Christian Instruction for the Family and the Congregation," *Interaction*, III (Jan. 1963), 10—14.

Sodergren, Carl W. "Christian Nurture Continuous . . . Confirmation at What Age?" *The Lutheran Companion*, CV (April 29, 1959), 8.

S[ommer, Martin]. "Why Children Should Take Catechetical Instruction and Be Confirmed," *The Lutheran Witness*, XXXIV (Sept. 7, 1915) 276, 277.

————. "Confirmation," *ibid.*, LIV (April 9, 1935), 129, 130.

Stählin, Wilhelm. "Religionsunterricht in der Diaspora," *Evangelisch-Lutherische Kirchenzeitung*, XI (June 15, 1957), 184—187.

in the Lutheran Church

Steege, Herm[an] A. "The Preparation of Confirmands, or the Instruction of Catechumens," *Concordia Theological Monthly,* III (May 1932), 351—368.

Strasen, Martin. "Techniques of the Annual Roll Call," *American Lutheran,* XXIII (March 1940), 22, 23.

Streng, William D. "The Age for First Communion," *The Lutheran Quarterly,* X (Aug. 1958), 255—262.

Stürmer, Karl. "Nur ein Festessen? Von Mannbarkeit, Jugendweihe und Konfirmation," *Evangelischer Pressedienst,* Feb. 18, 1961, pp. 9, 10.

Stump, A[dam]. "Newly Confirmed Church Members," *Lutheran Quarterly,* XV (April 1885), 232—243.

Stump, Joseph. "A Brief History of Catechization," *Lutheran Church Review,* XXI (Jan. 1902), 66—75.

T., C. B. "On the Rite of Confirmation," *The Lutheran Observer,* I (Jan. 2, 1832), 163—165.

Thiel, Wulf. "Der Katechumenat der Kirche," *Evangelisch-Lutherische Kirchenzeitung,* V (Aug. 31, 1951), 245—247.

"Timely and Sensible," *The Lutheran and Missionary,* I (Nov. 21, 1861), 13.

Thomas, Wilhelm. "Die Grundlage der Konfirmation ist die Taufe!" *Evangelisch-Lutherische Kirchenzeitung,* XIII (March 15, 1959), 91—93.

"Ueber das Alter unserer Kinder bei ihrer Confirmation," *Der Lutheraner,* XXXIII (Jan. 1, 1877), 3—5.

"Verständnis und Ordnung der Konfirmation: Stellungnahme des Theologischen Ausschusses der Vereinigten Evangelisch-Lutherischen Kirche Deutschlands zur gegenwärtigen Diskussion über die Konfirmationsfrage. Vom 16. Oktober 1958," *Evangelisch-Lutherische Kirchenzeitung,* XIII (Feb. 15, 1959), 56.

Vogel, Arthur A. "Note on the Gifts in Baptism and Confirmation," *Anglican Theological Review,* XXXVIII (Oct. 1956), 276—285.

Von Schenk, Berthold. "Confirmation and First Communion," *Una Sancta,* XIV (Pentecost 1957), 3—7.

Waech, O[swald] A. "Advancing in Evangelism: Confirmation," *Advance,* II (March 1955), 22, 23.

Wedel, Alton F. "Basic Fallacies about Confirmation," *The Lutheran Witness,* LXXX (March 21, 1961), 127.

Weidmann, Carl. "Ordained for Christian Action, *Una Sancta,* X (SS. Philip and James 1951), 2—10.

Weissgerber, Hans H. "Zur Geschichte der Konfirmation im 16. Jahrhundert," *Evangelisch-Lutherische Kirchenzeitung,* IX (May 15, 1955), 157—160.

"What Does Confirmation Mean to Us?" *Lutheran Standard,* LXXI (March 15, 1913), 161.

"From a Wider Field," *The Northwestern Lutheran,* XLIV (Feb. 17, 1957), 53.

Wiencke, Gustav K. "Confirmation in Historical Perspective," *The Lutheran Quarterly,* VII (May 1955), 99—113.

———. "Crisis in Confirmation," *The Lutheran,* XLIII (Sept. 13, 1961), 11—15.

Abbetmeyer, C. A.
111 fn., 122 fn.
Absolution 19—21, 35,
52, 168
Achelis, Ernst C. 20 fn.,
30 fn., 31 fn.,
40 fn., 43 fn.,
65 fn., 69 fn.,
70 fn., 87, 92,
93 fn.
Adam, Johann 31 fn.
Aepinus, Johann 49, 50
Africa 146 fn.
Age for confirmation 46
to 49, 54, 56, 57,
75, 82, 87, 88, 91,
92, 97, 99, 125 to
128, 140—142,
144, 147—149,
165, 170, 171,
173, 177, 182 to
192, 204—206
Agenda; see also Church
Orders
Finland 84
Germany
Hesse 73
Mansfeld 24 fn.,
28 fn., 58 fn.
Pomerania 51—54
Schleswig-Holstein
79, 80
United Evangelical
Lutheran Church
of Germany 145
Württemberg 79,
101
Sweden 83, 84
United States
Augustana Evangel-
ical Lutheran

Church 109,
110 fn., 111 fn.,
112, 114 fn.,
118 fn., 120 fn.,
123 fn.
Buffalo Synod
111 fn., 117 fn.,
119 fn., 121 fn.,
122, 123 fn.,
179 fn.
English Evangelical
Lutheran Church
in New York
103 fn.
English Synod of
Missouri 111 fn.,
120, 123 fn.,
179 fn.
Evangelical Lu-
theran Church
108, 111, 114 fn.,
118 fn., 120 fn.,
123 fn.
General Council
109, 110 fn.,
114 fn., 117 fn.,
118 fn., 121 fn.,
123
General Synod
103 fn., 104 fn.,
109, 114 fn.,
116 fn., 117,
121 fn., 125 fn.,
131 fn.
Iowa Synod 38 fn.,
118, 123 fn.,
126 fn., 127 fn.,
129 fn., 137 fn.,
175 fn.
Löhe 38 fn., 108,
110, 114 fn., 115,

116, 118 fn., 119,
123, 125, 126,
128, 129, 137 fn.,
175 fn.,
Lutheran Free
Church 110 fn.,
111, 114 fn.,
118 fn., 120 fn.,
123 fn.
Missouri Synod 108,
109, 110 fn., 111,
114, 116, 118 fn.,
120, 121 fn.,
123 fn., 124, 176,
179 fn., 185
National Lutheran
Council 108, 111,
112 fn., 114 fn.
New York Minis-
terium (Synod)
103 fn., 104 fn.,
117
Norwegian Evangel-
ical Lutheran
Synod 108, 111,
114, 118 fn.,
120 fn., 123 fn.,
136
Ohio Synod 105,
108, 109 fn., 110,
111 fn., 114 fn.,
116, 117 fn., 118,
119, 120 fn.,
121 fn., 122 fn.,
123 fn., 130, 131,
136, 179 fn.,
180 fn.
Pennsylvania Minis-
terium 101—104,
106 fn., 107,
109 fn., 110 fn.,

114, 116, 117,
119, 121 fn., 122,
125, 128, 130,
174 fn.
Synodical Confer-
ence 5, 108 fn.,
109 fn., 110 fn.,
111, 112 fn., 116,
120, 121 fn.,
123 fn., 176 fn.
Tennessee Synod
106, 109 fn.,
110 fn., 118 fn.,
119, 124, 180 fn.
United Lutheran
Church 109,
110 fn., 111 fn.,
117, 121 fn.,
123 fn., 180 fn.
United Norwegian
Lutheran Church
108, 111, 123 fn.
United Synod of the
South 109 fn.,
112 fn., 117 fn.,
120, 174 fn.,
175 fn.
Wisconsin Synod
109, 110 fn., 114,
116, 118 fn., 120,
121 fn., 123 fn.,
176
Alexander of Hales 14
Allegheny Synod 105
American Evangelical
Lutheran Church
185 fn.
American Lutheran
Church 132,
149 fn., 184 fn.
"American Lutheranism"
97, 105
"American religion" 147
Anabaptists 29—31, 34,
36, 45 fn.
Anderson, O. B. 111 fn.
Andreae, Jacob 41
Andreae, J. Val. 67
Andrén, Carl-Gustav
20 fn., 27 fn.,
46 fn.
Anrich, Gustav 30 fn.
Ansbach 24; *see also*
Church Orders

Apology of the Augsburg
Confession 16,
38 fn.
Arminianism 96
Arndt, Joh. 65
Arnkiel, Trogillus 71, 72
Aquinas, Thomas 14,
39 fn.
Asia 146 fn.
Atkinson, James 16 fn.
170 fn.
Augsburg 28
Augsburg Confession 16,
172
Augsburg Interim 47, 48
Augustana Lutheran
Church 132, 151,
185 fn.; *see also*
Agenda
Augustine, St. 40
Austria; *see* Church
Orders

Bachmann, Joh. F. 25 fn.,
43 fn., 48 fn.,
51 fn., 74 fn.,
82 fn.
Backenschlag 52, 54, 55
Baden 191 fn.
Balthassar, Aug. 54
Balthassar, Jac. H. 23 fn.,
24 fn., 51 fn.,
52 fn., 59 fn.
Ban, church 30, 33
Baptism 18—21, 24, 32,
36, 37, 39, 40,
42—44, 47, 48,
50, 52—56, 67,
69, 72, 77, 78, 81,
85, 86, 89,
90—92, 97,
107—109, 112,
115—117, 125,
127 fn., 140, 145,
146, 156—169,
172, 175—178,
180, 183, 192,
199, 206, 211,
212, 214—216,
226
Early church 13
Infant 14, 29, 67, 88,
143, 156, 157,

161, 162, 166,
168, 205
Postbaptismal prayer
7, 13
Roman Catholic
14—16
Baptismal covenant
104 fn., 107—109,
111, 112, 118,
146, 156—160,
165, 167, 171,
176, 179 fn.
remembering 42, 58,
68, 70, 75, 107,
160, 178
renewing 42, 58,
68—70, 72, 74,
75, 77, 86, 93, 97,
98, 102, 103,
104 fn., 108, 109,
143, 159, 160,
179, 183, 215,
223
Barth, Karl 143
Bastian, Herman 30 fn.
Bavaria 82 fn., 85
Belfour, Edmund 26 fn.,
57 fn., 134
Bells 81, 124
Bente, Fr. 117 fn.
Benze, Chas. T. 47 fn.
Bergstresser, P. 107 fn.,
117 fn.
Berlin 70, 71
Bernheim, G. D. 100 fn.
Blegen, Theo. C. 101 fn.
Blessing of holy water 38
Blessings
(Segenswünsche)
71, 80, 119, 146
Blow on the cheek; *see*
Backenschlag
Boehm, J. 100
Bohemian Brethren 30,
63
Bonaventura 14
Book of Concord 134;
see also Lutheran
Confessions
Bradfordt press, W.
100 fn.
Brandenburg 49 fn.; *see
also* Church
Orders

Braunschweig-Lüneburg 62; *see also* Church Orders
Bremen-Verden 79
Brentz, Johann 22, 23 fn., 24, 41
Bretall, Robert 88 fn.
Bretscher, Paul G. 189 fn.
Bretschneider, Karl G. 77, 78
Bridges, Matthew 213, 214
Brunnholtz, Peter 100, 134
Bucer, Martin 18, 20, 29—32, 34—39, 42, 43 fn., 45 fn., 46, 47, 69, 71, 90, 119, 120, 164
Buesching, A. F. 83
Bugenhagen, Joh. 17, 18, 22, 26, 45, 47, 48, 50, 51
Buytaert, Eligius 14 fn.

Calvin, John 57 fn.
Calvinism 96, 130
Canada 148, 150, 181, 229
Canon law, Roman 56
Caspari, H. 134
Caspari, Walter 20 fn., 23 fn., 30 fn., 31 fn., 41 fn., 43 fn., 45 fn., 49 fn., 50 fn., 59 fn., 64 fn., 66 fn., 73 fn., 77 fn., 79 fn., 80
Cassel 34; *see also* Church Orders
Catechetical examination 22, 24—26, 28, 33—35, 41, 45, 48, 51, 62, 63, 70, 71, 74, 79, 91, 98, 101—103, 104 fn., 120—122, 133, 136, 142, 145, 162, 173, 175,

211, 212; *see also* Confession of faith
marriage 24 fn.
Catechetical instruction 18, 19, 21—27, 32, 35, 47, 48, 51, 53—55, 58, 62, 64—68, 71, 90, 91, 103 fn., 105, 107, 121, 126, 149—152, 162, 166, 167, 177, 179, 180, 182, 184, 187—189, 191, 193, 197, 198; *see also* Confirmation instruction
Catechetical sermons 20, 23, 25, 56, 64, 65; *see also* Sermons
Catechizing schools 132 fn.
Catechism 23, 24, 31 fn., 38 fn., 56, 63, 64, 66, 67, 72, 74, 83, 95 fn., 100, 101, 103, 105, 127 fn., 131, 133—136, 140, 150—152; *see also* Small Catechism
Catechismus; see Catechetical instruction
Celle Conclave 48, 49
Chemnitz, Martin 28, 41—43, 70
Chrism, 15, 27, 39 fn., 52, 54, 55
Chrysostom, John 16 fn.
Church discipline 29—38, 43, 47, 58, 73, 90, 120, 164
Church membership 19, 31—33, 37, 43, 44, 77, 78, 85, 88, 89, 91, 92, 102, 115—118, 127, 128, 141, 142, 145, 147,

160—162, 170, 174, 179, 180 fn., 215, 223
Church Orders 36, 40 fn., 59, 65 fn., 182; *see also* Agenda
Austria 34
Lower Austria 57
Denmark 26
Germany
Allstedt 56
Ansbach 56
Brandenburg 17, 18, 41, 45, 46, 50, 56 fn.
Brandenburg-Ansbach-Kulmbach 56 fn., 57
Brandenburg-Nürnberg 22 fn., 24 fn., 45
Braunschweig 24 fn., 41 fn., 57, 59
Braunschweig-Lüneburg; *see* Braunschweig-Wolfenbüttel
Braunschweig-Wolfenbüttel 41, 58 fn.
Bremen 22 fn.
Calenberg; *see* Braunschweig-Wolfenbüttel
Calenberg-Göttingen; *see* Braunschweig
Cassel 33, 35—37, 40, 41
Cologne Reformation 40 fn., 59
Goslar 22
Hesse 22 fn., 28, 34, 35, 39, 40, 45 fn., 70, 90
Hohenlohe 56
Hoya 59
Lauenburg 24 fn., 28 fn., 56 fn., 58 fn.

Liegnitz 24 fn.,
25 fn., 45, 46,
56 fn.
Lüneburg 75
Pfalz-Neuburg
25 fn.
Pomerania 28 fn.,
36, 50—52
Ratzeburg 61, 62
Reussischen
Herrschaften
Burggräfliche
25 fn., 27 fn.
Saxony 23 fn.,
24 fn., 25, 26,
56 fn., 58 fn.
Saxon Generalartikel
25 fn.
Schleswig-Holstein
75
Schwäbisch-Hall
25 fn., 231
Stralsund 52
Strassburg 24 fn.,
25 fn.
Waldeck 35, 36,
40 fn., 43, 45 fn.,
46
Wittenberg 23 fn.
Wittenberg
Reformation 17,
18, 47, 56 fn.,
58 fn.
Wittenberger
Consistorial-
ordnung 22 fn.
Württemberg 23 fn.,
24 fn., 56 fn.
Ziegenhain 31—34,
37
Russia
Mitau 81, 84
Sweden 27, 46, 57
Church visitations 59, 62
Civic education 81
Cleveland 107 fn.
Coiner, Harry G. 6
Communism 144
Concordia Seminary
Library (St. Louis)
100 fn.
Confirmation
Anglican 20
Early church 13

Eastern churches 14
Greek Orthodox 13
Lutheran
adult 17, 43 fn., 99
catechetical type
21—28, 50, 57,
67, 74, 78
compulsory 32 fn.,
81—85, 92, 93,
96
hierarchical type 21,
28—37, 69, 89
opposition to
21—23, 31 fn.,
41, 44, 46, 50,
73—75,
104—106, 139,
143—145, 175
pietistic type 21,
69—84
private 28, 61, 62,
71, 73, 173
rationalistic type 21,
76—84
reform proposals
88—93,
139—145, 149,
176, 177,
181—227
sacramental type 21,
29, 37—44, 51,
52, 55, 69, 77, 90,
106, 179
traditional type 21,
28 fn., 44—56,
149, 176, 177
Roman Catholic
13—16, 20, 21,
26—28, 37, 39,
41, 44, 46—50,
54, 55, 72
Confirmation certificates
116 fn., 123, 223,
224
Confirmation clothes
124; *see also*
Confirmation
robes
Confirmation instruction
9, 64, 70, 74, 76,
85, 92, 97,
100—103, 126,
129—132, 140,
141, 144, 145,

148, 163, 166,
177, 191, 199,
205, 206; *see also*
Catechetical
instruction
confirmation
instruction, post-
140, 165, 178,
184, 190, 193,
195, 196, 199,
205, 206—210
Confirmation robes 226,
227
Confirmation service
211—227; *see
also* Confirmation
rite
Confirmation stoles 226,
227
Confirmation workshops
3, 4, 146, 147 fn.,
148 fn., 153,
184 fn., 185 fn.,
189 fn.
Confirmor 136, 137, 162,
177, 178
Confession, private
19—21, 24, 35,
46, 49, 52, 173
Confession of faith 22,
24, 27, 32, 36, 42,
45, 47, 48, 58, 70,
72, 79, 87, 89,
91—93, 103,
112—114,
120—122, 142,
145, 146,
161—163, 176,
178, 179, 182,
212, 213, 215; *see
also* Catechetical
examination
Confessor's fee 73
Conversion 67—71, 76,
97, 102—104,
107, 121, 170
Counter-Reformation 64
Cruciger, Caspar 47, 48
Crypto-Calvinistic
Controversy 25

Deacons 73
Deism 95

Deinzer, Joh. 38 fn.,
137 fn.
Denmark 23 fn., 26, 57,
74, 83, 133,
146 fn.; *see also*
Church Orders
Diehl, Wilhelm 28 fn.,
31 fn., 33 fn.,
34 fn., 38, 39,
45 fn., 50 fn.,
59 fn., 62, 70 fn.,
71 fn., 73 fn.,
76 fn.
Dietrich, Conrad 66,
134, 135
Dietrich, Veit 16
Doberstein, John W. 152
Doerne, Martin 22 fn.,
28 fn., 37 fn.,
38 fn., 45 fn.,
69 fn., 72 fn.,
84, 85 fn., 87 fn.,
90 fn., 140—142,
183 fn., 190 fn.
Dresden 28, 70
Duus, Olaus F. 101 fn.

East Germany 144
Ecclesiastical Estate 63
Eckstein, Richard 145 fn.
Eels, Hastings 29 fn.
Eielsen, Ellin 133
Eisenschmid, G. B. 78 fn.
Elizabeth Friderica
Sophie von
Bayreuth 64
English Evangelical
Lutheran Synod
of Missouri
213 fn.; *see also*
Agenda
Englishmen 99, 100
Episcopalians 104 fn.,
106
Erasmus, Desiderius 20,
32, 35, 42
Ericis, Ericus 63
Erlangen School 89—91,
168
Ernsberger, C. S. 105 fn.
Ernst, August 31 fn.
Erskine, Dr. 105 fn.
Eugene IV 15

Europe 13—93,
139—146,
181—184
Evangelical Church in
Germany 146
Examination; *see*
Catechetical
examination

Fälber, Leonard 30 fn.
Fahlenius, Jonas 75
Falckner, Justus 100 fn.
Falckner Swamp, Pa.
99 fn.
Falkenstein 61 fn.
Faustus of Reji 14 fn.
Fehn, Helge 216 fn.
Finland 63, 64, 74, 75,
84, 93, 146; *see
also* Agenda
First Communion; *see
also* Lord's
Supper
Early Church 13
Lutheran 21, 24,
25 fn., 26, 27, 32,
35, 36, 42, 44, 46,
49, 51—58, 61,
63, 64, 67, 73 to
75, 88, 90—92,
98, 106, 113, 120,
121, 125, 126,
129—131, 136,
142—144, 146,
147, 149, 162,
163, 167, 170,
172—174, 178,
180, 183, 184,
187—189, 191,
192, 213, 226
Roman Catholic 15 fn.
Francke, Aug. H. 72
Frankenmuth, Mich,
110 fn., 122
Frankentrost, Mich.
110 fn.
Frankfort on the Main
28, 69
Franklin, Benjamin 100
Frederich August II 64
Freistadt, Wis. 127
French Invasion 62
Friedburg 61 fn.

Frör, Kurt 14 fn., 143 fn.,
146 fn., 147 fn.,
216 fn.
Flacius, Matthias 41, 49,
50, 72
Floral wreaths 81
Florence, Council of 15,
39
Flowers 124
Fürbringer, Ludwig 107,
110 fn., 126 fn.

General Council 135; *see
also* Agenda
Georg II 62
Gera 28
Gerber, Christian 73
Gerberding, G. H. 136
German law 56
German Lutheran
Churches in New
York, United
104 fn.
Germany 15—93, 98,
139—146, 183;
see also Agenda;
Church Orders
Gesenius, Justus 66—68
Getz, Arthur H. 152 fn.
Gilbert, W. Kent 151 fn.,
198 fn.
Gill, Joseph 15 fn.
Girgensohn, Herbert 152
Gnesio-Lutherans 50
Goerss, Daniel F. 111 fn.
Gotha 61 fn.
Graebner, Theo. 115,
128 fn.
Graff, Paul 25 fn., 39 fn.,
40 fn., 61 fn.,
62 fn., 64 fn.,
67 fn., 72 fn.,
74 fn., 75 fn.,
76 fn., 77 fn., 78,
79 fn., 80 fn.,
81 fn., 82 fn.,
84 fn.
Gratian, Decretals of
14 fn.
Greiffenhagen Synod 52,
53
Greifswalder Ministerium
54

Greifswald, Synod of
23 fn., 24 fn.,
51 fn., 59
Grimsby, Henry P. 150
Grossgebauer, Theophil
67—69, 159
Gruber and May 133
Gründler, Georg 143

Halle, 72, 74, 97
Hamburg 21, 28, 67, 139
Hamel, Johannes 143,
144
Hamina 84
Handclasp 80, 123, 168
179, 180 fn., 216
Handschuh, Joh. Fr. 98
Hanser, A. T. 129 fn.
Hansen, Emil 23 fn.,
24 fn., 43 fn.,
49 fn., 54 fn.,
59 fn., 61 fn.,
72 fn., 73 fn.,
82 fn., 86 fn.
Hareide, Bjarne 147 fn.
Harkey, Sarah 103 fn.
Harms, Claus 82 fn., 85,
86
Harnack, Theodosius 89
to 91
Hartwig Synod 105
Hauschildt, Karl 143,
147 fn.
Hausmann, Julia 225
Health education 82
Hefentreger, Joh. 43 fn.,
45 fn.
Heinecken, Martin J.
149 fn., 190 fn.
Helmbod, Ludwig 76
Helsinki, 147 fn.
Henkel, David 133
Hesse 21, 28, 29, 31, 32,
34, 37, 62, 63, 68,
69, 71, 73, 82; see
also Agenda;
Church Orders
Hesse-Darmstadt 62, 76
Hildeburn, Chas. R.
100 fn.
Hippolytus 13 fn.
Hofgeismar 146 fn.
Höfling, Joh. W. F.

23 fn., 49 fn., 89,
116, 177
Hoh, Philip 150, 151
Home; see Parent(s)
Hooper, Nebr. 122 fn.
Horine, John W. 136
Hugo of St. Victor 14
Hunnius, Aegidius 65
Hymn(s) 49, 75, 76, 80,
81, 86, 98, 123,
124, 127, 131,
213, 216, 224,
225
Hyperius, Andreas 40,
65, 66

Iceland 28 fn., 74 fn.
Instruction; see Cate-
chetical instruc-
tion; Confirmation
instruction
Iowa Synod 135; see also
Agenda
Irish 99
Irvin, Donald F. 152

Jerome, St. 41
Joachim II 17
Juusten, Paavali 63

Kaftan, Th. 136
Kansanaho, Erkki 23 fn.,
24 fn., 27 fn.,
63 fn., 64 fn.,
74 fn., 75 fn.,
84 fn., 93 fn.,
146 fn.
Karg, Georg 24, 56 fn.
Kaye, Bishop 106 fn.
Kenny, J. P. 15 fn.
Kierkegaard, Sören 87,
88
Kliefoth, Theo. 40 fn.,
57 fn., 72 fn.,
75 fn., 81 fn.,
82 fn., 179, 211,
215 fn.
Klessmann, Ernst 143
Kline, J. J. 99 fn.
Knipstro, Johann 51 fn.
Krause, L. F. E. 127
Kraushaar, Otto 110 fn.
Kreider, Harry 104 fn.
Krotel, G. F. 134

Koch, Peter 100
Koehler, Robt. T. 150 fn.
Koepchen, Paul K.
150 fn.
Krauss, E. A. Wm.
191 fn.
Kuegele, Martin F.
131 fn., 132 fn.
Kügele, Friedrich 116
Kuester 65, 71
Kunze, John C. 104 fn.
Kurtz, Benj. 103 fn.,
104 fn., 125, 131
Kurtz, Wm. 99 fn.

Lampe, G. W. H. 13 fn.
Langemack, Gregorio
51 fn.
Large Catechism 19, 157
Latvia 82, 128
Laurelius, Olaus 63
Lauterbach, Anton 33 fn.
Laying on of hands 15,
16 fn., 17 fn., 30,
32, 37—48, 50 to
52, 54, 55, 58, 61
to 63, 84, 89—92,
98, 102, 118, 119,
127 fn., 146, 179,
216, 224
Lebanon, Pa. 99 fn.
Lection 214
Leo XIII 15 fn.
Leipzig 28
Leipzig Interim 47, 48,
51
Liegnitz 44, 49 fn.; see
also Church
Orders
Lilja, Einar 63 fn.
Lindblom, Jacob A. 63,
83, 134
Lindemann, F. 135 fn.
Lindemann, J. C. W. 136
Lindow Register 56
Littell, Franklin H.
30 fn.
Loccum 146
Löhe, J. K. Wm. 38 fn.,
108, 115, 118,
121, 122, 124 to
126, 127 fn., 135,
175 fn., 191; see
also Agenda

Lord's Supper 19, 20, 22, 24, 34, 36, 40, 44 to 46, 48, 51—54, 56, 62, 66, 69, 71, 81, 87, 89, 91, 97, 104 fn., 116, 117, 125—127, 145, 148, 149 fn., 156, 167—178, 180, 182, 186, 187, 199, 202, 206, 211, 212, 216, see also First Communion
Löscher, Valentin 73, 74
Lose, Peter 30 fn.
Lowrie, Walter 88 fn.
Lübeck 28
Lührs, Albert 134
Lund, Emil G. 134 fn.
Luther, Martin 23, 32, 33 fn., 45, 47, 151, 158, 159, 169, 170—172, 213
    catechetical instruction 18, 19
    confirmation 16—18, 20, 22
    Roman confirmation 15—17
    writings 13, 15 fn., 16, 17 fn., 18, 19, 23 fn., 38, 158, 170, 172; see also Small Catechism; Large Catechism
Lutheran Confessions 16, 25, 156; see also Apology of the Augsburg Confession; Augsburg Confession; Book of Concord
Lutheran Church in America 148, 149, 151 fn., 185 fn.
Lutheran Church — Missouri Synod, The 131, 132, 134 to 136, 149, 150, 151 fn., 213
Lutheran Hymnal, The 202, 214, 225 fn.

Lutheran World Federation 146, 147 fn., 153
Lynch, Kilian F. 14 fn.
Lyon, Council of 15 fn.

Maasel, Richard G. 4, 134 fn.
Mann, Wm. J. 134
Magdeburg-Lund 61 fn.
Mahrenholz, Christhard 36 fn., 174 fn.
Major, Georg 47, 48
Manschreck, Clyde L. 49 fn.
Marbach, Supt. 31 fn.
Marburg 40 fn.
Marburg disputation 29 fn.
Marriage 81
Marx 87
Mass 29
Matthie, Johannes 63
Maurer, Wilhlem 14 fn., 15 fn., 20 fn., 35 fn., 39 fn., 42, 43 fn., 52 fn.
Mayer, E. A. 122 fn.
Mayer, Philip F. 133
Mecklenburg 61 fn., 73
Meissen 48
Melanchthon, Philipp 16, 18, 19, 46—49, 55
Memory verses 71, 80, 123, 124
Mencel's Zirkularschreiben 25 fn.
Mertz, Georg 65 fn.
Methodism 96, 104 fn.
Metzger, George 136
Meyer, Carl S. 5
Miller, Arthur L. 4
Missouri Synod; see Lutheran Church — Missouri Synod, The
Mitau 82 fn., 84; see also Church Orders
Morris, John G. 133
Muehlenberg, Henry Melchoir 97—100
Mueller, Arnold C. 132 fn., 150 fn., 185 fn.

Nagel, William 51 fn., 53, 54, 143
Nassau 62
Natorp, B. Chr. 78
Neale, John M. 214
Neunhauser, Burkhard 15 fn.
"New measures" 104
New Germantown, N. J. 99 fn.
New Hanover, Pa. 99 fn.
New York 103 fn., 133
New York Ministerium (or Synod) 95 fn., 103—105, 133, 134; see also Agenda
Nicolai Church, Berlin 70
Nicolai, Erasmus 46
Nicum, Johann 95 fn.
Niebergall, Alfred 142, 143
Nolde, Otto F. 151, 152
Nordic Wars 63, 74
North Carolina 132 fn.
Norway 74, 83, 133, 146
Nürnberg 28
Oath; see Vow
Objectives 5, 131, 196 to 204
Oehler, V. Fr. 67 fn.
Oemler, Chr. W. 78
Ohio Synod 103 fn., 104 fn., 105; see also Agenda
Oley Mountains, Pa. 99 fn.
Onoltzbach 24
Orange, First Council of 14 fn.
Ordination of laity 89, 227
Örebro, Council of 27
Orthodoxy, Lutheran 25, 27, 61—67, 73, 134
Ostfriesland 61 fn.
Otto, Count 59

Parent(s) 18, 19, 24, 26, 32, 35, 42, 45, 49, 52, 54—56, 62, 63, 66, 91, 92,

107, 121, 130,
139, 144, 145,
163, 168, 173,
177, 178, 182,
186, 189 fn., 190,
192, 193, 195,
197, 199, 204 to
206, 212, 215
Parisius, Th. L. 77
Payne, Ernest A. 143 fn.
Pennsylvania, Historical
Society of 100 fn.
Pennsylvania Ministerium
97, 101, 103 to
105, 134; *see also*
Agenda
Peter Lombard 39 fn.
Petri, Laurentius 57
Pfaff, Ch. Matthew 72
Pfeffinger, Johann 48
Philadelphia 100
Phillip of Hesse 29, 31,
33, 34
Pietism, Lutheran 28, 61,
68—77, 82—84,
86, 93, 96—98,
101—104, 106,
107, 114, 116,
118, 123—125,
159, 160, 183,
212, 213, 223
Pikestown, Pa. 99 fn.
Pirna 33 fn.
Pistorius, Johannes 46
Plague 62
Pomerania 49 fn., 50 to
54, 56, 59, 62;
see also Agenda;
Church Orders
Pontoppidan, Eric 74,
133, 134
Prayer(s) 25 fn., 27, 32,
36—40, 42, 43 fn.,
46—49, 53, 58,
61, 63, 84, 91, 98,
102, 104 fn.,
127 fn., 146, 173,
178, 179, 211,
216, 231
Prenter, Regin 158, 159,
167, 168
Privileges 19, 77, 81, 84,
89, 91, 92, 119,
123, 137, 144,

146, 160, 168,
174, 179, 180 fn.
Pro Armenis 15
Providence, Pa. 99 fn.
Prussia *Befehl* 22 fn.
Prussian government 54
Prussian Union 54 fn.
Pseudo-Isodorian Decre-
tals 14 fn.

Quistorp, Johann 73
Quitman, Frederick H.
95 fn., 133

Racine, Wis. 148 fn.,
153, 184 fn.
Rambach, Johann J. 76,
213 fn., 214
Rationalism, "Lutheran"
44, 50, 54, 71,
76—88, 95,
104 fn., 106, 118,
123, 128, 161,
183, 223
Ratisbon Colloquy 46, 47
Ratzeburg 61, 62
Reading 66, 71
Regensburg 28
Rendtorff, Heinrich
87 fn., 92 fn.,
140 fn.
Renunciation of the devil
48, 103, 159, 164,
165, 179 fn., 215
Reu, J. Michael 23 fn.,
24 fn., 25 fn.,
31 fn., 34 fn.,
35 fn., 38 fn.,
39 fn., 40 fn.,
43 fn., 56 fn.,
65 fn., 66 fn.,
71 fn., 74 fn., 76,
100 fn., 113, 135,
136, 163
Revised Standard Version
151
Revivals; *see* "New mea-
sures"
Rhabanus Maurus 14 fn.
Richter, Aemilius L.
19 fn., 22 fn.,
23 fn., 24 fn.,
25 fn., 29 fn.,

32 fn., 34 fn.,
36 fn., 38 fn.,
40 fn., 43 fn.,
45 fn., 56 fn.
Rietschel, Georg 28 fn.,
40 fn., 45 fn.,
51 fn., 74 fn.
Rights; *see* Privileges
Ringstrom, Martin T. 112
Rite of confirmation 5,
22, 26—28, 32 to
38, 41—46, 50,
52, 53, 54, 56 to
59, 62—64, 67,
68, 74, 81, 82,
85, 89—91, 98,
101, 102, 104 fn.,
106, 108, 111,
130, 136, 141,
145, 168, 174 to
177, 211, 215 to
223
Rite of initiation 30—32
Rock County, Wis. 133
Röbbelen, Karl A. W.
122
Rohne, J. Magnus 133 fn.
Rohnert, Wilhelm 90
Roschen, Arnold 99, 100
Rostock 73
Rott, Wilhelm 31 fn.,
39 fn., 50 fn.
Rowan County, N. C.,
99, 100
Russia 28, 81, 82, 84;
see also Church
Orders

Sacraments of faith 38
Sahlfeld, Georg Fr. 84
St. Louis, Mo. 124 fn.
St. Nikolaus Church
(Strassburg) 31 fn.
Sarcerius, Erasmus 41
Saubert, Johann 67
Sauer, H. G. 135 fn.
Saxony 64, 74, 79;
see also Church
Orders
Scandinavia 26, 27, 50,
61—63, 92
Schafft, H. 140 fn.
Schaumberg-Lippe 61 fn.
Schleiermacher, Fr. 77

Schleswig-Holstein 54 fn., 59 fn., 61 fn., 72 fn., 82 fn.; *see also* Agenda; Church Orders
Schlez, J. F. 78
Schmauk, Theo. E. 99 fn.
Schnabel, George 30 fn.
Scholl, Wm. N. 105
School(s) 24, 32 fn., 55, 65 fn., 66, 81, 82, 84, 90, 96, 126, 128, 130—132, 144, 145, 147, 171, 182, 184 to 187, 189, 190, 192, 193, 196, 223, 224
Schreiner, Helmuth 139, 140
Schuette, Walter E. 109
Schuh, H. J. 136
Schultze, Victor 43 fn., 45 fn.
Schuppius, Joh. Balth. 67
Schwan, Henry 134, 135, 150
Schwarzburg 61 fn.
Schwenkfeld, Kaspar 29, 30 fn.
Sehling, Emil 18 fn., 22 fn., 23 fn., 24 fn., 25 fn., 26 fn., 27 fn., 28 fn., 41 fn., 42 fn., 45 fn., 46 fn., 47 fn., 50 fn., 51 fn., 52 fn., 53 fn., 54 fn., 56 fn., 57 fn., 58 fn., 59 fn.
Seidel, Chr. T. 79
Seiler, Georg Fr. 77, 78, 83
Serenius, Jakob 74
Sermon 53, 78, 81, 86, 97, 98, 116 fn., 122, 124, 145, 214, 215; *see also* Catechetical sermons

Service Book and Hymnal 202, 214, 225 fn.
Sextro, H. Ph. 78
Sheatsley, C. V. 103 fn.
Sheneman, Lloyd E. 149 fn., 189 fn.
Shuttleworth, F. K. 186 fn.
Small Catechism 19, 23 to 25, 34, 63, 67, 74, 100, 106, 114, 127, 130, 131, 134—136, 151, 169, 182, 201, 203
Smith, Henry P. 186 fn.
Social debut 82
Sodergren, Carl W. 148 fn.
Solinus, Gregor 18 fn.
Songs; *see* Hymns
Sonntag, Karl G. 79, 80
Spener, Philip 68—73
Sponsor(s) 18, 19, 24, 32, 34, 35, 45, 48, 54—56, 73, 81, 97, 104 fn., 107, 108, 121, 137, 145, 149, 159, 162, 164 to 166, 182, 212
Stauch, John 103 fn.
Stephani, Heinrich 80
Stettin, Synod at 51, 52
Stöcker, Adolf 87, 93
Stohlmann, J. E. 134
Strassburg 29—31, 45 fn.; *see also* Church Orders
Strassburg Debates 30 fn.
Strassburg synods 31 fn.
Streng, Wm. D. 148 fn.
Stump, Joseph 135
Sunday school 105, 130, 190, 193
Suomi Synod 185 fn.
Surrender to Christ 29, 32, 36, 37, 58, 102, 120, 164
Svebelius, Olaus 63, 83, 134
Sverdrup, H. U. 134
Sweden 26, 27, 46, 57,

63, 74, 75, 83, 84, 133, 146; *see also* Agenda; Church Orders
Synodical Conference 216; *see also* Agenda

Tanner, Jacob 150
Tennessee Synod 131 fn.; *see also* Agenda
Tertullian 13 fn.
Teuscher, Harold J. 4
Thirty Years War 61, 62, 66, 69
Time of confirmation 25, 32, 35, 52, 58, 59, 82, 99, 128, 129, 131, 174, 175, 225, 226
Trappe, Pa. 99 fn.
Treatise on the Power and Primacy of the Pope 16
Trent, Council of 15
Trinity Lutheran Church (Mequon, Wis.) 127 fn.

United Evangelical Lutheran Church of Germany 146; *see also* Agenda
United Lutheran Church 117, 132, 184 fn., 185 fn.; *see also* Agenda
United Evangelical Lutheran Church 132, 184 fn.
United States 21, 95 to 137, 146 fn., 147 to 153, 155, 171, 181, 184, 190, 229; *see also* Agenda
Urseth, Hans A. 134 fn.

Vaccination 82
Velthusen, Johann C. 78, 100 fn.
Vietor, Heinrich 40 fn.
Vilmar, Aug. F. C. 90

Vischer, Lukas 20 fn., 39 fn., 64 fn., 71 fn., 143
Von Helmuth, Mercurius 69
Von Hofmann, Johann Chr. 89, 90, 92
Von Rode, Paul 51 fn.
Von Schenk, Berthold 148 fn., 156 fn.
Von Wolff, Christian Freiherr 83 fn.
Von Zezschwitz, Carl A. 49 fn., 89, 91, 136, 177
Von Zinzendorf, Count Nicolaus 100 fn.
Vow 18, 20, 29, 30, 32 to 34, 37, 43, 47, 58, 70, 72, 78—81, 82 fn., 87—89, 91—93, 102, 103, 108—112, 118, 123, 124, 128, 137, 142, 144, 146, 159, 164 to 166, 179, 180 fn., 183, 187, 215, 223; *see also* Baptismal Covenant
loyalty to the Lutheran Church 64, 103 to 106, 110, 111, 112 fn., 114, 128, 165, 166, 215, 223
oath 35, 72, 79, 80, 111, 128, 165, 179 fn.

Wackernagel, Philipp 76 fn.
Waech, O. A. 114 fn.
Walther, C. F. W. 109, 110 fn., 111 fn., 126, 129
Walther, Michael 134
Wangerin, Walter M. 151 fn.
Weissgerber, Hans H. 25, 36 fn., 37 fn.
Wette, Martin de 17 fn., 18 fn.

Wichern, Johann 86, 87, 91
Wiencke, Gustav K. 151
William of Auxere 14
Williams, George H. 29 fn., 30 fn.
Williston, Ralph 103 fn., 104 fn.
Wisconsin 101 fn.
Wittenberg Synod 105
Witzel, Georg 17
Wolbrecht, Walter 5
Wolffianism 83
World War I 139
World War II 140, 142

Yelgava 82 fn.
Yelverton, Eric E. 57 fn.
Youth dedication 78, 143

Zion in New York, English Lutheran Church 103 fn.
Zismers, B. F. 107 fn.
Zorn, Carl M. 176 fn.
Zwinglian theology 36